PROFUNDITY

Jean Gabbert Harrell

PROFUNDITY

A Universal Value

The Pennsylvania State University Press
University Park, Pennsylvania

Library of Congress Cataloging-in-Publication Data

Harrell, Jean G. (Jean Gabbert), 1921–
    Profundity : a universal value / Jean Gabbert Harrell.

        p.   cm.
    Includes bibliographical references and index.
    ISBN 0-271-00849-0 (alk. paper)
    1. Aesthetics.   2. Depth (Philosophy)   I. Title.
    BH301.D46H37   1992
    111'.85—dc20   91–41518
                                                         CIP

Published by The Pennsylvania State University Press,
Suite C, Barbara Building, University Park, PA 16802-1003

Printed in the United States of America

It is the policy of The Pennsylvania State University Press to use acid-free paper for
the first printing of all clothbound books. Publications on uncoated stock satisfy the
minimum requirements of American National Standard for Information Sciences—
Permanence of Paper for Printed Library Materials, ANSI Z39.48–1984.

To the Memory of My Inspiring Grandmother
Emma Lundahl Bergson Doyle
San Francisco, 1860–Berkeley, 1941

Contents

Preface

More than the dictates of logic and scientific observation, aesthetic motivation drives human activities in such a central way as to take over whole human lives. It is these activities that we say "make life worth living," even when that aesthetic motive may be found in scientific investigation. But the aesthetic thrill in "Eureka, I have found it!" does not itself ground scientific discoveries, as the recognition that "all men are brothers" grounds profundity of aesthetic values. The sense of primal worth of all human life, lived out each day by healthy (and sometimes unhealthy) individuals, and found primarily through arts and religions, surely forces an acknowledgment of the importance of aesthetics that is quite contrary to its current low status in philosophical inquiry.

Recognition of this primal and pervasive aesthetic function has not been well served, if it has been served at all, by past academic philosophical aesthetics, especially not by "analytical" aesthetics. There, we have talked of instantiating p's and q's and have hoped to apply truth-functional thinking to analysis of aesthetic predicates. In the wake of recognition of a peculiar and mercurial function of aesthetic vocabulary that is quite compatible with Wittgenstein's insights into language use, and that appears to be always subjective and variable in time and physiological circumstance, we have yet offered definitions of aesthetic qualities in the terms of biconditional tautologies, as though this is the only acceptable way to be "clear about what we are saying." If there are many statements couched in aesthetic predication, then let us treat each as having truth-value separately, put them on a truth table, and show a tautological function.

Or, to make our inquiries compatible with those of analytical ethics, we have tried to cover all aesthetic predicates in the general statement form "x is good." Even if we find aesthetic "goodness," however, this tells us nothing about human choices that differ from one another within what pragmatists or hermeneutists see as an interpretative world that has a cultural history. So, it seems, anything or everything can be aesthetically "good."

Aestheticians have thus deserved their reputation, past and present, as pursuing a sham discipline, in effect a self-defeating enterprise, most or all of whose theses and countertheses are negative in character. We cannot find principles of aesthetic taste. We cannot define "art." We cannot connect psychology with logical analysis. And so the picture of the academic aesthetician is often that of a delighted iconoclast who, dusting his hands and with a gleeful smile, walks from the ruins saying "Look what I did!" What might originally have been an honest, though naïve, hope to penetrate the mysteries of aesthetic judgment has, in the name of academic expertise, reduced to a game-play, demonstrating only that those playing may indeed be clever fellows.

Philosophers have a way of setting up strictures, be they ontological, epistemological, or valuational, within which—in the name of logical entailment and consistency—they must work. Yet our own judgment of philosophical aesthetics is largely now viewed as an academic discipline that enlightens no one but those who have set up the strictures. Nowhere is there a more glaring discrepancy than that between philosophical analysis and the obvious permeation in the "real" world of aesthetic drive, from the most superficial to the most profound. This is not just in the pursuit of different "arts," but, as John Dewey was at pains to show, lying at the very roots of intelligent human activity. The paucity of relations between academic study and what whole cultures and generations thrive on is glaringly obvious. It reaches into most pressing human situations—into the identification of "crimes against humanity," into the loss among the impoverished and segregated of a rudimentary will to live, into complaint against blight of industrial places where millions are forced to subsist, into the defacing of the natural environment. But if Kant was right to identify aesthetic judgments as based on feelings, not concepts, then there can be no logical entailment in their justification. Feelings logically entail nothing. Without such entailment, what can philosophers hope to look for that would form an intellectual understanding or backup of what goes on daily and that, in the end, justifies the very fact of human life?

Academic study of aesthetics now seems to have reached a standstill.

Book publication in the field is almost entirely limited to anthologies, both historical and analytical, that acquaint the student with the strictures of the distant past or with analytical results of the recent past that are heralded by their makers as "progressive." In many cases, the valuational function of aesthetic judgments has been almost entirely lost, and when grounds of aesthetic value in older writings have been the center of inquiry, they have been primarily restricted to beauty, with the prevalent assumption that other aesthetic qualities can, one way or another, be subsumed under this general rubric. Care has not been taken to determine whether this assumption is correct, and it appears to have been largely this failure that explains the general failure of philosophical aesthetics to relate to primary human concerns that are other than things of beauty.

Such stagnation of academic aesthetics need not be. Escaping it, however, requires changes that are radically original. If we wish to maintain a close connection between academic study and the vital interests of human life, we ought to stop poring over the history of the subject and trying to operate consistently within time-honored strictures of the past. These strictures and assumptions, while interesting in themselves, should be abandoned in a way that yet enables us to remain within inquiries of "mainstream" philosophy that are compatible with the twentieth century. The subject of this book presents one way to accomplish this. The primary aesthetic valuational criterion of *profundity* is not taken to be a feature of judgments of beauty. We cannot find, moreover, in the past or present any suggestion that this issue ought to be pursued, nor has there been recognition of the extent to which references to profundity catapult us immediately into the most fundamental concerns of human life.

The title of this book may suggest to the reader just one more ho-hum academic analysis of aesthetic values. That is misleading. The isolation of one of many such values leads to a demonstration that the quality of profundity is not reducible to the others; it leads, as well, to a refutation of a total valuational relativism that is now almost universally accepted, both in aesthetics and in general philosophy. Zeroing in on an initially elusive fugitive, succeeding chapters in addition trace its relation to specific and primary human concerns, both humanistic and scientific, to constructive and sometimes astonishing results. Solutions are suggested to major issues in philosophy and in criticism of literature, music, and visual arts, as well as in religion, psychology, anthropology, and cognitive science. Curtains are opened on assumptions that need not have been made, on conclusions that are unnecessarily restricted, and on future progress heretofore not thought of. Most important, however, the book supplies the sort of intimate relation between a new direction of academic inquiry and major features of all human activity that past academic aesthetic inquiries have never had.

None of this supposes that we are here really doing metaphysics or epistemology. Let it not be said that the universal found in aesthetic judgment is really a form of Platonism or a detailing of Kant's forms of sensibility. Care should be taken to keep valuational concerns separate from those of metaphysics or epistemology, however often it is rightly said that "facts and values" are inextricably mixed. Facts and values may indeed be inseparable, but this does not mean that the establishing of beliefs and the establishing of valuations are essentially identical processes. Nor should it mean that separate inquiries into valuation should continue to be treated as secondary in importance to those of metaphysics or epistemology. Do the tables on this not ultimately turn when philosophy itself is finally judged not so much upon logical cogency as upon profundity of insight?

For their excellent reference suggestions and challenging discussions, I owe thanks to my colleagues, Marek W. Bielecki, Kathleen (McLaughlin) Blamey, Eugene D. Mayers, and Joaquin A. Zuniga, and to my good friend, the late Milton Charles Nahm. Thanks also to my sister, Marion Wilkerson, for guidance in navigating the voluminous writings of C. G. Jung.

Introduction

As a synonym of *depth*, *profundity* is a spatial, but nonvisual, metaphor. It is also a commonly used and maximally positive valuational criterion that often seems to function in a kind of "last-ditch-stand" way. That is, after all empirical or logical observations are in, and/or all other valuational grounds have been considered and either questioned or discarded, this criterion typically appears as a final resort, and a ground that is universally convincing (except perhaps to some philosophers who think that through their arguments they have made it go away). In a way, it slips into valuational reasoning under cover (perhaps it is better to say that it was there all along). Sometimes it pops out all alone, without argument, at a concert or at a particular performance of a Shakespearean tragedy. But its more usual silent accompaniment to sophisticated debate vitiates the relativist's conviction that all "values," along with all "facts" about the "world," result from interpretations relativistically determined via cultural or linguistic presuppositions that have a history.

However many other "values" may be shown to be relativistically based, this book develops a claim that, as a quality of immediate awareness, profundity is a valuational ground that is universal to humanity, ahistorical, and probably prelinguistic. It is time that philosophers intent upon drawing conclusions that apply to all human knowledge or to all human values, and coming to relativistic results compatible with skepticism, pragmatism, existentialism, phenomenology, hermeneutics, or deconstructionism, recognize the possibility that at least one major valuational criterion does not fit now-popular philosophical molds. Instead of talking in blanket terms about any and every "value," it is time that "the world so full of a number" of values should yield a counter-example through dissection. Paradoxically, a move away from the "universal" inquiries of philosophy will uncover at least one major valuational ground that is universal. If this universal is "subjective," it is so in the sense that it originates in humans; but it is not subjective in the sense that it results from "active" interpretation or freedom of choice within social contexts.

Production of "art" and its values has been assumed throughout past centuries to result from human interpretation and representation, rather than (as Plato has had it) from imitation of independently existent objects and qualities. The artist has been taken to be dependent upon three primary variables: sense perception, emotion, and social custom. It has been entirely fitting, therefore, to judge a work that is an imitation or copy to be inferior art, and "monkey see, monkey do" is a damning judgment. Rather than eulogizing means of imitation, it has been means of interpretation of materials at hand that have been commended and recommended. Primary among these are "imagination," "creativity," and "freedom of choice" or "freedom from rule." Thus, aesthetic value, whose main locus has been found in "art," has consistently been understood to be unjustifiable in a universal way. A particular judgment of a particular artist's work may be justified by reference to general social custom, but it is assumed that across cultures there is no universal rule governing art that can be shown to have determined relevant aesthetic value. Biologists may have identified certain invariant or universal features of human color perception, for example, but they have not yet in this way verified or justified particular color preferences. Thus, you may read that fashion "experts" have decreed that green is a "good" color for ladies this spring. Yet if, wishing to be "correct," you order a spring dress in green from your *couturière*, it is entirely permissible in *this* world for you to get one in red, "because Madame likes you in red."

Plainly opposed to this view of aesthetic valuation have been inquiries of the philosophical world centered in epistemology, logic, and philosophy of science. Generally prior to the twentieth century, philosophers evaluated their epistemological inquiries by a Greek model that placed highest importance upon acquiring knowledge, or "truth," about the space-time world. The consistent search was for grounds of knowledge of an "objective" world existing independently of any and every human mind, thus for universal grounds of knowledge independent of human interpretation of particulars. Although an evaluation of philosophy itself was clearly implied here, this was not, so far at least, an aesthetic evaluation.

Within this setting, when Alexander Baumgarten established what is now known as a branch of philosophy—the subject of "aesthetics"—his attempt was immediately dubbed by Kant to be "abortive" and "fruitless" (*Critique of Pure Reason*, A21; B36). Kant complained that Baumgarten's new subject could never yield "transcendental principles" (universal and necessary) upon which, in his opinion, scientific knowledge must be based. He thought that "aesthetic" inquiry would yield empirical psychology, which, he implied, would always be dependent upon contingencies of sense interpretation.

Consistent with Kant's original deprecating opinion (about which he later changed his mind), aestheticians have regularly been treated as second-class philosophical citizens. Grudgingly, it seems, the aesthetician has been admitted to the Inner Sanctum, provided he entered by the back door, sat in the rear, and didn't say anything. Most broadly, this reflected an opinion that the aesthetician was playing a losing game, that he could not find for the values and valuations of any social world a universal ground. In the beginning, his targets of inquiry—"taste" and "pleasure"—may have appeared ephemeral. What would an Indian or an African understand of pleasure or *le bon goût* in a world of powdered wigs, snuffboxes, and royalty saying "Let them eat cake"? Besides, the aesthetician kept losing his quarry: whether locating aesthetic value in such a "formal" principle as "unity in variety," or in "emotive" means of "expression," he kept reducing evaluations to descriptions of states of affairs. Even when twentieth-century aestheticians had tried to gain good standing by substituting "logical" methods for "psychological" ones, the net result was that they took up analysis of everything they could think of about "art" that sidestepped questions of value. Identifying their subject now as metacriticism, that is, as logical analysis of the language of art critics, they took up such issues as: Can a work of art be defined? What is the nature of artistic expression? What sort of object is a work of art (the "ontological" question)? How do we identify Beethoven's Fifth Symphony as itself and none other (the question of identity)? Even then on occasion they committed logical sin, as when they confused the ontological question with the question of identity.[1]

With the coming of pragmatism, existentialism, phenomenology, hermeneutics, and deconstructionism, however, the tables turned heavily on the rulers of the Inner Sanctum themselves. Each of these recent developments shares an intent to demonstrate that all of human knowledge is a product of interpretation, of interaction between variables both in human cognition and in "external" environments. Suddenly, Nietzsche has acquired a significance that in the past escaped accredited notice. He, after all, had produced a hybrid between philosophy and poetry. Consistent with their own methods, epistemologists, logicians, or philosophers of science would have found it too difficult to figure out what Nietzsche *meant*, and therefore how to judge him.

Instability of the Inner Sanctum, however, has not yet produced its complete collapse. Most recently, defenders of "artificial intelligence" (AI) have put a still-unresolved challenge to those convinced that no comprehensive account of human cognition can be given on the model of a computer program. As Terry Winograd and Fernando Flores put it: " 'Artificial intelligence' is an attempt to build a full account of human cognition into a formal system (a computer program)."[2] Prior to these authors' negative criticism of this attempt, such an account has, of course, brought forth vigorous counterargument from those already of existentialist persuasion. Consider, for example, the following argument from Hubert Dreyfus:

> If one thinks of the importance of the sensory-motor skills in the development in our ability to recognize and cope with objects, or of the role of needs and desires in structuring all social situations or finally of the whole cultural background of human self-interpretation involved in our simply knowing how to pick out and use chairs, the idea that we can simply ignore this know-how while formalizing our intellectual understanding as a complex system of fact and rules is highly implausible.[3]

This passage might as well have been written by John Dewey or Martin Heidegger, with some vocabulary shift here and there, but a large part of its challenge to artificial intelligence lies in the failure of AI to include "the role of needs and desires" in a comprehensive account of human cognition. In accord with the way in which "artistic" activity has consistently been interpreted for centuries, now values and valuations sneak back into a picture of "possible worlds," where previous philosophical concerns with "knowledge" and "truth" had most often explicitly excluded them. In this picture, moreover, we find a vocabulary long since debunked as "messy," "unclear," "metaphorical," even downright "meaningless." Freely now, words like *history* and *culture* appear without apology, as though no one had asked in the past, "What does *culture* mean?" To critics of AI, it appears to be assumed that if the message cannot be carried in this way, then it is not to be carried at all.

Yet it has been largely this feature of "messy" vocabulary that has led to the demise of the writings of John Dewey. To extremists in the Inner Sanctum, who would require translatability into symbolic notation and definitions in the biconditional format of a tautology, Dewey's language was inexcusable. He had been so intent on establishing "interaction" between "organism" and "environment" that logicians were hard-put to distinguish subject from object. If we asked whether Dewey was talking about felt qualities or qualities of objects, he would have to say that he was talking about both, which, to the scientific mind, made his whole polemic muddleheaded. Muddling, of course, was one way Dewey tried to put his principal point that all human cognition was a result of interpretation within his proverbial "problem situation" of how to get out of the woods. This did not reduce to such a question as how to win at chess, where established and inflexible rules play in the background as guides to all possible moves—however limitless those possibilities may seem. Nor, had Dewey been familiar with computers, would it have reduced to a question of how to program a computer. Getting out of the woods was his metaphor for a solution to a problem behind which there was no established and inflexible rule of appeal.

Thus, for Dewey, aesthetic value was found at the "consummatory" point of any human inquiry whatsoever, including science, when we typically exclaim: "Eureka, I have found it!" It was that indeterminate feature of cognition, underscored in the grappling with "needs and desires," that called for recognition of aesthetic value as an integral feature of cognitive activity, and also for a theory locating artistic success in "freedom from rule." This is probably why a contemporary writer like Richard Rorty overrides technical logical difficulties of Dewey's language when he finds Dewey's general insight "edifying."[4]

The effect of Dewey's account of the origin of all "aesthetic" value, however, only underscored the relativistic opinion about all human values and valuation extant in Western thinking at least since the time of David Hume and exacerbated by recent twentieth-century analytical trends. As a precursor of philosophies now bent on defeating AI, it did not—any more than do they—lead to the slightest questioning of a relativistic valuational stand. Nor is there suggestion of AI defenders that that phase of human cognition called "aesthetic evaluation" is even relevant to their account of cognitive process. Essentially, then, the relativistic status of aesthetic values and valuation goes unchallenged on all fronts.

Although the advertising executive may have told his new employee to look for "creative" ideas, he has the logical principle of contradiction on his side when he fires his ambitious underling for submitting an ad that reads: "New! Improved! Grandmas' Old-Fashioned Cookies." The underling should have known by simple logic that it will not do to tell the public that it ought to buy one and the same product that is new and improved, but that is not new and cannot be improved upon. The pragmatic employee might argue, however, that the addition of real vanilla to the company's standard recipe has brought its cookies closer to what everybody's grandma used to bake, so where's the contradiction? His employer may fire him anyway for back talk, but, in the empirical world of aesthetic delights, the underling should have the whole army of pragmatists, existentialists, phenomenologists, hermeneutists, Marxists, and deconstructionists 100 percent behind him. When we ask what made grandmas' cookies so good in the first place, we must admit that they were not all from the same recipe, that we were not all eating them on Christmas after an exciting trip over the river and through the woods, or that if we ate the cookies of the grandma who happens to live next door we might find them unfit for consumption. There can be no universal recipe for all grandmas' cookies, thus nothing analogous, say, to De Morgan's laws governing "or-gates" in computers. Too much of our nostalgia that centers in particular cookies varies in different experiences of different judges. To try to unpack the gestalt in order to say what makes your grandma's product so good beyond what your particular palate and memory tell you is to plunge into a vocabulary, so familiar to the art critic, that is ineradicably vague and "all over the map."

Recognition of vague vocabulary is a major condition lying behind general negative assessments of philosophy of value and valuation. When philosophers have sought definitions of what any "value" amounts to, or analysis of how any valuation is "grounded," relativistic vultures find easy prey. The words *value* and *valuation* can sometimes be found to function differently from what the resultant theories determine. Counterexamples abound in "demolishing" them. But it is one thing to question or discard theories about any and every value, or explanations of any and every valuation, and quite another to demonstrate that there is no *particular* value that is held by all humans, or no particular valuation that, at one time or another, all humans honor. If the superaltern is false, the corresponding subaltern need not be. Moreover, the situation is not analogous to the statement "All men are mortal," of which it is empirically impossible to find a refutation. If we think of an example that would force us to reject this statement as false, we need to be able to identify a man who will unquestionably live forever. The relativist who rejects a general theory of value or valuation, however, does not demonstrate that it is impossible to find a valuational instance that is not dependent on historical or cultural conditions. Quite the contrary, as we shall see in Chapter 1, when a die-hard relativist like Richard Rorty encounters a defense of "depth" in philosophy by Thomas Nagel, he tries to argue it away. Amid much flailing, Rorty gets rid of Nagel's counterexample to total valuational relativism by setting up a straw man.

Argument that there *is* no such thing as an exception to radical relativism is far from restricted to infighting among academic or "professional" philosophers. The unequivocal tenor of the following quotation from the literary critic George Steiner may have presumed authority of certain philosophers behind it, but as an assertion of a truth so apparently obvious as to require no demonstration whatsoever it is also typical of art criticism generally.

> [In literary criticism] the act and art of serious reading comport two principle motions of spirit: that of interpretation (hermeneutics) and that of valuation (aesthetic judgment). The two are strictly inseparable. To interpret is to judge. No decipherment, however philological, however textual in the most technical sense, is value-free. Correspondingly, no critical assessment, no aesthetic commentary is not, at the same time, interpretative. The very word "interpretation", encompassing as it does concepts of explication, of translation and of enactment (as in the interpretation of a dramatic part or musical score) tells of this manifold interplay.
>
> The relativity, the arbitrariness of *all* aesthetic propositions, of *all* value-judgments is inherent in human consciousness and in

human speech. Anything can be said about anything. The assertion that Shakespeare's *King Lear* "is beneath serious criticism"
(Tolstoy), the finding that Mozart composes mere trivia, are
totally irrefutable. They can be falsified neither on formal (logical)
grounds, nor in existential substance. Aesthetic philosophies,
critical theories, constructs of the "classic" or the "canonic" can
never be anything but more or less persuasive, more or less
comprehensive, more or less consequent descriptions of this or
that process of preference. . . .

To be "indwelt" by music, art, literature, to be made responsible,
answerable to such habitation as a host is to a guest—perhaps
unknown, unexpected—at evening, is to experience the commonplace mystery of a real presence. Not many of us feel compelled
to, have the expressive means to, register the mastering quality of
this experience—as does Proust when he crystallizes the sense of
the world and of the word in the little yellow spot which is the
real presence of a riverside door in Vermeer's "View of Delft" or
as does Thomas Mann when he enacts in word and metaphor the
coming over us, the "overcoming of us," in Beethoven's op 111.
No matter. The experience itself is one we are thoroughly at
home with—an informing idiom—each and every time we live a
text, a sonata, a painting.[5]

Undoubtedly a great deal of such radical relativism derives from
recognition that human values and valuations are based on emotions
whose literary expression gives evidence of irrationality that, in Ion's
case, was masquerading as wisdom, but by Socrates' analysis was better
identified as "divine inspiration." Then, too, when aesthetic qualities
attach to sense perceptions, we must acknowledge that humans are
notoriously subject to "sensory fatigue." After a while, you can't smell
the perfume any more. The bottle must be corked and put away for—
how long?—before that old magic will return to promise a night of
passion.
    Those intent on extending linguistic insights of Ludwig Wittgenstein
to matters valuational may argue from another, less biological perspective
that function of all vocabulary that we identify as valuational or use
valuationally is determined by the way "we" speak and cannot be
transferred across the board to any human culture whatsoever, past or
present. We are then cautioned to look to language "use" or "usage." If

we do, we should realize that human language has a background and is a product of interpretation within culturally variable circumstances. Once more, however, we shall have to argue similarly as Rorty argues against Nagel, that the words *deep* or *profound* are themselves products of interpretation within our culture, and that their evident reference to something universal in human experience across cultures is either misleading or mistaken.

Not wishing to set up a straw man in turn, I propose to begin this inquiry into *profundity* by analyzing use or usage of the word. This should indicate that "x is profound" is not totally irrefutable, as Steiner would have it, and that not "anything can be said about anything." I follow the Wittgensteinean suggestion, however, aware that objections to inquiry into use and usage have recently been voiced in a quite persuasive way. The following extended comments of Brand Blanshard are especially well taken:

> [Language analysts thought] they could accept as the test of appropriateness standard usage itself. They could say that if you penetrated behind the irregularities of ordinary speech you would find a meaning which was itself proof against confusion and sufficient to rectify all irregularities. Ordinary usage, sensitively discriminated and faithfully followed, was as good a test as we could hope for. No less an authority than Wittgenstein was reported to have said, "Philosophy must not in any way, however slight, interfere with the ordinary use of language; in the end, philosophy can only describe it." This sounded strangely like Moore as interpreted by Malcolm. Indeed Antony Flew in introducing the first series of essays on *Logic and Language* thanks "that apostle of commonsense and linguistic propriety, Professor G. E. Moore. For it has been Professor Moore who has made philosophers see how easy it is to slip into nonsense by even apparently trivial deviations from standard English . . ."; and in introducing the second series he asks, "How else could one investigate the concept of knowledge than by studying the various correct uses of the word 'know'?" "Philosophical questions," wrote Dr. Macdonald, "are not factual but verbal; philosophical problems can be solved by understanding how language is ordinarily used, how certain uses of it have provoked these problems and how it has been misused in many alleged solutions." Such language became common among writers known to be careful in weighing their

words. *"Knowing what a thing is,"* said Professor Austin, "is, to an important extent, knowing what the name for it, and the right name for it, is." Mr. Strawson remarks in passing that he takes "the philosophical problem of truth" to be the same as that of "the actual use of the word 'true' ". "There would be no need for philosophy", writes Mr. Urmson, "if language were not inadequate". Professor Hart writes, summing up on the transformation in philosophy: "Not only has much changed in philosophy in the intervening thirty years [since 1919], but the most important of the changes has been the replacement of the traditional philosophical conception of language as simply the vehicle in or by which an internal non-symbolic activity of thought about or knowledge of objects is expressed or communicated, by a conception of language as logically inseparable from what is meant by 'knowledge' and 'object' ". And Professor Findlay has made it delightfully clear that the new gospel is for him a full-blooded affair, not one of dry leaves only: "to me, at least, the question 'What shall I say to speak well?' is as solemn and important as the old question: 'What shall I do to be saved.' "[6]

Blanshard gives several reasons for his disagreement with these philosophers' expectations:

1. Examining language usage lays a ground for clarifying and answering epistemological questions, but only "facts" can finally supply such answers.
2. Language of "practical men" does not reach the subtlety of philosophers' speculative issues. "The philosopher who settles speculative issues by appeal to ordinary usage is really enabled to do so by endowing it with ranges of meaning not its own."
3. It is extremely unclear just what "ordinary usage" means. "What is needed for . . . analysis . . . is not a general resolution of meanings into word habits, but a more sensitive psychology and metaphysic."
4. "Ordinary usage is full of ambiguities."
5. "The appeal to ordinary language confuses correctness with truth . . . [and the business of the philosopher] is to discover truth."
6. "Ordinary usage may mislead, distort and deceive. . . . Good usage . . . will always lead us into conformity with fact, since if it does not, it is not good usage."[7]

How do Blanshard's criticisms apply to an analysis of use or usage of the particular word upon which we concentrate? First, *profundity* is admittedly vague and to some degree ambiguous, yet this will not restrict a general analysis of its valuational function to "word-habit," or prevent us from relating it to "a more sensitive psychology and metaphysic." Nor does our proposed breakdown of this term in Chapter 1 threaten to "mislead, distort or deceive" or lead us away from "conformity with fact." Referring to number 2 above, however, what is perhaps most interesting when philosophers themselves evaluate their own work on the ground of profundity—as in devotees' judgment of the philosophy of Wittgenstein—is that they appear to step out of their sophisticated and refined vocabulary momentarily and themselves speak no more than the language of the "plain man." In this particular case, an ultimate positive evaluation of philosophy itself reverts to a criterion of general standard use. Philosophers have not apparently endowed *this* term with a "meaning not its own." Finally, however, the primary result of our inquiry into *profundity* is precisely to uncover something that is true about the world that humans inhabit.

When *deep* or *profound* function valuationally, they also function metaphorically. Initially, our broad task is recognized as one of elucidating a metaphor. Now, analysts of "ordinary language" may have offered definitions of what any metaphor is, but, in accord with their shunning of rules and universals, they have hardly laid down recipes for elucidating particular metaphors. Indeed, any particular metaphor would be looked upon as emerging without recipe from "creativity" or "imagination." And when a word originally used metaphorically becomes a part of common usage, it is often called a "dead metaphor," not simply because it is now commonplace but because it has also lost its value. Metaphors are often thought to be "marvelous" because they create new meanings; but when their meanings become commonplace, then their valuational function is lost. *Profundity* or *depth* certainly are articles of common speech. It has apparently ever been so, yet their valuational function (taken as synonyms) appears not to have been lost or to have changed over time. Rather than once having created a new meaning, and thus having once been something "marvelous" on that account, *profundity* or *depth* (used metaphorically) point to something fundamentally valuable to humans that is not new, but rather is so old as to appear primordial. And calling attention, as these words do, to something that has for the most part lain hidden or forgotten, their reference is as vague as anything can be.

For our purposes the legacy left us by philosophical analysts of metaphor is not particularly helpful. Together with the conviction on all philosophical fronts of total valuational relativity, we are left with little reason to pursue an analysis of *profundity* at all. Perhaps in matters of ethics philosophers' inquiries into things of value are still relevant on practical grounds, since moral actions in many cases can lead to what is outrageous, carrying a death penalty or at the very least a stint in jail. But aesthetics? Ha! For after working hours. For escaping boredom. For affording the social prestige of an art connoisseur. Even though we must admit that profundity, like moral virtue, is a serious matter, it is not a moral virtue and its loss lacks the force of what is morally outrageous. (I suspect, however, in certain extreme cases its total, permanent loss may produce suicide, which, in turn, is to humanity intolerable.)

Avaricious gurus abound, who profess to hold the secret to profundity in the "meaning of life"—provided that you are not too old to achieve lotus position and have a lot of money. But if you *are* too old, you are also privy to their ploys. Then, there are religious proselytizers who will tell you that you have just been sitting in the wrong pew. Yet no matter what the brand or mix, there is ever a ground for doubt, succinctly expressed by John Huston:

> It seems to me, honey, like superstition. I don't see any difference between the rituals and dogma of the Catholic Church and the Heart of the Congo or the Sepik river. Have you watched the Ayatollah's return to Iran, the hysterical symptoms and the way he was carried by the crowd? It's the same thing. There's something wanting in their spiritual makeup that requires people to believe in something.[8]

It may not be the belief, however, that is profound, but what the belief should lead to. That calling voice of an imam for whole communities to resume once more the fetal position five times daily, mound after mound, row upon row, facing toward Mecca, may lead these humans to recognition once more of a universal value in their origin that is momentarily forgotten in the bargaining exchanges of the marketplace. The minister or priest of Christian belief may lead his sermon to its capstone in prayer of semifetal position—heads bowed, eyes closed, hands forward of the body, knees bent to force a kneeling or sitting position—for what? To find once more what is profound, and to ask then for eternal life. Humans may function without any fixed "beliefs" at all, religious or otherwise, and still know what they mean when they find "profundity" in the music of Beethoven, in the tragedies of Sophocles, or in the philosophical grand scheme of Spinoza. What spells perhaps the ultimate irony is devotees' recognition of Wittgenstein's insight into the dependence of metaphysical and epistemological language upon culturally established speech—the same devotees who then, on that account, use the universal criterion of "profundity" to place their prophet top on the philosophical totem pole. In their practice, they deny their philosophical persuasion, and lend credence to J. N. Findlay's final judgment:

> A wildly metaphysical way of speaking may still be preferable, logically, to our ordinary accounts of things. For ordinary language is the breeding-ground of every metaphysical system: it is only innocuous because it holds them *all* in germ, in which state they may cancel out each other's defects, but do not develop any of their compensating excellences. It is clear, finally, that to live and talk without philosophic examination is a mode of life not "liveable by a human being"; it is much better, plainly, to be Socrates dissatisfied and confused than the ordinary speaker competent and satisfied.[9]

1

Looking for Universal Value

I

A quick way to negate any claim to fact or value is to say that it is "merely subjective." With respect to "facts," this is at least to say that the claim is not reliable; with respect to "values," it is at least to say that the claim is not worth notice. The distinction of "mere subjectivity" is most often contrasted with that of "objectivity," where "objectivity" refers to what is independent of any and every mind or judge—as when we speak of "scientific objectivity" or the "objectivity" of Platonism. But this common contrast obscures ambiguity in both "objectivity" and "subjectivity." "Merely subjective" refers to what is dependent on a particular mind or minds. However, as Kant was at pains to show, we can also point to a knowledge claim or valuation that is dependent upon the way any and every mind is taken to operate, thus to a cognitive or valuational subjective universal. Correspondingly, we can refer to a knowledge claim or valuation as "objective" that has only limited inde-

pendence of minds or judges, as when we find a need to make Madame's
opinion of flattering colors more objective by bringing it into accord with
the general opinion of fashion "experts."

As in epistemological skepticism, where analysis of the reliability of
factual claims is made in terms of origin of knowledge, in valuational
relativism analysis of worth is most often made genetically by reference
to origin in valuational process. Perhaps the most stinging feature of
valuational relativism, however, stems from a logical rather than from an
empirical failure—that is, from failure to distinguish between argument
that demonstrates subjectivity of *particular* judgments, and argument that
demonstrates that there is no valuational subjective universal. From
repeated recognition that particular valuations are based on contingencies
both of a subject (for example, his emotional state) and of environmental
conditions, we jump to the conclusion that there is no objective universal
ground that is independent of any and every mind or judge whatsoever.
This conclusion may be perfectly true. But it bypasses the possibility that
there may yet be discoverable a valuational ground that is, to be sure,
dependent on minds or judges, but that is also dependent upon the way
any and every one of them operates, thus upon a subjective universal.
The primary point to note in usage of *profundity* is that it functions as
just such a subjective universal.

As J. N. Findlay has seen especially clearly, valuational *justification*
proceeds from a particular valuation to a general or universal taken to be
its ground. But a ground that is universal need not be a ground that is
objective in the broad sense of the word. Before arriving at relativism in
epistemological matters, philosophers of almost any persuasion have
apparently long since agreed that relativism is the only way to go in
valuational matters. This conviction, however, has not generally been
based on denial of objectivity in valuational judgments but on denial of
their universality. In the following extended summary from *A History of
Six Ideas*, Władysław Tatarkiewicz indicates this especially well:

> In the light of the new theories, the old ones have seemed
> mistaken. The Pythagorean theory, according to which beauty
> depends exclusively on proportion and number, for so long attrac-
> tive to philosophers and artists, was only a partial truth; as a
> general theory of beauty it is inadequate and seems mistaken;
> unless one narrows the ordinary concept of beauty or broadens
> the ordinary concept of proportion.
>
> The Platonic theory that there exists an idea of beauty that we

know and make use of, and through which alone we can recognise beauty, is a mistake; one that was recognised for a mistake fairly quickly, although for centuries it did not cease to have its votaries.

Another Platonic theory—that art is morally harmful—likewise is an error.

The Aristotelian theory of *katharsis*, viewing art as a purgative: an ambiguous theory lending itself to many interpretations, partially valid but as a general theory of art an error. The Aristotelian attempt at creating a general theory of tragedy—an error.

The Neoplatonist theory of "*claritas*"—is too ill-defined and unsufficiently functional for a theory. Likewise the scholastic identification of "*claritas*" with "form", or the theory that a thing is beautiful when its essence shines through its material appearance. This theory, created by 13th-century Albertists, had—not without reason—only a brief life.

The Renaissance "*concinnitas*"—a beautiful theory, but applicable rather only to classical art, and inadequate with regard to Gothic or baroque beauty.

The theory of poetry developed by 16th-century Aristotelians— worked out by them in such detail—nevertheless, both in general concept as in many of its specific observations and prescriptions, is an error.

The literary and art theory of the 17th-century French academicians is a flagrant error.

The mannerist "*agudeza*", the theory according to which the only true beauty resides in subtlety and refinement corresponds to only a limited range of works; as a general theory of literature and art it is a mistake.

The system of fine arts elaborated by Charles Batteux, the first system in history to be accepted in principle by 18th-century theoreticians, was, however, amended, altered—and at last treated as an error.

The first conception of aesthetics as a science, springing from Alexander Baumgarten's assertion that aesthetics is the science of sensory cognition (*cognitio sensitiva*), was criticised and treated as an error already in the 18th-century.

The aesthetics of von Schelling and Hegel were great theories full of splendid ideas, but as a whole were a great error: not enough facts, too much construction.

The countless theories of literature and of the arts created by

writers and artists in the 19th and 20th centuries, the realisms
and naturalisms, expressionisms and formisms, have accorded with
certain currents, with a certain moment in history, with a certain
group of artists—but as general theories of art they have been
unsuccessful and have been rejected by other currents, moments
and groups.

By the same token philosophical theories of beauty, art and
aesthetic experience, devised and developed by newer aestheticians—the hedonisms, illusionisms and theories of empathy—
have been important as partial observations; nevertheless, they
have met with criticism and as prospective universal aesthetic
theories have been treated as errors. In fine—nearly as many
mistakes as theories. They are to be found not only in early
theories, with which anonymous aesthetic reflection first com-
menced, but also in the latest, more mature theories of scientific
aesthetics.[1]

The essential objection to all of the foregoing theories is not that they
failed in objectivity, but that they failed in universality. Yet if we look at
the way in which people habitually talk, we cannot rest in consigning
the apparent universal reference of *profundity* to unthinking cliché that
has somehow hung on over a very long, though indeterminate, period.
The reference is found in many languages other than English—in Latin
(*de profundus*), in French (*profondeur*), and in German (*die Tiefe*). If
Wittgensteineans finally judge their prophet's work as *profound*, surely
they do so in all seriousness, although perhaps in some convoluted way
they might agree that *profundity* should itself be subject to understanding
through analysis of language use. Moreover, we repeatedly find in art
criticism judgments of profundity that, far from being unthinking repetitions of cliché, are not only given as universally understandable but as
ultimate and irrefutable. Consider excerpts from comments about the
music of Beethoven made recently by Herbert Blomstedt, conductor of
the San Francisco Symphony:

It is a cliché to say that Beethoven's appeal is universal, but this
is in fact true. Cultures that are just beginning to make contact
with Western music, for example, generally approach it through
Beethoven: It is his work that attracts them most. Even today,
audiences in Japan still respond to Beethoven with incredible
interest—in Tokyo you can play the Ninth Symphony evening

after evening and fill any hall. . . . No composer but Beethoven has written music of such universal appeal. . . . It is purely and directly human. Like all good music, it is, in a way, strictly abstract, but it also mirrors the soul and touches all human sentiment. . . . When the drama is over, we feel that it has touched our souls and echoed our own experience. A bond is created among all those who heard the same performance.[2]

Although Blomstedt does not use the word *profundity* here, he might as well have used it. This one word not only refers to a quality universally understood, but at one stroke it obscures the very distinction between subject and object. Blomstedt has here not only made an aesthetic evaluation of Beethoven's music, he has stated what he regards to be an objective fact about it. In blurring the distinction between description and evaluation, he has left it quite unclear whether he is talking about a quality felt by listeners at a concert—thus to something "subjective," or to a quality or property of the music itself—thus to something "objective," or finally whether he is at once referring to both. Metaphors are said to draw unusual relations between things ordinarily separated from one another. In the case of *profundity*, the usual separation of subject and object itself is muddled. In this it should prove to be a logician's nightmare.

Obscuring as it does the distinction between subject and object, we might think that the word *profundity* would be grasped at happily by process philosophers as encompassing in one stroke of "ordinary language" what they themselves have required volumes of sophisticated analysis to expose. But, for one thing, process philosophers have concentrated on epistemology and metaphysics, with only a few troubling to ask how "values" and "valuations" fit into their pictures of what some call "possible worlds." Within the process of "interpretation" through interaction and mutual dependency of "subjects" and "objects," it has been assumed for the most part that "values" and "valuations" have, so to speak, "gone along on the ride," and that the origin of "subjectivity" of values is without need of explication. Even when an explicit attempt has been made to analyze the origin of "aesthetic" value, however, as in John Dewey's *Art as Experience*, subjects and objects have not lost their distinction. They have only lost their supposed separation and mutual independence. In the case of *profundity*, on the other hand, the very distinction between subject and object is blurred, thus making it from a language analyst's point of view a doubtful candidate not only for instantiation in predicate calculus but for process philosophy as well. With regard to deconstruction, *profundity* already comes deconstructed, but, with regard to process philosophy generally, subjects and objects do not lose their distinction from one another as they do in "profound" moments of human experience.

Still another major trait of *profundity* must be mentioned. Not only does the word refer to a subjective universal and obscure the subject-object distinction, the metaphorical use of *deep* most often also refers to something that is not visually accessible. In the literal use of *deep* we have a spatial determination, but of something that generally cannot be seen from the surface. What is deep may become visible if we dig down far enough, but then, from that new vantage point, the thing is no longer deep. *Profundity*, in the metaphorical use of *depth*, is of something that is hidden from view. At best, depth can be regarded as a negative visual metaphor, relating to vision only by what it (usually, at least) is *not*. This may help to explain why in our maximum positive evaluation of architecture we either say that a structure is beautiful or great. A building from bottom to top, from all sides and at any possible angle, is too obviously and completely visible for the metaphor of profundity to be appropriate. We may say upon viewing the stained-glass windows and soaring buttresses of Chartres Cathedral that we are "profoundly moved." But we do not call the cathedral edifice itself profound. Where vision is our primary medium, our aesthetic judgment tends to maintain the subject-object distinction characteristic of epistemology, thus bifurcating and to some extent weakening the valuational function of *profound*. In the case of auditory art, on the other hand, when we say that Beethoven's Ninth Symphony is profound, we mean not only that it "moves" us profoundly but that the work itself is profound.

The lack of connection with visual perception that functions so prominently, and probably necessarily, in epistemological matters suggests, fourth, that *profundity* looks back to a point of human origin that is previsual, but not preauditory. This, then, identifies it as dependent upon some kind of memory, memory of a once-conscious state in which a difference between a "subject" and its world was not clearly drawn. The primary value found in the subjective-universal function of *profundity* appears to be rooted in a rudimentary recall, which we are not aware of as *being* a recall, and recognition of an intrinsic value in the biological fact of life established previsually, therefore probably prenatally. This recognition will be of a condition that is simple and context free. It appears to carry with it an awareness of what Kant termed a *sensus-*

communis (KdU ¶40), an awareness of a common humanity that yields at certain unusual moments the sudden utterance—as though it needs to be said once more—"All men are brothers." If there is accompanying this any visual image that can be expressed in language, it will be of vague, faceless masses of humanity—of "whosoever, wheresoever," or, again in Kant (KdU ¶6), of *jedermann*. And if there is an involved emotion for which we have a name, it will be that of "love."

In all this, *profundity* appears to have yet two more connotations. What appears free from context does not appear to be a result of interpretation, and therefore does not appear as a representation or an expression. Rather, it appears to be something found or recognized. Moreover, the quality of profundity does not vary in degree. We do not have more or less of it. Either we have found something profound or we have not.

No sooner is the quality recognized and honored in such observations as Blomstedt's than it is countered that profundity is a sometime thing, a temporal nonconstant, subject to primary psychological variables of emotion, memory, and sense perception, as well as to pluralistic environmental circumstances in which they function. Once more, the enumerating of varying conditions of recall or occurrences of particular emotions seems to reaffirm that no valuation can possibly be context free. Then the greater the number of contexts possible and the greater the complexities that appear within which valuations occur, the larger the question looms: Can there really be any valuation that is simple and free of context? The question is surely now more empirical than it is logical.

We want to fashion our understanding of human history on the model of the life of an individual—from birth, through maturity, to death—and then to say with Thomas Wolfe, "You can't go home again." Well, what was this experience that the audience had at a performance of Beethoven's Ninth, anyway? A mirage? In finding that Beethoven's music is "universal" is Blomstedt only expressing a wish, and not really saying anything true about it at all? Distinguishing a subjective universal as a logical possibility is one thing. But in the empirical world of human psychology, multiplicities, complexities, and contingencies appear to be inescapable, and also to be permanent blocks to turning back the clock to exactly repeat the past.

Another feature of our empirical world that is prevalent, if not inescapable, however, is found by those who say, in effect, that you *can* go home again, perhaps depending upon use of a certain drug or some kind of meditation that often blocks out vision. Thus, Jamaican Rastafarians, who smoke marijuana seven hours a day and listen to reggae, find a

disclosure in an immediate awareness that all of the ways men find to
segregate themselves from one another—through wealth, skin color, or
political power—are spurious, and that all men are brothers. In their own
way they blend ethical with aesthetic value in what they take to be
Christian insight. If in this way they find profundity, however, to the
proverbial "common man" with twenty-twenty vision the picture is
incomplete. Philosophers have had a fondness for naming this man
"Jones" (he may or may not exist). Now pejorative words like *primitive*
and *rudimentary* crowd in to displace *profound*. What to the Rastafarian is
of supreme value becomes to those immersed in the "everyday world" no
such thing. Profundity is still revered by Jones, all right, but it needs
pragmatic backing—so say the philosophers who take themselves to have
refuted Platonism. Even to Nietzsche, the man who knows things profound is the one who has fought, suffered, and lost, and who, "hardened
and torn," acquires through this a wisdom that backs, not primitivism,
but "true" profundity. Especially to students of literature and philosophy,
the requisite of *wisdom* in finding profundity must seem obvious, as it
must to those who, perhaps less often, find the quality in visual art (as
Rudolf Arnheim has found it in Picasso's *Guernica*).

It can be shown, however, that wisdom is neither a necessary nor a
sufficient condition of profundity. Consider excerpts from Brand Blanshard's analysis of the concept:

> [Wisdom] involves intellectual grasp or insight, but it is concerned
> not so much with the ascertainment of fact or the elaboration of
> theories as with the means and ends of practical life.
>
>   . . . Common opinion is . . . at one with . . . philosophy; it
> regards the judgment of values as a field in which wisdom may be
> preeminently displayed. It must admit, however, that this judg-
> ment is of a peculiar kind; it seems to be intuitive in the sense
> that it is not arrived at by argument nor easily defended by it.
> One may be certain that pleasure is better than pain and yet be at
> a loss to prove it; the insight seems to be immediate.
>
>   [Still] man's major goods are rooted in his major needs, and
> since the basic needs of human nature are everywhere the same,
> the basic goods are also the same. No philosophy of life that
> denied value to the satisfactions of food or drink or sex or
> friendship or knowledge could hope to commend itself in the long
> run.
>
>   . . . The judgment of the wise man may carry a weight out of

all proportion to that of anything explicit in his thought or argument. The decisions of a wise judge may be implicitly freighted with experience and reflection, even though neither may be consciously employed in the case before him. Experience, even when forgotten beyond recall, leaves its deposit, and where this is the deposit of long trial and error, of much reflection, and of wide exposure in fact or imagination to the human lot, the judgment based on it may be more significant than any or all of the reasons the judge could adduce for it.[3]

Features of this account of wisdom coincide with certain characteristics of profundity. Profundity, too, appears to be a quality that is intuited immediately and to be something not easily broken down by specific arguments about particular problems or theories. Moreover, some fundamental "concern for the human lot" may also be found in profundity. (I shall later try to draw through this quality a rudimentary connection between ethical and aesthetic judgments.) Again, those who find profundity in the writings of Wittgenstein undoubtedly find a "significance" in them beyond "any or all of the reasons [that they] could adduce for it." But the following points mark crucial differences between wisdom and profundity.

1. If wisdom is taken to be a necessary condition of profundity, it is surely not a sufficient condition. There is no guarantee that a wise man will utter profundities. In this way, possession of wisdom does not explain or justify judgments of profundity.
2. We may have evidence of wisdom in certain particular utterances of the wise man, such that these utterances are said to express or represent his wisdom. Profundity is not expressed or represented. If we agree that profundity is an immediate, intuited quality, it still appears to be something found or recognized, rather than expressed or represented, either through language or other means.
3. Wisdom varies in degree. Of the biblical Three Wise Men, one might have been wiser than another, and one of them might have been wisest of all. Profundity does not vary in degree.
4. Profundity signals a greater universality of grasp than we find in wisdom, something that transcends the particulars that the wise man within his culture has sorted through and comprehended in one way or another. Wisdom is not a subjective universal.
5. Although both wisdom and profundity are backward looking, wis-

dom appears to have been more recently established than profundity. Epictetus's wise counsel, "If you kiss your own child or wife,
say to yourself that you are kissing a human being, for when it dies
you will not be disturbed" (*Encheiridion* ¶3), may be traced to the
Stoic doctrine of natural law, and also to political conditions of the
time. In contrast, profundity references appear to have no point of
establishment in human history, no point of establishment within
a particular culture. The "profound" insight that "all men are
brothers" is of no determinate historical origin and thus appears to
go backward to man's universal biological-psychological beginnings.
Blanshard's note that "no philosophy of life that denied value to
the satisfactions of food or drink or sex or friendship or knowledge
could hope to commend itself in the long run" bypasses the cultures
we could point to that, in one ascetic way or another, have in the
name of wisdom denied the value of every one of these. Of course,
we can also point to persons who have denied that all men are
brothers. Still, this does not change the ahistorical character of
references to profundity as contrasted with those to wisdom.

6. I will show far more extensively in Chapter 3 that wisdom is not
even a necessary condition of profundity. We do not require that
Beethoven's Ninth Symphony emerge from its composer's wisdom,
or somehow reveal wisdom in any of its performances. If we follow
Nietzsche, we may think that in order to produce a profound
composition Beethoven needed to have suffered, and indeed some
such argument has been extensively presented by J.W.N. Sullivan.[4]
This, however, may be dismissed as Romantic nonsense.

II

In the fourth of his Carus Lectures, delivered at the December 1985
meeting of the American Philosophical Association in Washington,
D.C., Hilary Putnam raised certain problems about valuation, primarily
in ethics. He thought at one point that some of the philosophy of Charles
Sanders Peirce might be of help. To justify turning to the ideas of Peirce,
Putnam evaluated him as perceiving "the depth of individual problems
. . . [with] great flashes of genius." Although this procedure appeared
somehow to be methodologically circular, the lecturer smiled at his
audience and they appeared not to object. It was as though Putnam had

constructed a house that was to encompass the entire world and had then found that the passageway to the Valuation Room was somehow blocked. It was as though he had said to himself: "I think I'll step outside for a moment. After all, the house that Peirce built is just across the street. Perhaps I can borrow his plans." It was as though Putnam's house both did and did not encompass the whole world.

Although Putnam's judgment of Peirce's philosophy was apparently aesthetic, as his judgment of Peirce himself as a "genius" also seemed to be, his criterion had broader applicability than do the other more commonly recognized "aesthetic" predicates *beautiful* and *great*. We would hardly have expected Putnam to justify borrowing Peirce's plans by saying: "Peirce's philosophy is beautiful and Peirce was a genius"—surely his audience would have objected. *That* judgment does not reach far enough afield from judgment of art works or of nature itself. Nor would we probably have expected Putnam to justify borrowing Peirce's plans by saying: "Peirce's philosophy is great and Peirce was a genius" (although in a recent collection of essays on Peirce we find reference to his "growing reputation as America's greatest philosopher and one of the great philosophers of all time").[5] When Mortimer Adler's *Great Books* series (a collection containing major writings in science, philosophy, and literature) was published in 1952, considerable question was raised about the appropriateness of judging the primary value of these writings on the aesthetic criterion of greatness. For Putnam to say what he *did* say, however, seemed to carry just as strong a positive and unquestionable evaluation as it might have carried at any point in Western intellectual history.

The feature of "depth" in Peirce that Putnam stressed seemed to be the same as that observed by J. N. Findlay in his own references to Peirce's "genius." It is that of an insight into a certain apparently universal trait of human inquiry that seems to carry with it a positive intrinsic value. In speaking of how we "approve" of "beliefs," Findlay finds that they

> must be found to "fit in" with the whole coherent web tied to our compulsive experiences, and to do so however far this may be extended and developed, and to persist up to its limit. Seen in this connection, correspondence means no more than that a belief will correspond to a fact or to a reality if it can be sustained to the limit of inquiry, and will become ever firmer in the process, again a principle that we owe to the genius of Peirce. . . . If belief, by its nature, seeks accommodations with compulsive experience,

it must, by its nature, seek to make such accommodations as
detailed and deep-going as possible.[6]

It is clear that neither Putnam nor Findlay has simply identified Peirce
as an exceptionally wise philosopher. Findlay's acknowledgment of his
"genius" is in Peirce's insight into the leading of particular beliefs to a
"whole coherent web" that extends to an indeterminate "limit" as a
requirement of human cognitive process ("belief, by its nature,
seeks . . ."). Putnam's acknowledgment relates to Peirce's recognition
that rational activity of an individual is identified with a "community of
investigators." Thus, stressing problems of ethical value, Putnam considered the universal principle "All men are brothers," even though he did
not recognize that it is not a peculiarly ethical principle. At these points
both philosophers, however, find "depth" of philosophical insight in an
essentially Kantian understanding of human cognition as moving, in the
verification and justification of particular beliefs and valuations, toward
metaphysics and a universal ground of value that is context free.

The value here, however, is clearly not ethical. Whether it is properly
called aesthetic may be an open question. We may prefer to think of
depth as a fundamental value found by philosophers that is established
before both aesthetic and ethical values, and from which, perhaps, the
latter derive. Or, we may regard judgments of Wittgenstein's or Peirce's
philosophies on the ground of profundity much as we regard the pro-
nouncements of wise men—as having a final or primary merit that is
aesthetic rather than logical ("a significance . . . beyond any or all of the
reasons that [could be] adduce[d] for it"). We may wish to say that
identifying Einstein as a genius in authoring the theory of relativity is
not an aesthetic judgment, but that identifying Michelangelo as a genius
in creating the ceiling of the Sistine Chapel is. Such differences undoubtedly result from the vagueness of the word *aesthetic*. Suffice it to say that
when process philosophers now draw a close analogy between identification of all knowledge, scientific or otherwise, as a product of human
interpretation and the almost universal identification of artworks as
products of interpretation, the distinction between which products are
properly called aesthetic and which are not becomes increasingly difficult
to draw.

With the current domination of philosophy and general cultural
criticism by epistemological and valuational relativism, we may wonder
how Putnam, Findlay, or, even in their convoluted way, Wittgensteineans would have dared to promote profundity. How have they thought

they could get away with it? So prominent is the conviction that the past philosophical search for universals has been a mistake that many now herald the death of philosophy itself. Indeed, Richard Rorty has been determined not to let one of the more recent defenders of "depth," Thomas Nagel, get away with it. It is interesting to watch how, in the process, Rorty sets up a straw man, and to wonder, consequently, whether any pragmatic or existentialist argument against profundity is bound, one way or another, to stub its toe.

In his book *Mortal Questions*, Nagel defends a greater importance of certain fields and issues in philosophy on the basis of "depth." "There are no problems deeper and more important than those in metaphysics, epistemology, and philosophy of language that lie at the center of the field" (Preface, ix). Primarily in these areas, a certain rudimentary trait of human minds is exposed: to move from "subjective" views of a world of facts and values to an "objective" grasp that explains and justifies them. "Even if one admits to the world facts or values involving a particular point of view, it is tempting to assume that something's being so from a particular point of view must consist in something else's being the case from no point of view." Some philosophers may adopt a view of the world that is totally subjective (as in idealism) or totally objective. However, "the deep source of both idealism and its objectifying opposite is the same: a conviction that a single world cannot contain both irreducible points of view and irreducible objective reality—that one of them must be what there *really* is and the other somehow reducible to or dependent on it. This is a very powerful idea. To deny it is in a sense to deny that there is a single world."[7]

Nagel is not at all clear about how "values" can be interpreted as features of an objective world seen "from no point of view," such as might ground C. I. Lewis's distinction between the "inherent" value of objects and the "intrinsic" value of simple likings and dislikings.[8] Nagel notes that "the pursuit of objectivity . . . involves a transcendence of the self, in two ways: a transcendence of particularity and a transcendence of one's type. . . . Objective transcendence aims at a representation of what is of value in itself, rather than *for* anyone."[9] This may identify any value attached to a universal as intrinsic, but it does not of itself account for any *value* viewed from no standpoint at all. Indeed, a primary difficulty that Nagel observes in his analysis of "absurdity" found in human life, for example, is precisely in a lack of any value of human life in an "objective" account of the world.

Although Nagel's own identification of depth in philosophy is based upon a Kantian generalization about the presumed way in which any and every human mind functions, he identifies the universal with the objective, and does not even logically distinguish the possibility of a universal that is subjective, unless "transcending one's type" means transcending a point of view that is universal to humanity—that is, the human type. (But we do not know what a point of view that is universal to all humans would be.) Judging from his own analysis of "mortal questions," it thus seems that Nagel would have to identify his own judgment of philosophy itself as subjective (i.e., as deriving from human minds), but still without any particular point of view—as a context-free universal. Thus it seems unavoidable that Nagel, if only implicitly, acknowledges that the valuational criterion of "depth" in philosophy is a subjective universal.

Richard Rorty's essential argument against Nagel's criterion, however, is that it is not an objective universal. Like Nagel, he identifies what is universal with what is objective. Classifying Nagel as an "intuitive realist," in part because he establishes the "depth" of metaphysics intuitively, Rorty does not deny that we have intuitions of "depth." He holds only that their testimony can be interpreted as not what it seems— in other words, that we do not accept this testimony of intuition. "We have been educated within an intellectual tradition built around such claims"[10] to the disclosure of "depth" in philosophical matters. Spotting the Kantian influence in Nagel's tracing of depth to a human search both for universality and objectivity of knowledge, and recognition of an ultimate limit in its success, Rorty then reminds us of Kant's eighteenth-century philosophical stage with its Cartesian backdrop. To the extent that Nagel finds certain intuitions to be probably prelinguistic, he adds that Wittgenstein would surely not be convinced. Rorty sums up his own case:

> The issue is one about whether philosophy should try to find natural starting points that are distinct from cultural traditions, or whether all philosophy should do is compare and contrast cultural traditions. . . . The intuitive realist thinks that there is such a thing as Philosophical truth because he thinks that, deep down beneath all the texts, there is something which is not just one more text but that to which various texts are trying to be "adequate." The pragmatist does not think there is anything like that. He does not even think that there is anything isolable as "the purposes that we construct vocabularies and cultures to fulfill" against which to test vocabularies and cultures. But he does think that in the process of

playing vocabularies and cultures off against each other, we produce new and better ways of talking and acting—not better by reference to a previously known standard, but just better in the sense that they come to *seem* clearly better than their predecessors.[11]

In his application of pragmatism to philosophy itself, Rorty has reduced philosophical profundity to wisdom. Now "depth" in philosophy must vary in degree, depending upon how those "playing vocabularies and cultures off against each other" make new vocabularies and cultures "seem" better. And those who dub Wittgenstein's philosophy profound must have their prophet turning over in his grave, asking, with Jesus, "Who do men say that I am?"

The core of the difference between Rorty and Nagel lies in the existence and meaning of "natural starting points." This distinction appears to be based upon a biological model of any human being that originates without a cultural history. Are we to think of human cultural and philosophical history on the model of a particular human life, where at some presumed biological beginning consciousness is prelinguistic, where cognition is intuitive rather than conceptual, and where all intuitions are presumed to be identical "givens," rather than products of interpretation? Or are we to plunge *in medias res* and base an analogy between biological life and culture only on a state of perpetual and sophisticated adulthood with all its complexities and interpretative differences?

For the pragmatist, we cannot go backward to find what is "better" in the past. The wise man profits from recognizing inadequacies in old solutions used to solve new and unforeseen problems. If the Rastafarian finds solution to present moral dilemmas through the combined use of marijuana and a certain kind of dynamic music, far from being a step toward wisdom, his apparent retreat to a primordial state of awareness can only be interpreted as a cultural "cop-out." Moreover, it can be shown that the *value* of what he finds lies in its relation to his own present social and moral dilemmas, as when he sings "Black man, you better know yourself, before your back gets against the wall."[12] (Whether this relation marks the *sole* source of value, however, is a part of the point at issue about *profundity*.) From Rorty's view, Nagel's inquiries into "mortal questions" may show a pragmatic recognition that these questions are alive and well near the twenty-first century and still in pressing need of answers. But "natural starting points" upon which "deep" philosophy is based have no objective existence independent of human cultures. To this, however, Nagel could well respond that he has never really claimed otherwise.

Rorty does not argue that the philosophical search for universals cannot be warranted in any culture; only that when it is warranted and worthwhile, it derives from nonobjective cultural conditions. In *Philosophy and the Mirror of Nature*, where he develops his polemic most extensively, his observations appear to come straight from John Dewey:

> There would not have been thought to be a problem about the nature of reason had our race confined itself to pointing out particular states of affairs—warning of cliffs and rain, celebrating individual births and deaths. But poetry speaks of man, birth, and death as such, and mathematics prides itself on overlooking individual details. When poetry and mathematics had come to self-consciousness—when men like Ion and Theaetetus could identify themselves with their subjects—the time had come for something general to be said about knowledge of universals.[13]

III

Philosophers' concerns with universals, both pragmatic and nonpragmatic, have been almost exclusively those of epistemology and metaphysics. In *Philosophy and the Mirror of Nature*, Rorty takes up the question of "values" in only three places (and briefly each time), implying that an adequate account of "values" can be made exactly parallel to that of "facts," though nowhere does he demonstrate this. Again, in his essay that includes comments about Nagel's *Mortal Questions*, there is also pragmatic criticism of the epistemological aims of logical positivism that bypasses the positivists' analysis of valuational vocabulary as "emotive language" and beyond their "scientific" purview. Does Rorty think that the positivists got it right on *these* questions? We do not know, but perhaps for him it does not matter. At the same time Rorty clearly recognizes that the issue Nagel raises about philosophical "depth" is a valuational one. Yet not once does he suggest that pragmatic criticisms of past epistemology or metaphysics may not apply equally well to theories of value and valuation.

Rorty is far from alone in skipping over an explicit accounting of the subjective and cultural origins of all values and valuations. In a summary concluding paragraph of an essay demonstrating what he terms "an historical epistemology," for instance, Marx Wartofsky suddenly refers to "value systems," along with "beliefs," "ideologies," and "world views," although nowhere previously does he suggest how such "value systems" come to be or whether they are established in any way differently from "beliefs."

Wartofsky concentrates on an account of sense perception that is contrary to those basing human perception on invariant biological "starting points." His essential thesis is that "the very foundation of what is distinctively human in perception is its character as a socially and historically achieved, and changing mode of action; and [it is] thereby invested with a cognitive, affective and teleological character which exemplifies it as a social, and not merely a biological or neurophysiological activity. What is more, it is not an activity *of* the perceptual system or of a specific sense-modality, but an activity of the whole organism."[14] If Wartofsky has convinced us, however, that prior modes of representation and "symbolic embodiments or objectifications of modes of action" determine human sense perceptions, rather than vice versa, we still have no connection established between sense perceptions and questions of ethics, for example, such as likely dominate "value systems." We do not have even hinted a demonstration that "value systems" themselves at any time determine what our sense perceptions tell us about the way the world is. Wartofsky does find that some sense perceptions are "aesthetically" contemplated, or regarded in a "disinterested" fashion, but this he takes to be a sometime effect of established perceptions, rather than a cause of them, and also, as he puts it, "off line." Moreover, even though some perceptions are determined "affectively," this hardly demonstrates "value systems" to be their originators. From Wartofsky's account it is far from clear whether established social "value systems" have anything to do with the "affective" quality of sense perceptions or their sometime-"aesthetic" features.

Some pragmatic or existentialist neglect of possible differences between epistemic and valuational matters may result from simple dodging of a needed demonstration of invariant correlation between them, roughly following advice given to a lady whose skirt hem is uneven: "Walk fast and no one will notice." More likely, however, it rests in large part upon a long-standing and pervasive conclusion that is taken to be no longer in need of demonstration: human values and valuations are capricious, irrational, or without universal basis of justification. This opinion may come from crazy-quilt sources: from testimony of artists who could not say "whence came" their works of "genius," from failure of those very past aesthetic theories summarized by Tatarkiewicz, from the wildness of Romanticism, from recognition of simple sensory fatigue, from the mercurial character of memory, from judgments that the logical positivists at least were right on the "emotive" nature of valuational language, from Socrates' distinction between knowledge and Ion's "divine inspiration," and from mathematical and physical science, which has never had anything to do with matters of value. Surely, when pragmatists, hermeneutists, or existentialists now bring their sights into line with valuational relativism, they depend upon a tradition that is older than theirs. To relativistic epistemologists, at least, aestheticians could have said with the American Indians, "We were here first."

Thus, perhaps to Rorty it goes without saying that if the pragmatist denies the veracity of intuitions about universals in epistemological matters, this could always have been denied about values and valuations. Thus, Wartofsky can end his essay by noting: "A history of human perception needs to investigate the historical changes in social praxis. . . . In this sense, the history of technology, of science and of art *become* [italics added] relevant contexts."[15] Thus, those who argue against claims for artificial intelligence find a congenial arena in interpretative theories of art. In detail, however, there are primary unanswered questions.

As C. I. Lewis lamented, philosophers have routinely ignored the role of memory in epistemology. How well, on that count alone, can their theories transfer to questions about artistic or aesthetic value? As the *Encyclopaedia Britannica* gives out its accounts with authority, the article on Marcel Proust informs us that in his opinion "the artist's task is to release from the buried world of unconscious memory the ever living reality to which habit makes us blind." The contributor then judges *A la recherche du temps perdu* as "one of the profoundest and most perfect achievements of the human imagination."[16] For philosophers who have ignored the role of memory in their epistemological theories, we have here an uneasy fit indeed.

Again in epistemological concern with sense perception, examples have been taken almost exclusively from visual sources. There is an apparently automatic assumption that vision is our primary sensory means to knowledge about the space-time world and that other media, such as hearing, do not offer significant contrary information. In his book *Perceiving*, Roderick Chisholm's concentration on the blue cabin on Mount Monadnock appears to be typical, and his brief references to hearing do not suggest that auditory perception might change his general conclusions at all. Such assumptions about hearing from an epistemological point of view appear to be entirely well taken. Information gathered from auditory sources is generally cruder, far less exact and complex than that taken from sight. (In jungle warfare, for example, a sound assumed to be made by a close-in sniper can, in the darkness, cause comrades to kill each other.) How does this relate, however, to the primary valuational criterion of *profundity* as a spatial, but nonvisual, metaphor? This particular value, at least, simply does not fit epistemologists' concentration on visual perception. It is as though Blomstedt's audience is in another world where seeing is entirely beside the point. From a pragmatic, existentialist, or hermeneutical general view, "facts and values" appear to be always inseparable; yet, on the question of visual origin, the particular value of profundity maintains a significant and probably permanent split between them.

Suffice it to say that a glaring difficulty in evaluation of philosophy itself from a pragmatic or existentialist base lies in a pervasive failure to demonstrate anything like a constant correlation between accounts of origins of knowledge and origins of human values and valuations. At present, we have at best general demonstrations that both products of knowledge and of art are results of human interpretation; hence, we are often said to live in many "possible worlds" of indeterminate limit. It behooves us to take a special look at two philosophers who have carefully laid their valuational cards on the table—one pragmatist, John Dewey, the other nonpragmatist, J. N. Findlay, who notes that what he has to say about "values and intentions" is "either such as would be felt (though not always obeyed) in every possible world, or my whole treatment is a mistake."[17] Perhaps in one or the other of these general accounts we can find a home for profundity. If we do not find it in either one of these authors, we may conclude with better reason what has often been concluded before: that general attempts to define or account for any and every human value or valuation whatsoever are better left untried, and that more detailed, piecemeal approaches, such as that undertaken in Chapter 3, are far more enlightening.

2

General Theories of Value: John Dewey and J. N. Findlay

I

The distinction of "possible worlds" was originally made by logicians as a reference to counterfactual conditionals, their relation to truth-functional and modal logic, and to the analysis of "dispositional predicates." The antecedent of the conditional "If I had been inspired, then I would have painted a great picture" is contrary to the fact that I was not inspired. It also identifies a "disposition" term—that is, committing us to accept as true that I *would* have painted a great picture, given that I had been inspired. A connection other than that of strict implication obtains between the antecedent and the consequent. "The peculiarity of dispositional predicates," Nelson Goodman observes, "is that they seem to be applied to things in virtue of possible rather than actual occurrences. . . . The problem . . . is to explain how dispositional predicates can be assigned to things solely on the basis of actual occurrences and yet in due accordance with ordinary or scientific usage." Goodman notes, however, that talk about possible entities and possible worlds "need not transgress the boundaries of the actual world. What we often mistake for the actual world is one particular description of it. And what we mistake for possible worlds are just equally true descriptions in other terms. We have come to think of the actual as one among many possible worlds. We need to repaint that picture. All possible worlds lie within the actual one."[1]

The logical and extensional distinction of possible worlds as counter-factual conditionals has gained ontological import, however; Goodman, in *Ways of Worldmaking*, notes:

> The alternative descriptions of motion, all of them in much the same terms and routinely transformable into one another, provide only a minor and rather pallid example of diversity of accounts of the world. Much more striking is the vast variety of versions and visions in the several sciences, in the works of different painters and writers, and in our perceptions as informed by these, by circumstances, and by our own insights, interests, and past experiences. Even with all illusory or wrong or dubious versions dropped, the rest exhibit new dimensions of disparity. Here we have no neat set of frames of reference, no ready rules for transforming physics, biology, and psychology into one another, and no way at all of transforming any of these into Van Gogh's vision, or Van Gogh's into Canaletto's. . . . Since the fact that there are many different world-versions is hardly debatable, and the question how many if any worlds-in-themselves there are is virtually empty, in what non-trivial sense are there, as Cassirer and like-minded pluralists insist, many worlds? Just this, I think: that many different world-versions are of independent interest and importance, without any requirement or presumption of reducibility to a single base.[2]

Although Goodman's illustrations undoubtedly include valuational as well as factual determination of some "visions" or "world-versions," the primary reference of "possible worlds" that is compatible with his logical distinction remains one of descriptions of ways the world *is*, rather than of ways the world aesthetically ought to be. Goodman does determine "rightness" of world versions in terms of what is "fit," but this is in reference to

> rightness of descriptions, representations, exemplifications, expressions—of design, drawing, diction, rhythm. . . . The differ-

ences between fitting a version to a world, a world to a version, and a version together or to other versions fade when the role of versions in making the worlds they fit is recognized. And knowing or understanding is seen as ranging beyond the acquiring of true beliefs to the discovering and devising of fit of all sorts.[3]

Thus, an understanding of cognition as a process or practice in accord with what is fit appears to relate to aesthetic judgment only as that judgment is reduced to one of a "fit" or "right" state of affairs. Within Goodman's extensional logic of dispositional predicates, and his understanding of "worlds" through the "discovering or devising of fit of all sorts," he has yet to suggest how one pattern is chosen over another equally fit possibility, or why one "devised" possibility that has not been thought of by anyone else stamps the deviser as a "creative genius," who at the moment, at least, seems to have discovered the best of all possible worlds.

Goodman's particular account of "possible worlds" is of worlds that emerge cognitively through description, representation, exemplification, or expression in accord with a logic of symbols. Any one or all of these functions, however, may yield possibilities that are dull as well as inspired, cliché as well as novel, shallow as well as deep. When the study of "aesthetics" is centered on origin of aesthetic values, or justification of aesthetic valuations, we are thus provided with little suggestion that we might ever find a relation between the fields of aesthetics and cognitive science. More central, however, is that through a theory that is entirely one of symbol function we have no basis to explain the value of profundity as a quality that is not expressed or symbolized.

It appears far more fruitful in seeking a basis of judgments of the particular value of profundity to look to theories that acknowledge the origin of all human values in a broader concept of cognitive function than Goodman's, and to empirical theories that are nonobjective, at least in the most general sense that all values are taken to originate in or to be caused by human minds. This will mean that they are not only logically intensional but are intentional as well. They will be "psychological," however, in broad or narrow senses of the term.

Those who have defended profundity in philosophy itself all appear to have been influenced (whether directly or through others) by Kant's recognition in the first and third *Critiques* of a certain trait of the human mind that keeps trying to frame a metaphysic even though it knows that it can never succeed. This trait also tries for universal justification of aesthetic evaluations even though they only rest in an imperative that demands agreement from everyone, but also in one that can never in fact be satisfied. They appear to presume or recognize an *intention* common to the human mind that moves from the particular to the universal, and that is identifiable independently of particular times and places, particular ontological stances, or particular aesthetic judgments. In this sense it will be a function that is context free and universal. J. N. Findlay's theory is psychological in the broad sense that it is thus intentional. He argues no invariant relation of valuations with sense perception, however, though sense perception may most often be centrally important. On the other hand, John Dewey's account of aesthetic value is empirical through and through and is couched in the vocabulary and concepts of early American psychology. This is a psychological account in the narrower sense of the term. It rests upon an understanding of mind function that is always dependent upon present and varying circumstances, thus of one that is never free of context.

Findlay's book is eclectic in origin. It is neither "idealistic" nor "naturalistic" in the usual senses of these terms, but it is based upon a far more comprehensive analysis of human consciousness than is found in Dewey's understanding of conscious experience. Neither of these theories entirely succeeds in accounting for all features of *profundity* as they are detailed in Chapter 1, although they do account for some of them. A primary flaw with both is in their inadequate treatment of memory. Here the authors are far from alone. Even C. I. Lewis, who appears to have been right in his complaint about neglect of memory by epistemologists, himself neglected memory in his account of valuation.[4]

II

Pragmatic theories of value are accounts of value emergence. Dewey's theory of the emergence of aesthetic value through interaction of the "organism with its environment" makes no attempt to locate any value as existing independently of human action within an environment. It is thus subjective in both the narrow and broad senses of *subjective*: human valuation is dependent upon the operation of particular minds, and in some respects it is also dependent upon operation characteristic of any and every mind. In this regard, Dewey's understanding of aesthetic value is compatible with profundity recognized as emerging from common human experience, as essentially social in origin.

Dewey regarded art as a language, not in the narrower sense that works of art are symbols, but in the broader sense that these works, together with other factors, communicate, via aesthetic experience, "life meanings" in a clarified, concentrated, and intensified form. If art were related to aesthetic experiences *only* as symbols are related to their referents, we would have to say that the meanings of aesthetic experiences are not supplied, even in part, by art products, and this is clearly not the case. In Dewey's view, this did not exclude the possibility that symbolic references may be incorporated in aesthetic experience. It simply indicated to him that artistic communication is not synonymous with symbolic relation, and that some more comprehensive analysis of aesthetic experience is needed in a demonstration that art is, in an expanded sense, a language. So far, we have compatibility with an understanding of the particular quality of profundity as a quality that taps something universal in human understanding and that is not something symbolized.

Single sense organs in human perception, such as the eye or the ear, never, in Dewey's opinion, function alone. "If the eye is the organ primarily active [in perception of color], then the color quality is affected by qualities of other senses overtly active in earlier experiences."[5] Moreover, none of these sensory coordinations can occur without the cooperation of motor habits that are similarly dependent upon past experiences. "Motor and sensory structure form a single apparatus and effect a single function" (AE, 255). On this point, Maurice Merleau-Ponty's view of the coordination of sense perception with the entire body is very like that of Dewey.

Judging from what we now posit of prenatal development of sense perception, Dewey's account is at best an overgeneralization. Although presumably a fetus does not yet have visual perception, it does have perceptual auditory apparatus developed by its fifth month, and postnatal observations indicate that a fetus has been hearing for a significant time prenatally. But if a fetus has developed a "motor-sensory structure" before birth, it is difficult to understand what a specifically prenatal auditory-motor structure might be. Dewey often characterized functions of what he termed scattered and inchoate "native impulse" as typical of newborns, as though he thought that humans enter the spatial world without any established motor habits or any prior sense perception. He evidently understood all sense perception and all experience deriving from it to obtain postnatally in the space-time world. This is compatible with opinion of current writers like Rorty and Wartofsky that there are no "natural starting points" of human sense perception. Still, if Dewey was mistaken, this criticism is hardly fatal to his general pragmatic account of value emergence through human experience. It does, however, suggest that there may be some particular sense perceptions and values attached to them that are universal to humans, thus at least some sense perception that, historically speaking, marks a natural biological starting point.

Dewey regarded psychological functions as largely habitual. "The word habit," he noted, "may seem twisted somewhat from its customary usage. . . . But we need a word to express that kind of human activity which is influenced by prior activity, and in that sense acquired; which contains within itself a certain ordering or systematization of minor elements of action; which is projective, dynamic in quality; ready for overt manifestation; and which is operative in some subdued subordinate form even when not obviously dominating activity. Habit even in its ordinary usage comes nearer to denoting these facts than any other word."[6] When habits are latent, not yet active, Dewey also called them "attitudes" or "dispositions."

These acquired, "organized energies," these "sensitivities to certain classes of stimuli," these "standing predilections and aversions," sometimes actively dominant, sometimes latent and potential, take many forms (HNC, 25, 37, 42, 76). There are habitual motor and sensory activities; habitual desires and ways of seeking their fulfillment; habitual expectations, interests, memories, and associations; habits that are conscious and unconscious; habits that are emotive and affective; habits characterized by purpose, attention, inhibition, observation, imagination, and deliberation; and habits peculiar to individuals and habits of social custom. Most broadly, however, all of these habits are either "routine" or "intelligent," that is, they either function as repetitions of previous experiences or as "vital energies" or "forces" in the creation of new experiences.

In Dewey's opinion, established habits are never compatible with all aspects of the environment, and at some time this environment will frustrate their function. "When old habitual activity meets environmental obstacles, there arises within the organism demand for a changed environment, a demand which can be achieved only by some modification and rearrangement of old habits" (HNC, 53). Need, desire, or demand for a changed environment is perhaps the most immediate function of old habit that is faced with environmental obstacles. But other activities are also apparent. The greater the obstacles in the path of habitual activity, the more the organism becomes fully *conscious* of this activity, and of the situation in which it is found. "Consciousness (which marks the place where the formed disposition and the immediate situation touch and interact) . . . is the more acute and intense in the degree of the readjustments that are demanded, approaching nil as the contact is frictionless and interaction fluid" (AE, 266).

In the light of psychological observations made since the dominance of early American psychology, it would be as foolhardy to deny consciousness to the fetus as it would be to deny it all sense perception. Yet whatever consciousness or awareness it has does not appear to connect with Dewey's references to the challenges of the postnatal environment. The prenatal environment is apparently constant in all of its aspects, and any radical change in these may spell death to the fetus. Moreover, unless it has suffered a hearing loss, when a newborn responds to a playback of sounds of its mother's circulatory system it responds as do all other newborns. Within sixty seconds it is asleep. If it had not been conscious or aware of these sounds prenatally, we could hardly explain this invariant response. We need also to posit in the newborn a memory or recall of its prenatal state that might in some sense be considered a habit but that, far from eliciting a demand for a new environment, produces an immediate return to an earlier one. It may not be necessary to trace profundity in auditory art to anything prenatal, but, on the *possibility* that it can be so traced, we have now reached a serious difficulty in understanding emergence of the quality of profundity through Dewey's pragmatic account. The crucial problem, however, arises in his general treatment of the emergence of aesthetic value in human postnatal experience.

Among the most apparent habitual functions that cooperate with conscious activity are those of emotion, affection, attention, purpose, deliberation, and imagination. "Psychologically deep seated needs cannot be stirred to find fulfillment . . . without . . . emotion and affection" (AE, 257). Any extensive frustration of existing habits stimulates an emotive and affective response in the organism. Moreover, the very act of seeking resolution to an environmental obstacle implies seeking with purpose and with attention to the fulfillment of that purpose. "Roughly speaking," Dewey notes, "the course of forming aims is as follows. The beginning is with a wish, an emotional reaction against the present state of things and a hope for something different. Action fails to connect satisfactorily with surrounding conditions. Thrown back upon itself, it projects itself in an imagination of a scene which if it were present would afford satisfaction. . . . We have to fall back upon what has already happened . . . , and study it to see *how* it happened. This knowledge joined to wish creates a purpose" (*HNC*, 234–35).

It is intelligent habits that function in studying what has happened, seeing how it has happened, projecting in imagination a scene that would afford satisfaction, and thereby developing conscious purpose and attention. These habits, like routine ones, are acquired through past experience; unlike routine habits, however, they are active in adapting those existing habits that embody it to the present, novel situation. Intelligent habits are deliberative and imaginative. They "set up an attitude of criticism, of inquiry," predominantly characterized by "observation, remembering, contriving, and forecasting" (*HNC*, 77, 170). They function as experiments to determine "in imagination, not in overt fact, what the various lines of possible action are really like" (*HNC*, 190). Choice is "simply hitting in imagination upon an object which furnishes an adequate stimulus to the recovery of overt action" (*HNC*, 192).

To the degree that deliberation is rational, it "flexibly remakes old aims and habits, [and] institutes perception and love of new ends and acts." It does so by a process of selecting and combining, of "reinforc[ing], inhibit[ing], [and] redirect[ing] habits already working or stirr[ing] up others which had not previously actively entered in" (*HNC*, 192, 198).

Through resistances and resolutions of energies set up by conscious intelligent activity, old habits gain new order, new form. Prior experiences relevant to the solution of a situation are now neither dismissed nor "dwelt among as they have been in the past" (*AE*, 138). Memories, "though not necessarily conscious [now] feed present observations" (*AE*, 89); "needed disassociations are effected" (*AE*, 250); interests develop "push and centralizing tendency," and become the conscious and "dynamic force in selection and assemblage of materials" (*AE*, 66, 75, 95, 255). Emotions which, without the resistances of intelligent action, would have been mere "blind discharge of energy" are now both "stabilized and heightened" and color all imaginative action. "Anticipation . . . guides as well as stimulates effort," and desire is "converted into systematic plans" (*AE*, 62, 63). Suspense is built up toward the final resolution of opposing energies, "the attitudes of the self are informed with meaning," and "consciousness [that] . . . is turbid when meanings are undergoing reconstruction in an undetermined direction . . . becomes clear as decisive meaning emerges" (*HNC*, 55, 77, 98).

That phase of human experience which marks the resolution of opposing energies, and that gives clear meaning to the entire process undergone, Dewey calls "consummatory." It is this phase in the process of any human activity that gives the activity primary aesthetic value. And when consummation is emphasized above deliberation, or above other practical uses that the deliberation might have, this total activity, that includes deliberation as well as consummation, is termed aesthetic.

The consummatory phase of experience is predominantly marked by emotion and "intuition," intuition that is a "meeting [fusion] of the old and new in which the readjustment involved in every form of consciousness is effected suddenly by means of a quick and unexpected harmony, which in its bright abruptness is like a flash of revelation; although in fact it is prepared for by long and slow incubation" (AE, 266). It is through deliberative and imaginative activities that the meanings of old habits are selected, simplified, abridged, and condensed. It is through emotional intuitive consummation that they are finally clarified, coordinated, intensified, and concentrated. It is at this point that Dewey's analysis provides a good explanation of how, in an intuitive grasp of profundity, the very distinction between "subject" and "object" is blurred. This may be added to the other points of compatibility with traits of profundity noted above.

Consummatory experience always presents something new. In art, this means that unimpeded activity of routine habit is the very antithesis of aesthetic process, that artists cannot foresee in all detail the nature of their products before they are completed, and that appreciators must find through these products more than repetition of past experience. It means that, although both creators and appreciators of art products must go essentially through the same processes of selection, simplification, clarification, abridgement, and condensation, they must also add individually something of their own point of view and interest (AE, 54). This phase of Dewey's analysis does not explain the maximally positive value of profundity that appears to be primordially old and a context-free universal.

Although Dewey's understanding of aesthetic value is one characterizing experience of all humans, the content of that experience cannot be new if it is universal. "Intuition" at the consummatory point, resulting from fusion of "the old and new," is not the same as an intuitive sensus communis. Dewey's account cannot explain the fundamental value in the reiteration, as of something not new but always known, that "all men are brothers." By "psychologically deep-seated needs," Dewey may have meant needs that all humans have in common, such as those listed by Blanshard—for food, drink, sex, friendship, or knowledge. But Dewey did not provide an account of psychologically deep-seated needs in aesthetic experience as clearly universal to humans. However necessarily connected with "emotion" and "affection" they may be, he did not indicate that such needs are *recognized* by any or every individual (at least at one time or another) as needs common to humanity and worth satisfying *on that count*, regardless of the particular conditions of time or place. Moreover, where he specifically mentioned the emotion of love, it was "love of new ends and acts," which did not apparently relate to what is commonly termed "love of humanity" or "love of life."

Dewey's analysis presents us with a need to adjust discrepancy in vocabulary. From any pragmatic account, it seems that intuition of profundity as a context-free universal cannot be taken at face value, that the intuitive testimony is not what it seems. We thus appear to have two choices: either we side with Rorty's interpretation that "the pragmatist does not think there is anything like" a context-free universal, and thus deny the veracity of this particular intuition; or we conclude that the pragmatic accounts of Dewey and others who largely follow his analysis of aesthetic matters are overgeneralizations. Not all intuitive "flashes of insight," however "immediate" they may appear, are results of "long and slow incubation" throughout a Hegelian experiential challenge. We may here multiply rhetorical questions: Where in the quality of profundity is there evidence of the challenge, the upset of routine habits, the origin in complexity, the long and slow incubation of the final lightning intuitive flash, the ever-forward thrust to new solutions for new problems?

The present-future orientation of any pragmatic understanding of origin of human values and justification of human valuations not only rests upon a conviction that there is no biological "starting point" that henceforth governs, if only partially, what particular values and valuations will be. This orientation also rests upon a narrow and unilateral understanding of memory—of what human memory is and of how it functions. Dewey thought of memories as routine and devoid of value, aesthetic or otherwise, until they are somehow challenged by present problem situations. Their continued *significance*, therefore, is dependent upon an adjustment and change in them. It is clear that, for Dewey, you can't go home again and should not want to. His understanding of memory as a contributor to aesthetic experience was temporarily unidirectional, from past to present to future. The aesthetic import of a memory of times past, then, will depend upon how it "feeds present situations." It will not be taken somehow to contain within itself a primary and primal value established in the past and recalled without connection with present circumstances.

In this, Proust's hope to "release from the buried world of unconscious memory the ever living reality to which habit makes us blind" is clearly incompatible. We may note that what Marcel remembered in that famous passage in Swann's Way could not all have been originally experienced at the same time, as it was later brought back upon his present tasting of a madeleine dipped in tea. "The flowers in M. Swann's park, the water-lillies on the Vivonne, the good folk of the village and their little dwellings and the parish church and the whole of Combray and its surroundings" could not all have been experienced at once, and what of aesthetic value Marcel found in the total recall—the "shudder" through his whole body and the "all-powerful joy"—were probably nowhere experienced that way in his youth, though they were undoubtedly valued in other ways. Whatever telescoping effects memory of past events may have, however, we have yet to explain through a pragmatic theory of the emergence of value the source of the primary aesthetic value that Marcel found retrogressively and independently of his present circumstances. It was not the recall of past times that triggered new value in the present taste of the madeleine in tea, but vice versa.

There is yet another incompatibility between the quality of profundity and Dewey's account of value emergence. If profundity is a quality to which the complexities of the present "buzzing, blooming confusion" make us blind, when on certain auspicious circumstances it briefly shines through, it appears not only to be context free but also to be an essential simple. What "bond" did Blomstedt refer to that was created among all those who experienced the same performance of Beethoven's Ninth Symphony? The very one, so it seems, that repeatedly causes concertgoers to exclaim once more: "Music is a universal language." Even if *language* is taken metaphorically, what is intuited as universally understood also appears to be unanalyzably simple. This corresponds also with the frequent question about a great deal of "profound" music: "How can anything so unanalyzably simple be so moving?" This does not count out aesthetic qualities of "greatness" in highly complex forms of auditory art—contrapuntal fugues or African polyrhythmic drumming, for example. It seems that these complex forms do not lend themselves to the attribute *profound* nearly so well as do certain simple melodic turns, nor do those simple turns (that may reduce us to tears) alone lend themselves to the attribute *greatness* so well as do the complex forms. But we concentrate here on profundity, not on greatness.

In his article on Dewey in *The Encyclopedia of Philosophy*, Richard J. Bernstein notes:

The ideas contained in Dewey's *Art as Experience* . . . provided a surprise for many readers. Popular versions of his philosophy had so exaggerated the role of the practical and the instrumental that art and aesthetic experience seemed to have no place in his philosophical outlook. More perceptive commentators realized that Dewey was making explicit a dimension of his view of experience that had always been implicit and essential to an understanding of his philosophy. The meaning and role of art and aesthetic quality are crucial for understanding Dewey's views on logic, education, democracy, ethics, social philosophy, and even technology.[7]

If there is any correlation between a man's philosophy and his own perceptiveness, however, we could have found little in Dewey's own interests and aptitudes to correlate with those usually termed *aesthetic*. His colleagues and graduate students were well aware that music annoyed him. In the preface to *Art as Experience* Dewey observed that "I am somewhat embarrassed in an effort to acknowledge indebtedness to other writers on the subject. . . . My greatest indebtedness is to Dr. A. C. Barnes. . . . I have had the benefit of conversations with him through a period of years, many of which occurred in the presence of the unrivaled collection of pictures he has assembled. The influence of these conversations, together with that of his books, has been a chief factor in shaping my own thinking about the philosophy of esthetics. Whatever is sound in this volume is due more than I can say to the great educational work carried on in the Barnes Foundation" (*AE*, vii–viii). According to his students, Dewey was also notoriously dull in class, droning his lectures as he looked out of the window.

Thus, if "the meaning and role of art and aesthetic quality" were somehow providing an underpinning for Dewey's "views on logic, education, democracy, ethics, social philosophy, and even technology," we may wonder whence came his aesthetic insight. From Dewey's own comment, we visualize Dr. Barnes and his "pictures" as a chief source of enlightenment. This correlates well with Dewey's apparent empirical domination by visual perception in his examples, as of the instrumental value of the pots and pans of a Vermont kitchen, or of being lost in the woods. It even seemed to pervade his favorite jokes, as in the answer the Vermont farmer gave to a traveler's question of how to get to a distant town: "If I were you, I wouldn't start from here." Or in his story, recounted by Herbert Schneider, of how the Vermont farmer weighs a pig: First he finds an evenly shaped board and carefully lays it across the farm fence until it just balances. Then he puts the pig on one end and piles rocks on the other until they *just* balance. Then he guesses the weight of the rocks. (Dewey's favorite jokes were far from knee-slapping howlers.) In any event, it may be suggested that his stress upon environmental complexities and obstacles to reach a conclusion that does not accommodate an aesthetic value that is simple in origin, and that seems simple in intuition as well, may derive from such exclusive domination of visual perception as almost to identify the empirical with the visual.

It is probably true that at least some of the concepts and distinctions of early American psychology need updating, and that a possible valuational role of auditory perception may differ from those of visual perception. This much alone, however, does not appear fatal to Dewey's pragmatic aesthetic program. Yet in spite of this and in spite of the points of compatibility with certain features of profundity noted above, there appear conflicts that are fundamental and ineradicable. Dewey was led to deny from his pragmatism that there can be any intrinsic value. That the value of profundity appears to be intrinsic as well as universal and context free, that it fails to vary in degree, is nonvisual, and is in basis retrogressive, appear in rudimentary conflict with a general account that finds values to be instrumental, context dependent, visual in empirical origin, and present-future oriented. When it comes to a choice between the major features of the profundity metaphor and those of a pragmatically analyzed aesthetic experience, these extended discrepancies do not allow an exchange of one package for the other. However many aesthetic experiences we may find that fit Dewey's understanding, we must conclude that his account is at best an overgeneralization and does not provide sufficient philosophical backing for such prevalent undemonstrated assumptions about all of "human values" as those considered in Chapter 1. Contemporary authors may take exception in varying ways to Dewey's aesthetics. But on such fundamental features as the above, to the extent that they remain pragmatists the conclusion stands: *profundity* simply does not fit any pragmatic mold. Small wonder, then, that Rorty found a need to argue it away.

III

With acknowledgment of indebtedness to Franz Brentano and Edmund Husserl, J. N. Findlay's hope in *Values and Intentions* to present a picture

applicable to "every possible world" rests on an account of human
consciousness made independently of what consciousness is *of* and independently of different contents and objectives in different "orientations"
or "modes" of mind—specifically the modes of belief, action and endeavor, and wish and will. Just with regard to describing differences
between acts of believing and acts of judgment or opinion forming alone,
however, Findlay acknowledges that we are presented with "almost
insuperable problems for philosophical description."[8] Perhaps this is a
primary reason that his entire exposition is heavily metaphorical, as
though it is only by metaphor that any description of this difficult terrain
can be made at all. Findlay's resultant exposition, however, often becomes
virtually impossible to elucidate by paraphrase, and fair summaries of it
are extremely difficult to make. In spite of these difficulties, Findlay's
detailed and insightful account of consciousness, upon which his entire
subsequent analysis rests, is well worth a summary examination.

1. Consciousness, Findlay notes, is essentially "*dispersed* over a large
number of successive acts, which need not be close or continuous in
time" (VI, 34). He regards this view of mental life as "basically in
harmony with that of Brentano." He finds in the basic trait of dispersion
of consciousness reason for our "deep distrust" of philosophical explanations of mental life in terms of "built-in" forms that "seem not to square
with the looseness and openness favoured by empirical and experimental
approaches." Findlay does not, however, identify this dispersion of consciousness with "stream of consciousness," nor does he posit in it a
requirement of retention or memory of the immediate or distant past. In
this he sidesteps Husserl's distinctions of "retention" and "protention"
(*Phenomenology of Internal Time Consciousness*).

2. Besides its essential dispersion, consciousness evidences two "poles"
of what "is consciously clear, central, focal, relieved, regarded or emphasized, and what may by contrast be said to be obscure, marginal, in the
background, half-regarded or under-emphasized. Alternatively we may
state the opposition in terms of our own full conscious aliveness to certain
things and features of things, and our own ancillary half-aliveness to
other things and features which are, in no necessarily physical sense,
merely neighbouring" (VI, 47). We are cautioned, however, that if
something is singled out or taken note of or especially emphasized, this
may very well be something that is vague or problematic, such as an
"indeterminate sound maximally present to the mind" (VI, 48). Moreover, the distinction between "conscious aliveness" and "half-aliveness"

is not the same as that between active and passive consciousness, although "it has intimate interrelations" (VI, 50).

Findlay argues that this polar distinction is based on "the plainest of phenomenal differences."

> That by a metaphorical use of the words "clear", "obscure", etc., we should succeed in directing attention to the most basic feature of conscious experience is not at all remarkable; it is through the medium of metaphor that discourse first penetrates what are the unshowable reaches of the mind, though, once broached by metaphor, the unshowables lose their unshowability and the metaphors their metaphorical character. . . .

> If being consciously alive to anything involves, therefore, some position between the twin poles of the consciously clear and obscure, it involves also a position between the twin poles of yet another antithesis, which, following Husserl, we may call that between a *fulfilled* and an *unfulfilled* awareness. Conscious orientations have as their one extreme a state in which that of which they are conscious is fully and concretely present, actually apprehended or "given": at their extreme they have a state in which what they are *of* is merely indicated, foreshadowed, vestigially suggested, present merely in a reduced, attenuated or surrogative form. Husserl's metaphor of an "empty" conscious intention to which certain intuitive materials provide the appropriate "filling", hits the distinction as well as possible. For in both cases we have fundamentally the *same* consciousness, with the same scope and the same range of near or remote application, but in the one case it grasps, as it were, vainly in the void, whereas in the other case it is "fulfilled" or "satisfied". What it is important to stress is that *both* poles of the above antithesis are essential to anything that we should care to call "consciousness" or "awareness", and not only both poles, but also a continuous, restless shuttling between them. (VI, 51, 52)

In what appears to result from combining the first and second features of consciousness—dispersion and the poles of clarity and obscurity—Findlay links "profundity" of consciousness to the *duration* of fulfilled awareness. Thus he notes "the turning of the gaze in an actually or symbolically suitable direction, a real or symbolic manual exploration, an increase in

the force and accuracy of acts inspired by what we heed and a corresponding decrease in irrelevant activities, the profounder, more lasting effect
on the subsequent course of our performance, etc. etc." (VI, 51). It is
unclear at this stage of Findlay's exposition whether he takes this feature
of fulfilled consciousness to be more *valuable* than that of "ancillary half-
aliveness," but it is probable that, at least in an Aristotelian sense of
consciousness as working out its full nature, he does presuppose some
positive value in an extended fulfilled awareness over what might be
termed scatterbrained.

Findlay's understanding of the "polar" mode of consciousness is analogous to Dewey's references to "acute and intense" consciousness, or "fully
conscious" mental activity, as contrasted with "frictionless" or "fluid"
activity between organism and environment when there is no evident
problem situation. It does not, however, depend upon a relation to any
particular environmental condition in order to be identified, such that it
should be perfectly possible from Findlay's understanding for consciousness to be of an entirely nonproblematic situation and yet be "fulfilled."
Once more, however, he fails to consider any possible function of memory
in consciousness fulfillment, especially in the "profounder" one of extended duration, and he treats different modes of consciousness within
the frame of an ongoing present. The latter treatment appears to be less
psychologically plausible than Dewey's, but, on the other hand, Findlay's
account appears to run a better chance of explaining at least one feature
of profundity than does Dewey's, since it is given independently of any
particular environmental conditions and therefore as a function that is
context free.

All this, however, does not mean that Findlay regards consciousness as
entirely free from what is "present to sense."

> The paradigm case of fulfilment is of course the case of the direct
> "presence to sense". . . . There is a sense, too, in which sensory
> fulfilment may be said to be more "basic" and "fundamental" than
> fulfilment of any other sort, inasmuch as the most removed mental
> orientations all "point back", perhaps after a large number of
> intermediate stages, to possible illustration in terms of the deliv-
> erances of sense. The least palpable features of our inner experi-
> ence have a bond, tenuous and analogical, but essential, with
> what can be sensuously shown, and it is likewise obvious that
> there must be such bonds even in the case of the most refined
> abstractions of the natural and the philosophical sciences. The

particular form of our "sensibility" may be an empirical accident, but without something which at least in an analogous manner can fulfil our conscious references, there can be no such thing as "consciousness" at all. (*VI*, 53)

It is evidently one thing for sensa to be *present* in fulfillment of consciousness and another thing for sense perception to have been present at one time or another in the past, but not now, such that it "analogously . . . can fulfil our conscious references." But if present orientations "point back" or have "a bond tenuous and analogical, but essential," Findlay does not explain this occurrence by recognition of any such conscious function as Husserl termed "retention." How does such a "bond" emerge? How are analogies recognized?

Once more, Findlay observes that presence to sense "plainly provides the foundation for all identifications, for the notion of the *same* thing as the subject of a large number of distinct attributions, and hence, in the last resort, of the very notion of an *object* of thought or perception. For it is plain that it is in some sense possible to satisfy a large number of distinct mental references by means of what may be called the *same* sensory situation: while the impact on our senses remains in some sense unaltered, we can fulfil such varied intentions as those of 'something green', 'something smooth' . . ." (*VI*, 53, 54). But if this is in "some sense possible," Findlay does not tell us in what sense it is so. Again, he seems to overlook some needed reference to memory, at least in the limited meaning of retention.

Findlay distinguishes fulfilled and unfulfilled awareness from "*actual* and merely *dispositional* awareness. . . . There is a whole world of difference between actually grasping a pattern or meaning, even if not carried out illustratively, and being merely *able* to find one's way about it, or to develop it correctly, though the whole life-work of Wittgenstein has been devoted to its obscuration. . . . [It should be shown that] things which belong together profoundly, do not necessarily always go together in their actual existence . . ." (*VI*, 55). Once more, Findlay links profundity in conscious mental life to temporal constancy and pervasiveness of conscious content, but without reference to memory or retention. Rather, putting the first two "modes" of consciousness together, we get a picture of a dispersed consciousness through which all kinds of partially fulfilled awareness may hover or dart in and out, without ever establishing themselves as clearly relevant to the present focus. (I will, later on, compare this picture with that of parallel processing in artificial intelligence.) In anticipation of Chapter 3, which traces profundity judgments specifically to prenatal auditory perception, however, the following extended quotation should look like an unwarranted exaggeration.

> Just as the wide range of what we are aware of is chequered over by a constantly changing pattern of conscious clearness and obscurity, so it is also chequered over by a complex, ever-changing pattern of fulfilment and non-fulfilment. This is true even of the immediate situation present to our senses. When we *see* an object before us, there is a more or less clear segment of its features and dimensions of which we enjoy a *fulfilled* consciousness, while there remains a wide range of further features and dimensions of which we have only an *unfulfilled* awareness, a fact which may be the basis of many misleading sense-datum analyses, but which is none the less fundamental for all that. . . .
>
> We may here note, in general, that to recognize a close and necessary connection between unfulfilled conscious approaches and the corresponding fulfilment, is not to hold, with an earlier empiricism, that every unfulfilled notional awareness necessarily has an origin, at least as regards its elementary components, in some wholly fulfilled, empirical awareness. Much less will it commit us to that modern form of empiricism which not only holds that every unfulfilled notional awareness, at the price of having definite content, must necessarily terminate in a thinkable fulfilment, but which even goes further and holds that we must be able to *verify*, or go some distance towards verifying, every assertion involving an unfulfilled awareness. The content of an unfulfilled awareness is in fact, on this view, identified with all the infinitely many circumstances which bear on its verification, an extension which so strains the notion of meaning or significance as to destroy it altogether. (VI, 55, 56)

If we think in auditory rather than in visual terms, it can be plausibly shown that much of what Findlay says here is not always true. It can be shown that "infinitely many circumstances" do not always condition unfulfilled awarenesses, that some sense perceptions have few unfulfilled "features and dimensions," and that in accord with early empiricism there *is* a fulfilled sensory origin lying behind later unfulfilled awarenesses. It will be suggested, furthermore, that it is just this *sort* of essentially simple conscious "fulfillment" that lies behind valuational judgments of profundity, at least in the auditory domain.

3. There is another variable mode of consciousness which Findlay calls conscious "light," conscious "approach," or conscious "intent." This is connected with "aspects" or "moments" in which objects are viewed and often requires single words or verbal combinations to be recognized and studied. "I cannot say *how* something is appearing to my senses, or how it is being approached in my thought, except by making use of the words I would have applied to it, or used to describe it, had such application or description been called for" (*VI*, 60).

Like words, Findlay takes conscious lights to be universal or general, and hence may be "said to condense and 'telescope' the whole use of [a] word" (*VI*, 62). Some lights do not require words at all, but others, such as "universal" lights and those "which exploit such words as 'any', 'all', etc., probably require the aid of verbal symbols to fix them; it is only by formulating them verbally that we can come to have them" (*VI*, 66).

Borrowing heavily from Kant's "Analytic of the Beautiful" in the *Critique of Judgment*, Findlay later identifies aesthetic value primarily by back reference to conscious "lights" and "clarity."

4. Consciousness is sometimes "reflexive." There is a "presence of consciousness to consciousness" that is not something that always occurs, but is certainly "not rare or adventitious." This reflexive consciousness "involves the paradox of something actually had, that is also not had, and something present that is also not present, without any sizeable distinction to tone down this contradiction" (*VI*, 71).

Most interesting and pertinent to his later analyses of aesthetic judgments is Findlay's extension of mind's consciousness of itself-as-conscious in a universal "light" to existence of other minds. There is a tendency to " 'project' the findings of [mind's] inward turned researches 'outwards', to surround itself . . . with a supporting circle of 'other minds'. To be aware of objects as objects of consciousness . . . may be held to lead . . . to the thought of the possible presence of such objects to other possible conscious intentions, which are not to be found among those we now execute, and hence to the thought of other possible consciousnesses themselves. . . . [Moreover] other persons . . . give hardness and body to the interior society that we carry about with us and that we each intrinsically are" (*VI*, 70, 74). Findlay astutely notes here that the universal light of other consciousness precludes experiences of other minds as being anything other than themselves generalities or universals. Thus, "the one thing strictly incommunicable among disjoined minds is thought to be the *particularity* of their conscious references: what is 'this experience' for one can only be 'such and such an experience' for another" (*VI*, 73).

5. Finally, Findlay analyzes consciousness as having an implicit scope that "spreads out widely, perhaps indefinitely," beyond particular limits. Scope is thought of as "varying directions of relevant development" that "constitute a sort of sidelong intentionality additional to the straightforward: our states of mind are not only of this or that directly, but also of many things *implicitly* or *indirectly*. Of this we are sometimes aware reflexively: we may *feel* how our thought presses on beyond the bounds of what it principally illuminates. But since, for the most part, we neither feel nor know how our mind puts forth its 'cognitive energies', we judge of this sidelong intentionality only through its outcome, from the things and aspects that it brings to light" (*VI*, 75).

There is, Findlay notes, a *nisus* of consciousness, a "pressing on to a state of fulfilled awareness" that sometimes involves projecting reflections on inner experiences we are having "into the outward pantomime of others." There is a tendency "on the one hand to *impose* our conscious orientations on others, and on the other hand, to *conform* our orientations to theirs . . . , a tendency, therefore, towards an *impartial equalization* of the 'lights' in which things are viewed or thought of by different persons, or by the same person on different occasions" (*VI*, 89, 90). Findlay notes that increase in scope of a conscious "light," the rising "to a wider and wider universality," may be carried out "in the field of characters, relationships, etc., in the manner formalized in the higher functional calculus. . . . The whole line of advance . . . may be native to consciousness, but it could hardly be carried far without the use of symbols" (*VI*, 91).

The foregoing analysis of "modes" or "orientations" of consciousness forms a background for those states of mind having built-in endorsements, approvals, assessments of what is desirable, or preferences. Although Findlay does not put it this way, we may regard these as second-order modes, which he divides into three main types: modes of belief, modes of action and endeavor, and modes of wish and will. Without attempting a summary of his three chapters on these modes, it is notable that evaluation in each of them is found to be grounded in a process of universalizing. Thus, beliefs are seen to be grounded in "approvability" that is subject to norms, standards, or a "probable light" that can be "a real or true light only in the sense of a light for all believers" (*VI*, 115). Thus, "it is part of what we mean by a 'valuation' that it should have acquired a certain measure of fixity, and that it should have acquired this fixity by a process of careful trying out. The firmament of values cannot be peopled by passing meteors whose place and brightness changes rapidly: its contents must be constant . . . involv[ing] a movement towards the abstract and generic" (VI, 209). Thus, "hedonic" values existing in satisfactions of various wants and pleasures are justified as they are found to be "impersonal." "The impersonal attitude is essentially concerned with the universal, and with the particular as embodying the universal" (VI, 239).

Of special note here are Findlay's references to "sympathy for others" that emerges in an impersonal extension of personal sensory and emotional experiences.

> The would-be impersonal judge will . . . have to rise to the maximally vivid view of his object by employing every kind of imaginative or perceptual fulfilment. . . . Where spontaneous imagination fails, he will have to have recourse either to actually being in certain situations, or to hearing or reading of them in some detail. The fulfilments necessary will, further, have to be of the emotions, feelings and other experiences had, or possibly had, by the persons studied, and it is here that the techniques of sympathetic self-extension will be of supreme importance. Sympathy for the axiologist is a technique as indispensable as are observation and experiment for the scientist, and as little involving ultimate partiality or sentiment. For to the sympathy that immerses itself in the peculiar standpoint and interests of a given person, must be added the sympathy which immerses itself in the standpoint and interests of all other parties to the same transaction. . . .
>
> Our standard-setting impersonal reactions—how we feel that the detached, impartial, but also deeply sympathetic and understanding, person would feel—must also be affected by the tendencies native to the consciousness of objects. . . . One will tend, in particular, towards the regular extension of pattern, towards the filling in of gaps and the levelling of anomalies. The profound grasp of remote analogy from which spring most of the bridging hypotheses of science, will be no less significant in the realm of values. (VI, 168–69)

This interpretation of valuational justification stands in marked contrast with pragmatic instrumental accounts. On the basis of it, Findlay

himself holds instrumental values to be "merely instrumental" and linked
to "unserious wants." Thus, he finds that "unserious wants prolong
patterns impinging relatively externally on the conscious person—as
when we enter into other people's wants, or desire to impress them with
our sympathy, etc. etc. Such shallowly rooted wants thrive in consciousness and behaviour while a parent impulse sustains them, but languish as
soon as it languishes, and so are felt to be insincere, rootless in the
personality. Merely instrumental wants are among these rootless, evanes-
cent wants, and in all unseriousness and insincerity we in fact use a want
as a mere means to something else" (VI, 166). It is hard to find any
passage more contrary to Dewey's understanding of primary instrumental
value emerging from the most serious of problem situations. With its
basis in a universal human understanding that is context free, however,
the particular value of profundity is explained better by Findlay's stress
on universalizing of conscious states than it is by Dewey's account. Taking
shallow to be a contrary metaphor of deep, the above quotation is
reminiscent of Findlay's frequent use of profound in his elucidation of
fundamental and pervasive features of all human consciousness.

Beyond this, however, it is difficult to reconcile all of Findlay's varying
and sometimes inconsistent uses of deep and profound. For the most part,
he employs the terms in the way just seen: as having final reference to
what is universal to consciousness, especially to what is temporally
pervasive in its full function, and of which on occasion we are reflexively
aware. In many uses, however, these references appear free from emotional involvement, such that, for example, in reflexive awareness of
conscious activity we would not typically be said to be "deeply moved."
Findlay reserves a discussion of emotion and feeling for his analysis of the
mode of "action and endeavour" and the mode of "wish and will," both
of which are taken up after his analysis of "belief," where emotion does
not play a significant role. He also relates emotion to "values of welfare,"
one type of which he terms "hedonic"—those values linked to "pleasure"
and "liking."

The following observations come closest to our own understanding of
profundity:

> Obviously emotional life cannot be complete if its expansion ends
> in the voluntary, surface musculature: it must sink down to the
> deep, slow, hidden Lethe and Cocytus of our bodily life, and to
> the faint echoes which come up from their stirred depths. The
> direction towards emotionality is a direction towards detachment

from the exactly cognized object and the well-regulated response: it is a direction towards the personal *immanence* in which Tetens saw the specific differentia of feeling. Being such a direction, it must move towards the least practical, least object-bound of expressions, and these are no other than the disturbances of our inner bodily economy, and the barely describable sense-experiences issuing from them. It is in the queer language of the vitals, the formless changes of the breath, and the warm tides of the blood overstreaming their normal floodgates, that our emotional life has, and must have, its culminating expressions, even the preternatural calm of the religious ecstasy demanding an abnormal slowing down or arrest of these same processes. (VI, 168–69)

This expansive connection of emotion with things "deep," however, does not entirely square with Findlay's other identification of "depth" with "hedonic" values that are linked to individual pleasure and do not significantly differ from each other in point of comparative worth. Thus, in questions related to our satisfaction of wants:

Satisfactions cannot be ordered in a single lineal order of greater and less. There are, it is plain, satisfactions which are "deep", in so far as springing from wants radical and architectonic; there are satisfactions termed "broad", inasmuch as fulfilling a large range of interlinked wants; there are satisfactions classed as "lofty", in so far as springing from wants of a gratuitous, disinterested, admiration-evoking sort, and there are satisfactions "deeply felt", the "deeply felt" differing from the "deep" in its reflectively evident character: there are, finally, satisfactions classed as "exquisite", in so far as springing from some rare, little exercised or seldom adequately satisfied side of our nature. None of these differences are differences in anything other than our satisfactions, nor are any of them irrelevant to an impersonal assessment; a satisfaction may be *more* satisfactory along any of these distinct dimensions, nor is one of them a plainly prior ground of preference to another. (VI, 234)

These inconsistent accounts, first of depth as "culminating expression" of our "emotional life," and then of depth as having no priority of "preference" among satisfactions, do not appear to connect the term to a value that is aesthetic. According to Findlay, aesthetic value attaches to disinterested contemplation that is free from wants and their satisfactions, and free from concern with the "reality" or "existence" of its objects. Yet this cannot be entirely correct, since the term *deep* appears again related to the nonhedonic, contemplative light of consciousness that marks aesthetic value:

> There is a "value movement" from means to ends, which is merely a case of the operation of a deep-rooted conscious tendency on the special stuff of desire and practice. And the tendency towards disengagement must be strong by virtue of the sheer universality of the rational drifts in question: wherever we plan, wherever we consider, wherever we give orders or receive them, wherever we debate things with others, we of necessity follow the drifts of extending pattern, of equalizing cases, speaking for and with our fellows, etc. etc. Small wonder then that the form of such procedures "works loose" from its infinitely varied material, that from being instrumental it becomes final. . . . (VI, 218)

Here it is implied that what is deep is indelibly connected to the universal "light" of consciousness, and also, then, to the contemplative light that marks aesthetic value.

Not only does contemplation "tend towards detachment from cognitive interests" (VI, 241), or "refuse to develop [an] idea in a direction where it passes over into belief or disbelief" (VI, 234), but "by virtue of its withdrawal from, and subordination of, the merely personal, involve[s] an implicit aspiration, and an implicit claim, to 'speak for all' " (VI, 243). "It is the presence of something *to consciousness* that is important for this sort of satisfaction, not its incorporation into the fabric of reality. . . . Since our valuation is of a state of consciousness, and of an object only *qua* object of consciousness, it must obviously rate things more highly in proportion as consciousness is greater, in proportion, that is, as something is clearly, and not turbidly or confusedly, brought out" (VI, 245). Essential to all this is "sensory deliverance," even though a particular object of contemplation is not of an immediate sensory presence.

From Findlay's combination of ideas of Brentano, Husserl, Kant, and a bit of Hume, we now have a picture of depth that may either be thought of as an extreme degree of different values—hedonic, aesthetic, or other—or as itself a value of maximum status standing above other values as a kind of metauniversal. Looked at in the latter way, profundity is presupposed in Findlay's very analysis of full-functioning consciousness; hence that analysis cannot be appealed to in order to *explain* the value of profundity, without circularity.

Findlay's analysis of human consciousness is clearly one that he takes to be true. Yet even if we discount an interpretation of profundity as a value inherent in all conscious process, and thus avoid circularity in its explanation, there are other subsidiary problems with Findlay's analysis. One relates to the manner in which he takes hedonic values to be "impersonalized" and "interpersonalized"; another concerns his under-standing of how sense perception and language relate to "universalizing" within "a primitive continuity of time" (VI, 138). If we look at conscious-ness as having a history, rather than as functioning in an ongoing present, we may obtain different understanding of conditions of conscious "fulfill-ment."

Recent psychological observations of newborn humans cannot be explained by standard thinking about sense perceptions and the origin of human communication in prior established language. For example, a four-week-old human can successfully imitate basic expressions it sees in an adult face; moreover, at least in smiling, it appears in a genuine though rudimentary way to be communicating with that adult. How does it know that its own facial expressions are the same as those in the face it is looking at? And how does it apparently recognize another human with whom it may communicate? Again, of all the sounds newborn humans hear, they are said to "prefer" human voices, and of all of these they "prefer" the sounds of their mothers' voices. Surely this is established prelinguistically, and is not compatible with Findlay's contention that "universalizing" an individual's feelings and the like is dependent on language or upon prior experience of sensory "presences" in a postnatal world.

Findlay may be correct in his identification of major features of consciousness. But who is to say that these features, at all times in mental life, function in relation to each other in a uniform way, such that it is possible to frame around and through them a general philosophy of mind and of valuation? Surely we cannot deny consciousness to the human fetus, at least in its later stages of development, nor can we deny to it sense perception, although prenatally that perception appears to be exclusively auditory and tactual. But let us suppose that there are also laid down in prenatal life neurological or DNA conditions of later visual perception as well, such as might explain the pattern identified by Carl Jung as a "mandala"—a pattern he found recurring in all human cultures,

and partly from which he posited the existence of a "collective unconscious." We might then find similarities between the collective unconscious and Husserl's idea of intersubjectivity or Kant's "moment of
universality," and yet be able to explain the former without need of
setting up a general theory of all human mental function or of all human
valuation.

Findlay's theory provides a better basis than does Dewey's for explaining the universal and context-free connotation of *profundity*, and thus a
better foundation for identifying profundity as an intrinsic, rather than
an instrumental, value. This understanding, however, does not provide
solid ground for Findlay's apparent assumption that profundity varies in
degree ("a satisfaction may be *more* satisfactory along any of these distinct
dimensions"). His analysis of consciousness, however, shares the same
ability as Dewey's to explain the dual reference of *profundity* to a property
of an object and to the feeling of a judge. Rather than tracing this as
Dewey did to interaction between subject and object, Findlay's distinction
of reflexive consciousness affords an explanation in a different way, as
where he notes "the 'deeply felt' [differs] from the 'deep' in its reflectively
evident character."

In Chapter 3, I propose to examine in relation to profundity-judgments
two particular sensory patterns that can be studied in isolation from other
features of human conscious life. The first is an auditory pattern that is
evidently established prenatally; the other is the particular visual pattern
termed by Jung a mandala, which he took to be biologically built in, but
which I believe can be more easily explained as environmentally established immediately after birth in all humans. Looked at within a context
that has a history, however, this suggests that features of conscious and
biological activity isolated by Findlay may function independently and/or
be interrelated in different ways at different times in human life, such
that, for example, awareness of a *sensus communis* need not be understood
as a universalization of reflexive self-consciousness. It also suggests a
possibility that certain sensory patterns established in early consciousness
are carried forward via some kind of memory into later phases in a way
that is not only incompatible with pragmatic analyses that are present-
future oriented but also with most hermeneutical analysis, and even with
Findlay's eclectic account of consciousness.

Findlay's ignoring even of Husserl's understanding of "retention" in
"internal time consciousness" appears to derive, in part at least, from his
determination to obtain an analysis of consciousness independently of
what consciousness is *of*. Consciousness is presented as existing *through*

time, but not *in* time looked at in a past, present, future orientation. If we ask how memory can be thought of as a mode of which we are conscious—as occasionally we are reflexively conscious of our being conscious—the mode of time of which we are aware is differentiated by past, present, and future. We seem thus forced to include reference to what memory is *of*, whether it be of something long past, or of something just noticed, or of something in between these. Now, if memory is indelibly linked to "depth," it conditions the judgment as in part dependent upon conscious content. Findlay's inconsistent use of *deep* and *profound* seems on occasion to slip in under cover, so to speak, some conscious content in the form of memory or retention. This is especially the case in the excerpt quoted above—"It is in the queer language of the vitals, the formless changes of the breath, and the warm tides of the blood overstreaming their normal floodgates, that our emotional life has, and must have, its *culminating* [italics added] expressions. . . ." One may well ask how such "culmination" occurs without some kind of memory. Again, in identifying judgments of depth as of a quality of hedonic satisfaction, along with those of the "lofty," "broad," or "exquisite," Findlay identifies what is deep with satisfactions "radical" and "architectonic." How, once more, are we to interpret recognition of what is far reaching or global without some presupposition of memory content?

It is only conjecture that Findlay avoids reference to memory in his account of modes of consciousness for the reason suggested. Suffice it to say that subsequent discussion of profundity presupposes memory *of* what might be termed a mode of consciousness at the originating point of human life. If a *sensus communis* is taken to emerge from this, that awareness of, and sympathy for, other minds will not have been explained by an account of consciousness taken to be free from anything that consciousness is *of*. It will be free from a claim that universality of human judgments derives from what is universal to consciousness in framing any "possible world."

The aim of this chapter is not to demonstrate that pragmatic or hermeneutical analysis, or Findlay's eclectic approach, is entirely mistaken. It is only to argue that attempts at general theories of mind and valuation that are designed to apply to all times and circumstances and that *can* result in total relativism, or total idealism, or a total theory of conscious activity, stand in the way of progress in understanding their subject when it is pinned down to a particular application.

3

Pinning Down Profundity

I

Toward the end of the movie *Ironweed* (1987), Helen Archer has carried a portable phonograph into a room that she has just taken in a boarding-house, and, as we discover later, a single unwrapped recording inside her coat, tucked under her arm. She tells the manager, who has brought in other luggage, that she is paying him for two days' stay "in case I don't die tonight." In the first of three scenes in the room, two of which are cutbacks from scenes of Francis Phelan, her companion in another part of town, we see her resolutely place the phonograph on a table, take the recording from under her coat, and place it firmly on the turntable. This recording is clearly a favored one that she has brought to a momentary retreat from her sordid world.

We have learned at the beginning of the film that Helen has been a singer and pianist on radio and stage, and in one scene in a music shop she has said to a little girl playing a piano that music is the "greatest thing there is in this life, you know. We ought to be willing to die for our music." There have been hints also that Helen is sick, probably from drinking too much wine over the years she has lived off and on with Francis, sometimes in this very room, often on the streets with other alcoholics, and we surmise from her comment to the manager that she may very well be going to die.

In the first cutback, Helen has turned on the phonograph and is seen taking items from a suitcase and placing them on a dresser as we hear the first strains of the third movement of Beethoven's Ninth Symphony. Just as the music moves into a well-known and favored passage (bars 24–42), we see her carefully place a picture on the dresser, presumably of family members, although their identity is obscure. We hear this stretch of the composition as we have probably always heard it, as an extended lullaby that exudes love—the love of a mother for her child at its most rudimentary, elemental point, in which there is no possibility of social denial, no proviso to withhold love in retribution for any sin. We see Helen take a robe from the suitcase, her face showing extreme pain. The phonograph has played the entire sequence through bar 42.

After the second cutaway to Francis, in the final cutback we see Helen, turned from the camera, washing at a basin, then in side and back view again as she turns toward the dresser mirror to comb her hair. The phonograph has been playing the same sequence again. She talks briefly to herself as we see her full-face in the mirror, but she finally goes down on her knees in severe pain, as the recording continues just past bar 42. The combination of this human image, either in pain or often faceless, the blurred photograph on the dresser of her unknown family members, and this melody of elemental and unconditional love makes musically sensitive viewers want to cry. It is not just that we do not want Helen to die, certainly not in pain. It is that, reduced ourselves by this music to such rudimentary recognition and recall, we do not want anyone to die, real or fictitious. No one. Ever.

It may have been William Kennedy, writer of the original novel and the screenplay, who selected this most appropriate composition of Beethoven, or perhaps it was director Hector Babenko or other associates. Whoever it was must have fully sensed the relevance of a quality that Herbert Blomstedt observed in responses of Tokyo audiences to this symphony: "You can play [it] evening after evening and fill any hall."[1] Our knowledge that Helen (as well as Francis) had, as one critic put it, "held on to a basic human decency" in spite of their dereliction is surely relevant. But it is the undistilled quality of human love present in this music, synchronized here with blurred or faceless photographic images, that momentarily sinks the particulars of these characters into a universality touching the profound. It is at such moments that words like *deep*, *rudimentary*, or *primordial* so predominate in any judgment that we scarcely remember the pronouncements of pragmatists or hermeneutists against the universality of any and every human value, or recall Richard Rorty's confident statement that "the pragmatist does not think there is anything like that."

What seems clear from recent technological advances is that there is at least one basic human "starting point" that is sensory in origin, although it is not visual. No general theory of value or of aesthetic experience will uncover it so long as human sense perception is treated without discrimination between different sensory media, and no empirical account of valuational origins will entirely succeed so long as visual perception is treated as being on a par with its primacy in epistemology. There are, and probably always have been in the history of art criticism, strong clues that not all sensory media function in aesthetic judgments exactly alike, that not any one of the major sense media is as good as any other in eliciting any judgment properly called aesthetic. Such clues, however, appear to have been overridden by the global aims of philosophy. If they had been taken up more consistently, they might still have gone down to defeat by those in zealous search for counterexamples, even for *per impossible* counterexamples. If we could not find a counterexample in one sensory medium, then why not find it in another? And if we could not find it in *this* world, then why not construct it in another? Progress, so it seems, depends upon technological advances in the twentieth century, together with a determination to include as relevant in philosophical analysis information about what, from a scientific view, is true both of human sense perception and of memory. Fundamentally, it depends upon drawing a connection between aesthetics and cognitive science, when the study of aesthetics is looked at as a study of grounding valuational judgments.

In my book *Soundtracks*, I attempted to trace profundity or depth in music to human experience had prenatally.[2] I posited that judgments of depth in auditory art are based on an unconscious recall, or partial recall (probably via hearing musical analogues), of a dynamic sound pattern that is heard by all unborn humans continuously during the last four months of development. Perhaps the exact duration can be questioned, but it seems clear that the fetus, whose auditory apparatus is completely developed by the fifth gestational month, has been aware or conscious of this pattern for at least two months before birth. I noted that in the prenatal state the fetus does not yet have visual perception or language, but does have auditory and, in a minimal way, tactual perception. Drawing from suggestions made by P. F. Strawson and by A. J. Ayer,[3] I presumed that the fetus is in a solipsistic or semisolipsistic state, such that it does not clearly distinguish itself as an entity independent from what it hears. If this is so, and if primary intrinsic value is found in the fact of being alive, I had an explanation of many of the features of profundity that I have enumerated in Chapter 1.

Without depending on a general theory of aesthetic value, I could explain why judges of music repeatedly fail to distinguish between qualities of an object and feelings of a judge. I could explain the strong emotional response called "being moved" that is different from the feeling ("Eureka!") expressed upon solving an unknown. I could explain why music is called a "universal language" although it has no semiotic function. I could explain why analyses of representation or of expression are irrelevant in analyzing the quality of musical depth. I could explain why none other than spatial metaphor is available to express the music critic's "aesthetic" message.

By analogy with the experience of Marcel (of Marcel Proust's *Swann's Way*) of a vivid recall of the looks of Combray and an "all-powerful joy" in that recall through tasting a madeleine dipped in tea, I did not regard the taste of a madeleine in tea to be either a necessary or a sufficient condition of Marcel's recall. He might have remembered Combray in some other way, and certainly it could not have been guaranteed that anytime he dipped a madeleine in tea the taste would bring back that particular memory and its "all-powerful joy." Similarly, I did not regard the experiencing of a musical analogue of prenatal sounds to be either necessary for even a partial recall of the latter or a guarantee of such recall. Still, there is a sense in which Marcel afforded an explanation of what he found, an answer to his own question: "Whence could it have come to me, this all-powerful joy?"

The auditory pattern I refer to is produced by the functioning of the human circulatory system; it has only been heard at a time when the hearer was entirely inside another human body. I analyze it as consisting of three phases. The first is a hammering sound apparently produced by the systolic phase of the heartbeat. The second is a rushing sound apparently produced by the coursing of blood through vessels. The last appears to be produced by the diastolic phase of the heartbeat and consists of two separate sounds, one slightly louder than the other, that are easily interpreted as tones at approximately E-flat to D-flat in the midrange of the piano. This pattern has been uniformly forgotten (in any conscious sense) by everyone. Upon hearing a recording of it, no one will say "I remember hearing that before I was born. Listen, Mama, they're playing our song." Moreover, the sound quality of the pattern cannot be reproduced in the spatial world of postnatal life. Sounds heard through a stethoscope are not close to it. It has only been available to study for approximately seventeen years, via a recording that was made internally just before the onset of a mother's labor. (The recording has been most easily available packaged in a stuffed bear and sold at shops selling clothing and furnishings for infants. The quality of the recording produced by different companies has varied.)

The response to a playback of this pattern is identical in all neonates. Barring such possibilities as that a neonate is in pain or extreme want, upon hearing this pattern again it is asleep within sixty seconds. It is reasonable to suppose also that the pattern carries with it a strong positive emotion, close to if not the same as what is later termed *love*—specifically, love of sentient existence. A newborn's intimate bond with its mother is probably established before birth, and it appears that the pattern carries an intrinsic emotional value, as does the very fact of being alive under conditions that are not faced with adversity.

It is unclear how long humans will respond to this pattern postnatally. That may depend upon how long or consistently the recording is used. In spite of humans' inability to remember it, however, and despite the impossibility of re-creating it in a world in which a hearer is no longer inside another human body, we may posit that something of the pattern and its intrinsic value is retained by a significant number of the population in what might be called nonreflexive or unconscious memory. We may also posit that analogues of the pattern made by humans via whatever sound instruments they have available will possess a built-in value and a strong emotional attraction that other nonanalogous patterns may lack. With this we should have expected that humanity would, apparently throughout its history, repeatedly ask: "How can something so unanalyzably simple be so moving?" For as long as we have been unable to remember in any conscious way, Eduard Hanslick's confident observation would have seemed beyond question: "This primitive and mysterious power will forever be hidden from us."[4]

It is this posited connection that I have argued elicits judgments of profundity in auditory art. The composer and appreciator of music, then, can be seen as in part motivated by a desire to get something back that they cannot remember, but that lurks tantalizingly, so to speak, behind an impenetrable veil. This interpretation looks at composers, in part at least, as imitators in much the way that Plato looked at artists. In this case, however, composers are not pretenders to truth, although they clearly traffic with the sort of strong emotional appeal that had, in Socrates' opinion, led Ion astray, or that identified poets in *The Republic* as "liars by profession" and dangerous to the state.

If this interpretation is correct, then we should be able to find clear analogues of the prenatal sound pattern, or of parts of it, in music of different cultures worldwide. In the auditory domain it is not possible to reproduce examples as Jung was able to do in demonstrating the "mandala" pattern in different cultures or in the art of his patients. Excerpts in musical notation cannot properly convey what must be heard in performance, and it is not practically possible to present a recording of excerpts that, to be fair to the claim, could run for hours. I offer below, then, examples from music and drumming sequences of different cultures as especially good ones, hoping that they will lend credence to my thesis.

AFRICA
  "Drums of West Africa" (Lyrichord LLST 7307), side 1, band 1 (Ghana)
  "Music of the Rain Forest Pygmies of the North-East Congo" (Lyrichord LLST 7157), side 1, band 3
AMERICAN INDIAN
  "An Anthology of North American Indian and Eskimo Music" (Ethnic Folkways Library FE 4541A), side 1, band 3
HAITI
  "Voodoo Trance Music, Ritual Drums of Haiti" (Lyrichord LLST 7279), side 2, band 6, and side 1, band 1
INDIA
  "Lower Caste Religious Music from India" (Lyrichord LLST 7324), side 2, band 2
MOROCCO
  "Islamic Mystical Brotherhood" (Lyrichord LLST 7238), side 1, bands 2, 3, 4, and side 2, band 2 (Moroccan Sufi music)
JAMAICA
  "Dub on the Pressure" (reggae) (Channel One Studios, Kingston, Jamaica), SUFF 002, side 2
JAPAN
  "Kajincho" (King Record Co., Ltd., Japan, K13A-546), side B, band 3 (for Kabuki dancing)

I take these examples to be analogues of the entire prenatal sound pattern, although the Japanese recording appears least close. But all of them make focal use of percussive sound, varying in quality and loudness according to the instruments available within the culture. All present short, cyclical, dynamic sequences that are repeated almost exactly over and over, ending either with a clear, whole-tone drop or a quick finish of two adjacently related drumbeats characteristic of the diastolic phase of the pattern. Some of them differ in pace from the original, being very much faster or very much slower. I do not, however, regard such variations to count against their status as analogues of the original pattern.

More recent than the long-playing recordings cited above, a 1991 audiotape from the New Dimensions Foundation in San Francisco—"The Rhythm Experience with Reinhard Flatischler and Heidrun Hoffman"— offers corroborating opinion. At the beginning of the tape, one narrator states: "Rhythm: it connects us all. Our early beginnings even before birth are filled with rhythm—the pulsating rhythm of our mother's heartbeat. As humans, we are naturally attracted to the rhythms beaten out on drums. Every culture on the planet has developed a particular sound, from the Cuban *conga* to the Japanese *taiko*, from the Indian *tabla* to the Brazilian *surdo*. Their rhythms speak to us, touching deep chords of resonance within our ancestral memories. There is a healing power in rhythm. . . ." (One may draw a connection between "healing powers" as restorers of full, unfettered life and judgments of profundity.)

Within the musical tradition of Western culture, we can find analogues in music before that of Beethoven—for example, in Renaissance dance music. But it has often been recognized that Beethoven's main contribution to classical composition of western Europe lay in his introduction of dynamics that were largely missing in the works of his predecessors. I do not regard it as coincidence that Beethoven's music is often described as having "something primordial about it." And I take it that what Blomstedt has said about it is not just the expression of a wish by one who, in good Kantian fashion, is trying—though in vain—to "speak for all." Blomstedt is not alone in making observations about the quality of this composer's work that I also take to be literally true. I have found one of the best illustrations of this in the *Coriolan* Overture, specifically as interpreted by George Szell with the Cleveland Orchestra (Columbia MS 6966).

This composition appears, from start to finish, as an analogue of the entire prenatal pattern, such that with this interpretation it is possible at more than one point to superimpose the recorded pattern on the overture in almost perfect synchronization. This is possible in part because Szell's interpretation is almost exactly up to pace, making allowances for some rubato along the way that the recorded pattern cannot follow. Such near synchronization could not be accomplished with a reading markedly slower or faster. For example, Carmine Coppola's interpretation of this overture, which for some reason he inserted into his score for Abel Gance's silent film *Napoléon*, was far too slow to allow any superimposition. Still, it is fair to say that the Beethoven overture provides an astonishingly close analogue of the original pattern.

Analogues of the last phase of the pattern—the "diastolic"—that lack the dynamic and percussive features of the original appear to be far more common in western European music than do those of the whole pattern, such as the examples presented above as characteristic of other cultures, and appear to be far less peculiar to certain individual composers. I find one notable exception to this in Asian music. Whereas in the above list of analogues of the entire percussive pattern the Japanese example appeared least close, composition that consists of not much more than the little diastolic figure, reiterated over and over, seems to be even more common in Asian music than it is in Western. An excellent example is found in the thematic music of *The Last Emperor* (1987), by composers Ryuichi Sakamoto, David Byrne, and Cong Su, that is clearly taken to be characteristic of Chinese and/or Japanese composition. Another is in the traditional Japanese melody "Oharabushi" (on CBS recording M335862, with Jean-Pierre Rampal and the Koto Ensemble).

This drop of a whole tone that either forms the theme of an entire composition or is the figure to which the composition constantly returns forms the primary tone structure of a lullaby. Presumably mothers intent on achieving the same result that is produced more quickly by the newly obtained recording have hit on this small figure as especially effective. Whether this stems from trial and error or from what might be called "mothers' intuition" need not vex us. The human voice is not a percussive instrument that can repeat the whole pattern, yet it is clear that the repetitious nature of this little two-tone figure works. Once more we may ascribe the strong attractiveness of the figure to the same origin as that of the entire pattern.

This figure is most characteristic of the adagios, andantes, largos, and lentos in what may be heard as glorified or transfigured lullabies. In some composers, such as Dvořák and Mahler, the figure appears so consistently, either as a main theme or as the point of constant return, as to make it characteristic of their entire oeuvres. These compositions seem more often to be judged "beautiful," "perfectly beautiful," or "lovely" than do ones heard as analogues of the entire pattern. The latter seem more consistently to be judged "profound" or "primordial," although surely no hard-and-fast lines can be drawn here. In both cases, however, where either the entire pattern or the final phase of it originates aesthetic value, the *creativity* of the composer now appears to be reduced simply to an ability to find new ways to execute the same thing that are yet compatible with particular cultural traditions. Here are some especially good examples of what I interpret as glorified or transfigured lullabies:

Albéniz: Suite Iberia: Evocatión
Albinoni: Adagio in G Minor
J. S. Bach: Orchestral Suite No. 3 in D Major, BWV 1068, Air
    Brandenburg Concerto No. 2, BWV 1047, Andante
Beethoven: Symphony No. 9, Op. 125, 3d movement, Adagio molto e
    cantabile
Bizet: Symphony No. 1 in C Major (playing throughout, but especially in
    the 4th movement, Allegro vivace)
Borodin: *Prince Igor:* Polovtsian Dances
Brahms: Piano Intermezzo No. 1 in E-flat Major, Op. 117 (with quoted
    heading above the score from Herder's "Volkslieder": "Schlaf sanft,
    mein Kind . . .")
    Piano Concerto No. 2 in B-flat Major, Op. 83, movements 2, 3,
    and 4
Bruch: Violin Concerto No. 1 in G Minor, Op. 26, *throughout*
Castelnuovo-Tedesco: Guitar Concerto No. 1, Op. 99, 2d movement,
    Andantino
Chabrier: Overture to *Gwendoline*
Chaminade: The Flatterer
Chopin: Nocturne in G Major, Op. 37, No. 2 (and pretty much
    everywhere else)
Debussy: Claire de Lune
Dvořák: Serenade in D Minor, Op. 44, Andante con moto
    Romance in F Minor, Op. 11
Falla: Nights in the Gardens of Spain, *throughout*
    El Amor Brujo: Pantomima
Gottschalk: A Night in the Tropics
Gounod: Petite Symphonie, 2d movement, Andante cantabile
Granados: Goyescas: Intermezzo

Grieg: Holberg Suite: Air: Andante religioso
Handel: *Xerxes*: Largo
    Water Music Suite: Air
Herbert: Souvenir
[Hymn]: Abide with Me
Liszt: Bénédiction de Dieu dans la solitude
Mahler: Symphony No. 9, 4th movement, Adagio
Massenet: Ballet No. 3, Espada (with some features of the entire pattern)
Mendelssohn: Symphony No. 3 in A Minor, Op. 56, *throughout*
Molter: Concerto No. 2 for Trumpet and Strings in D Major, *throughout*
Mozart: Piano Concerto No. 21 in C, K. 467, *throughout*
    Symphony No. 31 in D Major, K. 297, 2d movement, Andante
Offenbach: Tales of Hoffmann: Barcarolle
Pachelbel: Canon in D Major
Pierné: Ballet: *Ramuncho*, Second Suite
Prokofiev: "Classical" Symphony, Op. 25, 2d movement, Larghetto
Rachmaninoff: Trio Élégiaque in D Minor, Op. 9, No. 2
Ravel: Pavane for a Dead Princess
Rimsky-Korsakov: Capriccio espagnol, Op. 34
Rodrigo: Concierto de Aranjuez, 2d movement, Adagio
Rossini: *Overture to The Barber of Seville*
Saint-Saëns: Le Déluge: Prelude
    Piano Concerto No. 5, 2d movement, Andante
Schmitt: Soirs: Après l'été, Sur l'onde, Un soir
Schubert: Piano Trio No. 1 in B-flat Major, Op. 99, 2d movement, Andante
Schumann: Scenes of Childhood: Child Falling Asleep
Scriabin: Pieces, Op. 51, No. 5, Fragilité
Sibelius: Valse Triste
Smetana: My Fatherland: Moldau
Suppé: Overture 2: *The Peregrination after Fortune*
Tchaikovsky: Symphony No. 4 in F Minor, Op. 36, movements 2, 3, 4
Turina: La Procession del Rocio
Vaughan Williams: Serenade to Music
Verdi: Introduction to La Traviata
Vivaldi: Concerto for Violin in E Minor, RV 278, *throughout*
Wagner: *Tristan und Isolde*: Liebestod

Comparatively speaking, this list is short—the two-tone figure is literally found everywhere. It appears, however, that the strong aesthetic attraction of the little figure, the first tone a whole tone above the second, has been established independently of the contexts that each of these composers has fashioned for it. It seems that the figure can be heard piecemeal as independently attractive, like the frosting on a piece of cake, or taken out of a particular context of a different composition, and yet retain its aesthetic attractiveness or function—for all the fact that such transfer might change the "style" or "unity" of the invaded composition. In this respect, the *value* of the figure has been mistaken over the centuries as a product of a particular composer's interpretation of it. The value is not, as process philosophies would have it, created by the composer, and it is not dependent upon the composer's interpretative process.

Consider four different ways in which Beethoven, Bach, Mozart, and Saint-Saëns have developed the figure. The primary thing to notice is that it is constantly repeated, as though we have here hit on a universal musical aesthetic ultimate. In the third movement of the Ninth Symphony, Beethoven takes the figure in an ascending direction, repeating it by moving it upward stepwise. In the Brandenburg Concerto No. 2, Andante, Bach repeats it in an instrumental canon, with the figure as the only theme, stating it first in one instrument, then again through other instruments, registers, and harmonies, in "answer." In the opening bars of the second movement of his Violin Concerto No. 3 (K. 216), Mozart repeats the figure consistently stepwise downward. In the Andante of the second movement of his fifth piano concerto, Saint-Saëns repeats the figure pretty much in lockstep, moving then at points both above and below it in register and in harmonies.

There is another point favoring our interpretation of the source of aesthetic attraction of this "diastolic" figure as prenatal or perinatal in origin. The characteristic word used in description is that the attraction is one of *love*. This, however, is not romantic love (although movie-score composers may use the figure to forge such a connection), but what ought more accurately but more broadly to be called love of sentient life, as in the unconditional love of any and every mother for her newborn. Note, again, that the appearance of the figure in its many different compositional contexts often brings tears. This indicates even more plausibly that this aesthetic attraction is biological in origin. Even in Bach's instrumental canon, where greater comprehensive structure predominates, its distinctly haunting quality relates, only more indirectly, to human love of sentient existence.

It may be a puzzle how dynamic, percussive patterns of music consistently provoke an irresistible urge to dance. This connection of sensory and motor activity is most evident in "popular," non-"cerebral" music; it is not typically the case with classical composition. Although Beethoven's Fifth Symphony is full of the pattern, it does not provoke dancing, nor does his Ninth Symphony, whose four movements are all based on the two-tone figure. Yet observation of a clear connection between the dynamic musical pattern and dance is especially important for my polemic since, interculturally, dance appears as an indelible feature of music, and both are typically performed *communally*. Can we find any prenatal environmental condition, concomitant with the auditory pattern, that is motor, rather than sensory?

On the face of our own "objective" observations, our first answer may easily be no. The feet of the fetus may move in limited ways, as in kicking. But there appears to be insufficient space in its environment for broader motions that are characteristic of dancing. Moreover, our observations of a pregnant mother's body, or even her own observations about her condition, do not yield clear evidence that a fetus must be in concomitant motion with the movements of its mother's body. Yet a moment's consideration indicates that since the fetus floats in the amnion "bag of waters," it must be *swung* in varying directions as its mother's body moves from side to side, up and down, forward and backward.

A new electronic rocking bed, "Nature's Cradle," that imitates sounds and rhythms of the womb, and that is far more sophisticated than the old-fashioned cradle, has been devised by the company Infant Advantage in the "Silicon Valley" of California. Recently demonstrated for San Francisco news television (CBS, aired 10 and 11 July 1991) at San Francisco General Hospital, the bed moves in gentle alternately swinging-sideways and up-and-down motions, the movements being to some extent randomly patterned. The bed graphically imitates what is not generally visible to outsiders or to the mother herself. In conjunction with recorded prenatal sounds, "Nature's Cradle" has been used so far primarily as a treatment for drug-addicted infants.

It is easy, however, to move directly to videotapes of communal gatherings, such as church services using gospel music, that follow the prenatal pattern faithfully, and observe that although the feet of the congregants may not be moving, all their upper torsos are moving side to side in unison. Hand clapping, also in unison, often aids the percussive pattern. Faces show expressions of pure joy. Words sung may come out in a two-beat pattern, such as "Ho-*ly*, Ho-*ly*," or "Lord-*God*, Lord-*God*."

Although the torso and hand motions technically are not dancing, we need only to observe other cases where whole bodies must take *themselves* in swinging motion, rather than being taken by another body. Thus, the feet move, and we have dancing.

Analogues of the prenatal pattern and of dancing can be found cross-culturally in an annual Japanese summer festival during which food and prayers are offered for the happiness of ancestors' souls in the next world. Thousands of spectators watch a unique dancing style, *bone odori*, in which the dancers' bodies move up and down as their feet are alternately raised up and down again to the ground in a procession to the accompanying drummed prenatal beat. Excitement is high and is often likened to that of the Rio carnival. (Narrated on CNN, *International Hour*, 14 August 1991.) This festival is thought to have begun in a rural village about four centuries ago.

It does not appear to be accidental that such dancing is always taken to be an expression of joy or emotional exuberance, in recognition of the value of all human life. From the preceding observations, made graphic by "Nature's Cradle," we can understand how in such communal celebrations all participants are alike and at-one, individual differences among them never being less to the point.

II

In framing an explanation of the phenomena I have observed, I do not see any way out of positing the existence of unconscious memory. It seems clear to me that there are at least certain features of human valuation that J. N. Findlay's analysis of consciousness within an ongoing present cannot explain. We may wonder how my understanding of unconscious memory connects with Jung's positing of the existence of a collective unconscious, and also whether I am correct in placing auditory perception as prior in establishment in humans to conditions of visual perception.

The visual pattern of a mandala observed by Jung is one that he found recurring in every human culture. It was on the basis of this and other recurring "archetypes," primarily in mythologies and religions, that he posited the collective unconscious. The basic form of the mandala is a circle, or "wheel." Jung found that individual mandalas are frequently bounded by a square or other four-sided "quaternity," often symbolizing religious doctrine. Frequently, the interior of the circle is divided by a cross into four symmetrical sections. These sections are very often filled by depictions of petals, especially of the rose. The circular, stained-glass rose window of Christian architecture is a mandala. Jung's understanding of mandalas, "archetypes," symbolism, and the collective unconscious developed over a period of years, and not all of his writings on these subjects are entirely consistent or unambiguous. Here is a general summary that was written especially for the journal *Du: Schweizerische Monatsschrift*, six years before his death:

> The Sanskrit word *mandala* means "circle" in the ordinary sense of the word. In the sphere of religious practices and in psychology it denotes circular images, which are drawn, painted, modelled, or danced. Plastic structures of this kind are to be found, for instance, in Tibetan Buddhism, and as dance figures these circular patterns occur also in Dervish monasteries. As psychological phenomena they appear spontaneously in dreams, in certain states of conflict, and in cases of schizophrenia. Very frequently they contain a quaternity or a multiple of four, in the form of a cross, a star, a square, an octagon, etc. In alchemy we encounter this motif in the form of a *quadratura circuli*.
>
> In Tibetan Buddhism the figure has the significance of a ritual instrument (*yantra*), whose purpose is to assist meditation and concentration. Its meaning in alchemy is somewhat similar, inasmuch as it represents the synthesis of the four elements which are forever tending to fall apart. Its spontaneous occurrence in modern individuals enables psychological research to make a closer investigation into its functional meaning. As a rule a mandala occurs in conditions of psychic dissociation or disorientation, for instance in the case of children between the ages of eight and eleven whose parents are about to be divorced, or in adults who, as the result of a neurosis and its treatment, are confronted with the problem of opposites in human nature and are consequently disoriented; or again in schizophrenics whose view of the world has become confused, owing to the invasion of incomprehensible contents from the unconscious. In such cases it is easy to see how the severe pattern imposed by a circular image of this kind compensates the disorder and confusion of the psychic state— namely, through the construction of a central point to which everything is related, or by a concentric arrangement of the

disordered multiplicity and of contradictory and irreconcilable elements. This is evidently an *attempt at self-healing* on the part of Nature, which does not spring from conscious reflection but from an instinctive impulse. Here, as comparative research has shown, a fundamental schema is made use of, an archetype, which, so to speak, occurs everywhere and by no means owes its individual existence to tradition, any more than the instincts would need to be transmitted in that way. Instincts are given in the case of every newborn individual and belong to the inalienable stock of those qualities which characterize a species. What psychology designates as archetype is really a particular, frequently occurring, formal aspect of instinct, and is just as much an *a priori* factor as the latter. Therefore, despite external differences, we find a fundamental conformity in mandalas regardless of their origin in time and space.[5]

Elsewhere, Jung defined "personal consciousness" as a "superficial layer" resting upon a "deeper layer which does not derive from personal experience and is not a personal acquisition but is inborn. This deeper layer I call the *collective unconscious*. I have chosen the term 'collective' because this part of the unconscious is not individual but universal."[6] He found that the contents of the collective unconscious are "primordial types . . . , universal images that have existed since the remotest times." Jung also looked at "primitive man" as "rediscover[ing] by means of analogy" psychic forms. He clearly believed that what is "instinctive" in humans is established prior to experience in the space-time world, and found in the "unconscious psyche" of "primitive man" an "irresistible urge to assimilate all outer experiences to inner psychic events."[7]

Several similarities and differences emerge between the analysis of profundity in human experience that I have made by exclusive reference to the prenatal auditory pattern and Jung's identification of a universal sensory pattern that is visual and rooted in the collective unconscious. The first is found in differences between what I have termed unconscious memory and Jung's collective unconscious. It has been argued that the collective unconscious is an untestable hypothesis. As Alasdair MacIntyre succinctly puts it: "The question of whether the collective unconscious exists cannot be answered by any possible observation or experiment. That the existence of the collective unconscious is intended as a hypothesis seems clear from the fact that it is avowedly introduced to explain why the same symbols keep recurring in dreams, mythologies, and works of art. However, there are no predictions that we can deduce from this hypothesis other than the vague generalization that such symbols do and will recur—and this, after all, is what the hypothesis was originally intended to explain."[8]

In contrast, it has not been my procedure to begin by noting recurrent patterns in different musical compositions worldwide, then to take these patterns to be analogues of an *unobservable* mental "archetype," and finally to posit unconscious memory as a hypothesis to explain the analogical connection. My analysis provides direct evidence in the form of a recording made internally of a prenatal pattern (not identified as an "archetype") that has no corollary in Jung's analysis of the mandala. Moreover, unless perhaps some future genetic or DNA analysis of prenatal biology uncovers an invariant condition of mental archetypes, what Jung termed instinctive or inborn conditioning shows no promise of direct demonstration and verification. Nor does my positing of unconscious memory suggest any kind of prediction of future recurrence of certain musical patterns.

I do not need to posit any genetic condition or DNA in order to explain my observations. The responses observed in newborn humans to the prenatal auditory pattern can as easily be explained by their prenatal auditory environment as can human responses to their postnatal environ-ments. It is true that my explanation of the universal response as based on conscious memory of a recent prenatal state is "hypothetical." Perhaps that response is more properly thought of as a momentary return to a prenatal gestalt. Later creation and appreciation of pattern analogues, however, are clearly not based on conscious memory of the pattern, nor are they based upon a recapture of an entire prenatal gestalt. It is thus extremely difficult to avoid explanation by reference to unconscious memory as a condition of the recurrence, culture to culture, of analogues, either of the entire pattern or of its last "diastolic" phase. I do not believe, in sum, that my defense of unconscious memory is vulnerable to MacIntyre's criticism in the way that Jung's defense of the collective unconscious is.

There is another difference between my analysis and Jung's. Sometimes he identified particular mandalas as symbols of mythological or religious ideas—the Trinity, for instance. At other times he thought of a particular mandala as an *analogy* through which "primitive man rediscovers" a primordial mental archetype. It is quite unclear in such references how Jung regarded particular mandalas to be *symbols* of a primordial mental archetype. Rather than thinking of them as referring, as symbols refer, to a mental archetype, he seemed to regard them as repeating that archetype in visual form, or, indeed, as *identifying* it. I have not, on the other hand, regarded musical analogues as symbols of anything, but rather as imitations of a pattern that was always exclusively auditory. This raises yet another difference.

Jung appeared to believe that humans carry around with them at all times a specific archetypal casting of a collective unconscious. The only formal feature of unconscious memory that I posit, however, is of a particular auditory pattern. And I make no assumption that all humans in later years even retain it *un*consciously, although I am assuming that a significant number of them do. Some who would have responded uniformly to playback of the pattern—had the recording been available—will yet grow up tone-deaf and/or rhythm-dumb, in which case we would not want to say that they remember it in *any* sense.

In spite of all this, there is a close correlation between my understanding of the *value* of the auditory pattern and Jung's understanding of the value of the mandala. Primary valuational importance is found in both, as they posit what is literally universal to humans in a biological base. Thus, both stand in opposition to cultural valuational relativism. Both bear out what Findlay has put so clearly: justification of a particular evaluation proceeds by subsuming it under a universal, but under a universal that is clearly subjective in origin (i.e., that originates in activity of the human mind). Jung often put his valuational case in terms of restoration of mental health to individuals who were severely "disoriented." But his extended correlations between unconscious archetypes and religious or mythical beliefs and practices clearly founded the latter in a primary value of full-functioning human consciousness. This was especially the case in his extended inquiries into myths of a Great Mother and of a second birth. Within my more limited observations about aesthetic judgment of profundity, I, too, explain its various features as deriving initially from conscious recognition of intrinsic value in the fact of human life. This much is quite compatible with Findlay's distinction of "fulfilled consciousness."

I do not, as did Jung, assume that the guiding source of value must remain unconscious in order to retain its power. He noted that "healing effects" of painting mandalas must be guided unconsciously and occur "only spontaneously. Nothing can be expected from an artificial repetition or a deliberate imitation of such images."[9] Again, Jung found that "emotions are instinctive, involuntary reactions which upset the rational order of consciousness by their elemental outbursts. Affects are not 'made' or wilfully produced; they simply happen."[10] The bringing of unconscious archetypes into conscious deliberation produces precisely the religious practices and dogmas, the recurrent myths that, when *believed* in and consciously reiterated, lose the power of their origin when it remains in the unconscious. Thus, the rituals, the hourly, daily, or weekly observances, the standard rites, the reiterated beliefs and dogmas, fail by the very fact of their appearance in the surface consciousness of daily life. In contrast, I do not wish to make my observations dependent upon any such universal or sweeping divisions. Where what I would have analyzed as emerging from unconscious memory is brought into conscious recognition, I do not want to predict an inevitable loss of aesthetic value attending it. It seems to me that there are more varied conditions determining loss of value in what has become habitual or obvious besides the simple fact that it is conscious rather than unconscious. It seems to me, also, that audiences at a performance of Beethoven's Ninth Symphony who repeat once more that music is a "universal language" speak of what to them is fully conscious, with the conviction of those who have just observed it "before their very eyes," although, of course, they have seen nothing and are at a complete loss to explain their psychic state.

It is difficult to think of a prenatal biological conditioning of visual pattern in other than genetic terms. Now that we have obtained the recording of prenatal sounds, however, we can trace an auditory pattern source as biologically determined without making any assumptions about genes or DNA. We can now explain profundity judgments in just the same way as we explain human judgments in the postnatal world. If we are pragmatists, we can forge an explanation in terms of interaction between organisms and their environments, prenatal as well as postnatal. We do not need more genetic information than we already have. In establishing conditions of postnatal valuational judgments, however, we *do* need to posit priority of auditory perception over visual perception as we know it in human postnatal life. In this way we gain the primary condition of human valuation that has been sought from the beginning in objection to total relativism: a context-free universal by back-reference to which (via memory) we justify the particular and primary judgment of profundity. And rather than positing a genetic difference in prenatal conditioning of later visual perception, we might now suggest that what is initially *heard* prenatally as a cyclical pattern subsequently—perhaps very quickly—transfers postnatally, in a sensory gestalt, to what is *seen* as a circular pattern, most likely that of a mother's full breast. *Thus* we can later say that the *music* "goes round and round."

To suggest that the origin of the value of the mandala pattern is the immediately seen postnatal configuration of a mother's breast may well appear altogether mundane, perhaps ridiculous. To the adult "objective" observer, this plain and commonplace visual pattern hardly captures the weighty and mysterious features of mandala making, as does Jung's explanation through symbolism or those equally mysterious mental "archetypes." We should think, however, of how this image likely appears to a newborn, rather than to an adult or even to an older child who is no longer dependent at all upon what was originally the major source of life sustenance. Within a vigorous, sentient gestalt, in that circle image (with a center) the newborn has the *look* of the *sole* source of sustenance of human life. Surely therein lies a simple but plausible explanation of the universal value of mandalas that Jung observed.

This, then, finally suggests a different and broader explanation of the consistent appearances of mandalas, especially in their connection with religion and myth, from Jung's assertion that they are attempts at self-healing, however centrally important the process of healing may be. It also explains the universal appearance of mandalas without holding that they are "inborn" in some prenatal visual origin. It finds the basis to be in a memory return to a psychic state that is intrinsically and aesthetically valuable, whether it accompanies an attempt at self-healing or does not. It thus accounts for mandala making as well as music making among those who are not psychologically disturbed at all. This will stand in spite of Nietzsche's conviction that what is profound in music making emerges from upset, suffering, and a host of other Romantic ills. Perhaps we can now show with considerable objectivity that such Romantic claims are false. Execution of meritorious art, whether visual, auditory, or other, is undoubtedly difficult, as Mozart's abandoned, unfinished compositions and Beethoven's sketchbooks attest. Perhaps this stems in large measure, however, not from psychological instability or disorientation but from difficulties in clearing away years of accumulated obstructions and reconnecting with our human origins, wherein is embedded the profound.

III

The foregoing analysis suggests that in the auditory domain humans are prenatally brainwashed. If we have drawn no essential difference in this domain between prenatal and postnatal environments, we may be reminded of the theologian's confident prediction: "Give me a child before he is seven, and I will make him a Catholic for the rest of his life." In both cases, brainwashing appears to be analogous to computer programming. Indeed, we can come closer to accurate prediction in the former case than in the latter. The only time that response to the prenatal recording fails is when an individual neonate has suffered a hearing loss. On the other hand, one or another of the adults who were gotten before they were seven may have an independent thought along the way from a great variety of circumstances that leads them to renounce Catholicism. The situation may be far simpler with neonates than with the religiously indoctrinated. At least at first glance, however, both appear to fit analyses of computer programming, so long as it is looked at as based on a process of pattern recognition rather than as an exercise in problem solving. We may view a nursery full of neonates in their auditory domain as a room full of little robots, and we may view what might be termed "the mechanical Catholic" in a similar light. Uniform behavior appears in both cases to result from recognition or memory of an established pattern of hearing or thinking.

In their overview of analyses of computers and artificial intelligence, Terry Winograd and Fernando Flores note:

> The artificial intelligence literature of the 1970's heralded a move away from the traditional problem-solving orientation towards a new one centered around "frames" or "expectations." Programs based on "beta structures" (Moore and Newell, 1973), "frames" (Minsky, 1975), "scripts" (Schank and Abelson, 1977), "schemas" (Bobrow and Winograd, 1977) all deal with how a previously existing structure guides the interpretation of new inputs. The emphasis is on *recognition* rather than *problem-solving*. It has been claimed that these systems avoid the limitations of earlier approaches to representation and that they support "non-logical" kinds of reasoning that more closely approximate human intelligence.[11]

The authors then give the following summary from Marvin Minsky's 1975 article, "A Framework for Representing Knowledge":

> Here is the essence of the theory: When one encounters a new situation (or makes a substantial change in one's view of the present problem) one selects from memory a substantial structure

called a frame. This is a remembered framework to be adapted to fit reality by changing details as necessary. . . . Once a frame is proposed to represent a situation, a matching process tries to assign values to the terminals [the detailed features] of each frame, consistent with the markers at each place. . . . Most of the phenomenological power of the theory hinges on the inclusion of expectations and other kinds of presumptions. A frame's terminals are normally already filled with default assignments. Thus, a frame may contain a great many details whose supposition is not specifically warranted by the situation. These have many uses in representing general information, most-likely cases, techniques for "bypassing logic" and ways to make useful generalizations. [12]

Basing computer programming on a theory of pattern recognition, memory, and pattern matching presupposes that cognitive activity is an interpretative process. It reflects an attempt to bring understanding of artificial intelligence closer to functions of natural language than do context-independent logical systems, and to processes of generalizing within social environments having indeterminate boundaries. Most attempts to develop such programs have been made in the domains of interpretation of visual patterns and interpretation of ordinary language meanings. Their success has been modest at best, and primary arguments have been made against the possibility of ever matching artificially the apparently limitless experiential variables that all humans encounter prior to, or in conjunction with, their cognitive reflection or deliberation. From a philosophical standpoint, these are general arguments against extreme claims for AI as promising to explain all of human cognitive activity on the model of a computer program. In accord with existentialism, pragmatism, or hermeneutics, it is assumed that such activity must extend beyond the boundaries imposed upon it by any and every computer program. As Winograd and Flores note with respect to any such program:

In writing a computer program, the programmer is responsible for characterizing the task domain as a collection of objects, properties, and operations, and for formulating the task as a structure of goals in terms of these. Obviously, this is not a matter of totally free choice. The programmer acts within a context of language, culture, and previous understanding, both shared and personal. The program is forever limited to working within the world determined by the programmer's explicit articulation of possible objects, properties, and relations among them. It therefore embodies the blindness that goes with this articulation.[13]

We are not, however, putting such a general challenge to AI. What we are asking is whether and to what extent the model of a computer program based on a theory of pattern recognition can successfully explain the biological and psychological observations we have made in the domain of pre- and postnatal auditory experience. Clearly, many who are engaged in "cognitive science" believe that the algorithmic bases of computer programming can be applied to biological and psychological aspects of human cognition. For example, in analyzing the cognitive activity of musical composition and appreciation, H. Christopher Longuet-Higgins has developed algorithmic programs that "can be translated quite automatically into stave notation." But he has simultaneously analyzed *performance* of that notation in terms of a "perception" that involves an "interplay between the sounds themselves and the frame of reference created by the listener."[14] His inquiries into musical perception, however, are admittedly limited in many ways, perhaps the most important being that "they are powerless to deal with the perception of atonal and arhythmic music."[15]

In a review of Longuet-Higgins's book, Brian Rotman expresses hope for progress in AI beyond limited algorithmic studies:

> The brain appears to do many things at once, and runs on data that are often inaccurate, contradictory and massively redundant. Attempts to incorporate these features into a new model of computers—the so-called parallel processing machine—are where the future of computer science, and therefore cognitive science, is pointing. Of course, if these attempts are successful then a new and powerful scientific paradigm will emerge, one which, by patterning the architecture of computers on the neurology of parallel processes, will be in a strong, virtually irrefutable position to provide a "computational" model of the brain. But such a model will still leave untouched the question: can an adequate and convincing account of subjective experience emerge from a description of what is still, after all, only mechanism?[16]

Four major differences emerge from these accounts of the present status of computer programming and my analysis of postnatal auditory patterns in relation to prenatal experience. We may identify the prenatal pattern as a "frame," by reference to which a composer interprets varying tonal and rhythmic data that have been established within his particular culture. So far, we may seem to be in accord with AI analysis. The *ground* of the composer's choices—his determination of how his structure ought to go—has been taken, at least at certain times, to be valuational and emotional ("subjective," in Rotman's terms) in a way that computer functions are never taken to be. This is the first difference. Second, although I have explained initial responses of neonates to a playback of the prenatal pattern as a product of "recognition," this recognition yet does not appear itself to be a product of interpretation within a complex context that could yield variable responses. AI understanding of pattern recognition and of pattern matching presupposes that the program frame is always complex and that pattern recognition is a product of a primary process of interpretation, thus allowing the identification of "default assignments." Although this presupposes a memory function as well, the broad challenge to the AI community has been to devise computer programs that are sufficiently comprehensive to provide an overall "com-putational model" of the human brain. This is, in Rotman's opinion, what would put parallel processing "in a strong, virtually irrefutable position." In contrast, we have no need to look at prenatal auditory pattern "recognition" as a product of interpretation at all. We have no evidence that neonates are or can be interpreting anything within a frame in which there can possibly be "default assignments." Thus, rather than appearing in this case as a product of interpretation, recognition is understood as a separate or independent conscious process.

This does not preclude the possibility of analyzing postnatal composi-tional process as one of interpretation within social contexts. But as one ground of aesthetic *evaluation* of those interpreted possibilities, the initial pattern appears to be a "given," rather than a product of the composer's "creation." The result of a "profound" composition may be most often hard won, and perhaps, in accord with Jung, recognition of its source must always remain an unconscious one. This is not to say that recogni-tion thought of as a product of interpretation is not, in postnatal life, found in the sense in which cognitive scientists take it. Longuet-Higgins's explanations of auditory beats as interpreted in duple or triple meter, or his explanation of harmonic relations between tones as interpretations by reference to key signature, surely presuppose recognition of meter or harmonic intervals as products of interpretation within complex contexts.

But, significantly, Longuet-Higgins does not take up questions of "musical aesthetics" because they are "far too difficult and too controversial."[17]

At least in the auditory domain, looking at recognition as initially a mental process separate from interpretation discloses a third difference between my analysis and that of AI. If we liken the prenatal pattern to a computer program "frame," that frame is an essential simple that lacks complexities of context, such as would require the making of comparisons or choices that determine the interpretative process. Where the hope of progress in AI is found in developments in parallel processing, it exists within the recognition of the sort of fluctuating and diverse cognitive activity that Findlay pointed out in his distinction of the "mode" of clear and unclear, fulfilled and unfulfilled consciousness. Puzzles that we had in this regard at the end of Chapter 2 concerning the applicability of Findlay's mode to a "wholly fulfilled empirical awareness" (such as that of the neonate upon hearing the prenatal pattern) are only exacerbated by analogous evaluation in AI of parallel processing. Behind both distinctions lies the assumption that *all* of human cognition and neurological processes occur within highly complex contexts. My assumption, on the contrary, has been that there is nothing in the case of hearing the auditory pattern that the neonate interprets. This is because prenatal existence has been identical for all humans and is invariant, simple, and context free.

This leads to a final difference. The very introduction of complexity of sensory features to the adult world, such as might bring the biological-psychological world closer in line with computer programs, simultaneously produces a loss of universality in function. Computer functions are time independent in a way that biological-psychological functions are not. The most prominent source of inconsistent response, especially of aesthetic response to sensory patterns, is sensory fatigue. The neonate does not appear to suffer fatigue in hearing a playback of the prenatal auditory pattern, yet in later years no favored composition, upon constant repetition, is responded to in a constant way. One wonders if it is the *same* Tokyo audience that goes to a performance of Beethoven's Ninth Symphony "evening after evening." In contrast, no one will point out a computer that will function only until midnight, whereupon we must let it rest until Tuesday before it will once more perform predictably—for a while.

There are other factors that diminish universality of response taken as a time constant. Some individuals do not develop sensitivity in the auditory domain, and as older children or adults are tone-deaf, rhythm-dumb, or both. Again, certain culturally determined *ideas* can establish avoidance of at least certain forms of music that are clear analogues of the primordial pattern. For example, in the *Confessions*, Saint Augustine recalls: "So oft it befalls me to be moved with the voice rather than with the ditty, I confess myself to have grievously offended: at which time I wish rather not to have heard the music."[18] Augustine's judgment against the fleshly, therefore sinful, attraction of pure music—such as might send people out dancing and singing in the streets (never mind the words)—greatly influenced what has subsequently been considered suitable music for church service. Such music was to act as a handmaiden to words designed to turn a congregation's thoughts heavenward. It would lack that percussive, cyclical pattern that, if not exactly judged to be "profound," certainly would yield the less somber side of the same coin—the fleshly celebration well known as joie de vivre. Therefore, he who was gotten before he was seven, who knows the difference between "good" and "cheap" music, and who finds himself in the bar on Saturday night, having a beer with the boys and responding to rock 'n' roll on the jukebox, will have to go to confession. The closer he would seem to come to the robot-Catholic, the less he would be able to respond consistently to this music in the way he might have responded before the theologian got hold of him.

Finally, Findlay's analysis of fulfilled consciousness that nearly always has concurrent awareness of diversities in unfulfilled consciousness does not appear to apply to all times in the life of the human mind. Were he to have included memory among the modes of consciousness, he might have recognized that in cases of concentration, meditation, or perhaps drug-induced trance simplicity of conscious content might be traceable to the memory of earliest awareness that momentarily blocks out the "disorientation" of complexities. In the biological-psychological life of the mind, there appear to be retreats—the more infrequent, the more powerful—to what Proust calls the past "recaptured." Surely this is not a "real" retreat to childhood or to a prenatal state. But it does indicate a different pattern of consciousness from the process of a computer model. Computers have memories, too. But when they function in the whole program process, they do not thereby wipe out its current complexities; rather, they add to them. Thus, when the human mind is looked at in terms of its valuational functions, rather than its epistemological ones, we find only a partial and quite unclear match, at best, with current "computational models" of the brain. We thus find also in much more detailed terms what was brought out in Chapter 1: that serious question should be raised about the pervasive assumption that, as epistemology goes, so goes valuation. Findlay's attempt to obtain an analysis of human consciousness that applies equally to establishing beliefs and valuations was admirable. But, so it appears, his neglect of memory masked some serious and ineradicable differences.

IV

More than one strong objection may be raised to the tracing of profundity judgments, and the marked aesthetic value that they carry, to the sensory patterns indigenous to pre- and perinatal life. Especially from those whose central concern has not been music, or whose acquaintance with music has been only peripheral, the reaction to such a suggestion may be a horselaugh. On the other hand, the response of persons who have concentrated academically on music and who recognize the complexities and subtleties of different compositions in the work of different composers may be one of outrage or contempt.

We may face the challenge from devotees of "popular" music that all of jazz, rock 'n' roll, or hard rock follows the prenatal pattern quite clearly. Yet no one would call any of it profound. Consider a selective list (mocking our own of classical music):

The Janettes, "Sally Go Round the Roses" (*pace* Jung)
Marvin Gaye, "I Heard It through the Grapevine"
Martha and the Vandellas, "Dancing in the Street"
The Young Rascals, "Groovin' "
The Human Beings, "Nobody but Me"
Mitch Ryder, "Ginny Take a Ride"
The Archies, "Sugar, Sugar"
Edie Gormé, "The Bossa Nova"
Sammy Nelson, "Team Beat"
The Reflections, "Romeo and Juliet"

To this argument, the first response should be that musical mimicking of the prenatal sound pattern is not a sufficient condition of a judgment of profundity. It might be added that a great deal of this "popular" music is at a very fast pace—far faster than the original speed of the human heartbeat. Thus, it seems to complement better the joie de vivre that it accompanies. Moreover, the intrinsic value of unimpeded life can be found both in celebration of full, dynamic existence and in lament at its loss, as well, perhaps, as in a quieter religious ceremony of slower pace more likely to be called profound.

In contrast to the above illustrations we find in other examples of "popular" music a clear connection with religious experience. Bobby McFerrin's album *Medicine Music* (1990) is at bottom one way to renew contact with "God," and comes at a clearly adagio pace. Among this group of pieces, McFerrin's own "Sweet in the Mornin' " is most striking and unusual. As the chorus presents the prenatal pattern through the metaphor "sweet in the mornin'," repeated throughout the composition in a rhythmic, but not percussive, recapturing of a mother's giving love to new life, McFerrin's exquisite solo singing imitates an infant's crying and brings with the chorus that universal union in love of new life between mother and child. It is not surprising, then, to find that McFerrin identifies God with the feminine and that he provides in his "medicine music" an auditory illustration of what Jung explained as self-healing in his patients' painting of mandalas. McFerrin's "Sweet in the Mornin' " almost moves toward opera.

In what might be called "popular" religious ceremony, we find again in the African-derived music of Father George Augustus Stallings's Catholic services blatant imitation of the prenatal pattern, this time both vocal and instrumental, and dominated by percussion. Here the pace is faster than McFerrin's, but by no means so frenetic as that of much "popular" music. In an interview with Morley Safer on 60 *Minutes* (CBS, 7 January 1990), Stallings bluntly states that "you cannot have fire in the pew if there's ice in the pulpit." At that time Stallings had been suspended from the Catholic church by James Cardinal Hickey of Washington, D.C., in part at least because of the avant-garde nature of his dynamic, percussive religious fare. (Gregorian chant this is not.) Although Stallings traced Hickey's actions to racism in the Catholic church, the universal arousal of his parishes to this primordial pattern suggests a more fundamental reason that transcends the issue of racism. Here, once more, is found that open, rudimentary recognition through auditory means that all men are brothers.

In Kenneth Branagh's film of *Henry V* (1989), Patrick Doyle's score for the final sequences of the desperate clash of life and death in the Battle of Agincourt picks up the two-tone diastolic phase of the prenatal pattern and repeats it almost without variation for so long a period as to make us wonder if this is going too far.

In the soundtrack of the television movie *Murder in Mississippi* (aired nationally on NBC, 5 February 1990), a female soloist repeats the entire prenatal pattern over two full minutes, with hand clapping and heavy bass piano notes providing percussive force behind the voices of the congregation of a backwoods Mississippi church.

Every day, everywhere examples appear, linking the "best" and sometimes even the "worst" of popular idioms to a "primordial" origin. Rather than looking at different aesthetic qualities as *logically* separate, from the foregoing analysis of profundity is this linkage not just what we should expect?

Still, we can anticipate another primary objection to this whole enterprise. Does the aesthetic critic not have the entire history of Western philosophy to buttress a contrary conclusion? In the search for wisdom and logic, when we narrow it down to the arts, do we not have a clear indication that grubbing in biological facts of the origins of human life is the wrong way to go? Our intellectual heritage hangs heavy and intransigent. We all know the concertgoer who brings his own score, presumably to follow and better judge the conductor's or soloist's interpretation of a composition. Although he sits among the other concertgoers, he is, to them, isolated, alone and aloof. He is not among those who find themselves communally together and may likely find their common talk about "universal language" a lot of poppycock; if there is any humming and weaving and nodding of the head, it is his alone to do. The sway of intellectual heritage fights the common view.

There are, after all, long-established music theories that detail what structurally is going on in this art, at least in tonal composition, in a similar way as systems of logic purport to detail what is going on in human reasoning and to determine its permissible boundaries. Many have assumed that in the highly sophisticated literature of music theory we find the true, perhaps the only, basis of music's aesthetic value. The still-influential harmonic theory of Jean-Philippe Rameau, however, developed a system of music-score analysis in accord with his determination to link harmonic composition to mathematics. In his analysis of chords and chord progressions by roman numerals, arabic numbers, and a theory of "chord inversion," Rameau identified vertical relationships between their component tones and harmonic compositions as essentially blocks of successive chords. Unfortunately, this system of analysis did not yield a structural description of any score that was compatible with the way that score sounded in performance, and thus it was a poor candidate for explaining aesthetic responses to hearing music.

Heinrich Schenker's contribution to music-score analysis provided a detailing of harmonic relationships that appear on the score horizontally, thus of relationships that sound in performance as though they are "moving." "In contrast to the theory of counterpoint, the theory of Harmony presents itself to me as a purely spiritual universe, a system of ideally moving forces," Schenker writes in the Introduction to *Harmony*.[19] Although the aesthetic value of harmony in a "purely spiritual universe" was not, as for Rameau, determined by the dictates of mathematics, to Schenker it was onotologically tied to relations of tones of the tonic triad, which he termed the "chord of Nature."

Out of the many tones discernible in the overtone series of any given ground tone, Schenker picked the perfect fifth and major third and, with the given ground tone, combined these into a three-tone chord, calling it the chord of Nature because these tones (the major third is really flat) appear in the natural physical sound series. Looking at harmonic composition as a working out (*Auskomponierung*)—on the score essentially horizontally—of these tones in apparently limitless ways, Schenker described harmonic composition in terms of three levels: the background (the chord spanning and determining direction of the entire composition), the middleground (detailing of subsidiary "goals of motion" along the way), and the foreground (the composition as it appears note for note). Distinguishing details of motion from goals of motion, which were identified in their close connection with the defining locus of the tonic triad, details of motion functioned to lead to or away from the goals. Thus it was in the unity of "ideally moving forces" that Schenker found "a purely spiritual universe."

Any tones in stepwise relation to one another (i.e., one whole tone apart) were identified as goals, because of their connection with the primary scale or key guiding the composition as a whole. This analysis, however, finds a very different value in stepwise tone motion from the two-tone figure discussed above. My suggestion has been that the two-tone figure, found everywhere in harmonic composition and in nontonal music of other cultures, has been established as of aesthetic value independently of the compositions in which it may appear.

It is fair to say that all music theory that yields principles of music-score analysis is essentially logical, rather than biological. And certainly our analysis of profundity biologically does not preclude recognition of logical sources of aesthetic value for humans, such as those prompting Emily Dickinson's observation that Euclid, alone, had looked on beauty bare. It may well be, also, that Schenker would adamantly have located profundity in musical composition precisely in those unifying "ideally moving forces" of tonal composition. Indeed, he did find quite different reason in his deprecation of "music of primitive peoples [that] never developed beyond a certain rudimentary state."[20] Thus restricted, however, Schenker could only explain the persistence, the simplicity, and the repetitiousness of those "primitive peoples'" music through an observation that might well have been true, but that was nonetheless blinding to a more comprehensive explanation that our biological analysis affords: they had not then, and have not yet, "discovered" the "chord of Nature."

4

The Vogue of Creativity

I

I had been set on the box beside the coachman, we were going like the wind because the Doctor had still, before returning to Combray, to call at Martinville-le-Sec, at the house of a patient, at whose door he asked us to wait for him. At a bend in the road I experienced, suddenly, that special pleasure, which bore no resemblance to any other, when I caught sight of the twin steeples of Martinville, on which the setting sun was playing, while the movement of the carriage and the windings of the road seemed to keep them continually changing their position; and then of a third steeple, that of Vieuxvicq, which, although separated from them by a hill and a valley, and rising from rather higher ground in the distance, appeared none the less to be standing by their side.

In ascertaining and noting the shape of their spires, the changes

of aspect, the sunny warmth of their surfaces, I felt that I was not
penetrating to the full depth of my impression, that something
more lay behind that mobility, that luminosity, something which
they seemed at once to contain and to conceal.

The steeples appeared so distant, and we ourselves seemed to
come so little nearer them, that I was astonished when, a few
minutes later, we drew up outside the church of Martinville. I did
not know the reason for the pleasure which I had found in seeing
them upon the horizon, and the business of trying to find out
what that reason was seemed to me irksome; I wished only to
keep in reserve in my brain those converging lines, moving in the
sunshine, and for the time being, to think of them no more. And
it is probable that, had I done so, those two steeples would have
vanished for ever, in a great medley of trees and roofs and scents
and sounds which I had noticed and set apart on account of the
obscure sense of pleasure which they gave me, but without ever
exploring them more fully. I got down from the box to talk to my
parents while we were waiting for the Doctor to reappear. Then it
was time to start; I climbed up again to my place, turning my
head to look back, once more, at my steeples, of which, a little
later, I caught a farewell glimpse at a turn in the road. The
coachman, who seemed little inclined for conversation, having
barely acknowledged my remarks, I was obliged, in default of
other society, to fall back on my own, and to attempt to recapture
the vision of my steeples. And presently their outlines and their
sunlit surface, as though they had been a sort of rind, were
stripped apart; a little of what they had concealed from me became
apparent; an idea came into my mind which had not existed for
me a moment earlier, framed itself in words in my head; and the
pleasure with which the first sight of them, just now, had filled
me was so much enhanced that, overpowered by a sort of intoxi-
cation, I could no longer think of anything but them. At this
point, although we had now travelled a long way from Martinville,
I turned my head and caught sight of them again, quite black this
time, for the sun had meanwhile set. Every few minutes a turn in
the road would sweep them out of sight; then they shewed
themselves for the last time, and so I saw them no more.

Without admitting to myself that what lay buried within the
steeples of Martinville must be something analogous to a charming
phrase, since it was in the form of words which gave me pleasure

that it had appeared to me, I borrowed a pencil and some paper from the Doctor, and composed, in spite of the jolting of the carriage, to appease my conscience and to satisfy my enthusiasm, the following little fragment, which I have since discovered and now reproduce, with only a slight revision here and there. . . .

I never thought again of this page, but at the moment when, on my corner of the box-seat, where the Doctor's coachman was in the habit of placing, in a hamper, the fowls which he had bought at Martinville market, I had finished writing it, I found such a sense of happiness, felt that it had so entirely relieved my mind of the obsession of the steeples, and of the mystery which they concealed, that, as though I myself were a hen and had just laid an egg, I began to sing at the top of my voice.[1]

In this memorable passage from Marcel Proust's *Swann's Way*, the narrator, Marcel, appears to be schizophrenic. There is the "I" who is aware of himself reflexively, making observations about another Marcel who experienced a particular carriage ride between Combray and Martinville. In these observations we can find, at least in germ, almost every analysis that has been made of creativity. And who, we might assume, would be best able to understand the psychological process than one who had been through it successfully? Do we not have an advantage here over someone who came across the "little fragment" that Marcel wrote and "never thought of again" in which the reflexive Marcel is nowhere to be found? Would such a one judge the origin of this passage, especially its originality and charm, as justly as the Marcel who himself judged it? Here is the little fragment as he reproduced it:

Alone, rising from the level of the plain, and seemingly lost in that expanse of open country, climbed to the sky the twin steeples of Martinville. Presently we saw three: springing into position confronting them by a daring volt, a third, a dilatory steeple, that of Vieuxvicq, was come to join them. The minutes passed, we were moving rapidly, and yet the three steeples were always a long way ahead of us, like three birds perched upon the plain, motionless and conspicuous in the sunlight. Then the steeple of Vieuxvicq withdrew, took its proper distance, and the steeples of Martinville remained alone, gilded by the light of the setting sun, which, even at that distance, I could see playing and smiling upon their sloped sides. We had been so long in approaching them that I was thinking of the time that must still elapse before we could reach them when, of a sudden, the carriage, having turned a corner, set us down at their feet; and they had flung themselves so abruptly in our path that we had barely time to stop before being dashed against the porch of the church.

We resumed our course; we had left Martinville some little time, and the village, after accompanying us for a few seconds, had already disappeared, when, lingering alone on the horizon to watch our flight, its steeples and that of Vieuxvicq waved once again, in token of farewell, their sunbathed pinnacles. Sometimes one would withdraw, so that the other two might watch us for a moment still; then the road changed direction, they veered in the light like three golden pivots, and vanished from my gaze. But, a little later, when we were already close to Combray, the sun having set meanwhile, I caught sight of them for the last time, far away, and seeming no more now than three flowers painted upon the sky above the low line of fields. They made me think, too, of three maidens in a legend, abandoned in a solitary place over which night had begun to fall; and while we drew away from them at a gallop, I could see them timidly seeking their way, and, after some awkward, stumbling movements of their noble silhouettes, drawing close to one another, slipping one behind another, shewing nothing more, now, against the still rosy sky than a single dusky form, charming and resigned, and so vanishing in the night.[2]

What is perhaps most glaringly missing in this little fragment is information about Marcel's own *evaluation* of the extended situation producing it—information both of his upset at the "mystery" contained in the steeples and of his gaining power over this upset and mystery through developing "an idea . . . that framed itself in words in my head." We are reminded in minuscule of God in his omnipotence creating heaven and earth and finding them good, except that, rather than through metaphorical manipulation of ordinary mortals' language, God created ex nihilo. Implied in the story of Creation, however, is an intrinsic value in power, inherent in God and "His image" alike, to control what is wayward and arbitrary. Thus we find predictions of the future to be "marvelous," whether they are later identified to be pro-nouncements of quacks or those of scientific experts, as though somehow in knowledge of the future there is control over it. Thus also we find Marcel, at completion of his fragment, singing in triumph at the top of his voice.

The self-reflexive Marcel, however, gives us only a very general idea of the source of his mastery over an emotionally disturbing, although initially merely irksome, situation. Although he must clearly have been subject to the grammatical rules of his language and to certain standard use of vocabulary, Marcel's mastery could not, it seems, simply have resulted from his manipulation of preestablished rules and standards. Thus, we identify his creativity as a process producing something that is at once original and unpredictable. How this happened, then, remains essentially mysterious. There are those who would say that this must always be so about creativity. There are others, however, who would argue that if we knew all that might be known about psychological processes what appears mysterious would no longer be so. They might say that if yet a third Marcel had known all that could or might be known about his own intricate psychology, he might have been able to identify peripheries marking his individual style within which what he wrote on that carriage ride between Combray and Martinville could have been quite closely predicted.

Within the limited domain of computers, visual artist Harold Cohen has developed a program called AARON that turns out drawings peculiar to his own genre, creating what he might have drawn but also might not have exactly predicted. Cohen analyzes AARON as based on a paradigm of his drawing, rather than as a code for drawing an individual object. In one reporter's account,

> AARON is a theory in action. It takes only a single key on the keyboard, to set AARON to creating a drawing or a set of drawings. Plotted in ink on a printer, the drawings show lush, fantastic plants and chunky, androgynous people. In some, a figure crouches behind a bush; in others, feet peek out from beneath fanlike leaves.
>
> Like other artists, the program makes decisions based on artistic first principles. These include rules about the placement of shapes on a paper, rules about relative sizes of people and other objects, rules about an imaginary horizon, and rules about balance—rules most artists never stop to think about.
>
> But Mr. Cohen, who is a professor of visual arts at the University of California at San Diego, had to formulate and

articulate these rules so clearly that a computer could follow them. In effect, his artistic production over two decades has been 14,000 lines of code written in a standard computer language called C. . . .

Early versions of the program produced drawings that had the two-dimensional look of children's art, or of prehistoric graffiti. In the last two years, however, Mr. Cohen has taken AARON beyond primitive art—albeit a primitivism strongly flavored by Mr. Cohen's own interpretations—to a program that produces representational pictures that only Mr. Cohen might draw. No longer does the program seek to mimic a universal artistic sensibility: It now is particularly and uniquely Harold Cohen.[3]

In the film *The Age of Intelligent Machines*, producer and narrator Raymond Kurzweil interviews Harold Cohen. Here Cohen notes that "creativity is a relative term," but that "for a program to be completely creative it has to be able to modify its own performance." Elsewhere he has noted that it is easy to change a program in comparatively insignificant ways: "A little randomness and some long-term planning could do that." But Cohen finds that AARON falls short of creativity in his sense of being able to

change its own paradigms—which is to say, itself—changing its own understanding of what a drawing is. I mean by this distinction to stress the notion of significant change as opposed to arbitrary change, significance being measured by how much difference the change makes. . . .

My own view is that the most creative act of all is to leave the world with a new or significantly modified paradigm: to propose a new point of view from which more or different aspects of the world are revealed: to change (our apprehension of) the world. . . . I am forced to conclude that I can never claim AARON to be significantly creative until it is able to modify its own paradigms. It is not enough for it to make very good drawings . . . or even to make drawings that surprise me because I could not imagine that the program I wrote could do them (though that's as much as most human artists manage). It would have to be able to make drawings that *could not* have been made by the program as I wrote it and left it. *That* would be significant![4]

It might, then, be the case that Cohen can predict, at least within broad limits of the program's "paradigms," what AARON will "create." But this would assume a limit in use of the word *create* that lacks "significance" of creation when it is taken to be based on the breaking or transcending of paradigms. Not only in a computer program would *that* be significant. *That* would also be inexplicable, and therefore unpredictable.

This interpretation of a necessary condition of "significant" creativity is reflected in Carl Hausman's distinction between mere newness of numerical identity (say, that of a particular pencil), whose difference from others of its kind is small and insignificant, and what he terms "Novelty Proper," which evidences newness of kind. Hausman notes that Novelty Proper "is present in first occurrences of plant or animal species in biological evolution. The differences between an old and 'new' species are sufficiently radical and impressive for them to be discriminated as new kinds of life."[5] We presume, then, that he would agree with Cohen that a computer program cannot be significantly creative if it can only function within the paradigms laid out for it by its programmer. And we may also assume that Marcel's little fragment—surely satisfying Cohen's hope of "a new point of view from which more or different aspects of the world are revealed"—would also be judged by Hausman to have been unpredictable. Indeed, Hausman finds creativity to be paradoxical, because the radical novelty in created products is inexplicable by any standard means of explanation. Novelty Proper he finds to occur spontaneously. Any reasons that could be given to explain it, and therefore possibly to have predicted it, remove the novelty by denying its spontaneity.

Although Hausman does not name them as reasons for the unpredictability of a creative product, he lists three other conditions of creative acts that are quite compatible with Marcel's account of his own. Hausman takes creative production to require some kind of break in continuity with ordinary daily occurrences. This fits well Marcel's original wish to keep his pleasure in seeing the steeples upon the horizon in company with those other transient pleasures of "trees and roofs and scents and sounds . . . without ever exploring them more fully." Hausman also takes creative acts to "manifest some control and direction on the part of the [creating] agent. A process that is creative must include critical, attentive effort that is relevant to the new structure that issues from the process."[6] Compatible with this is Marcel's account: "And presently their outlines and their sunlit surface, as though they had been a sort of rind, were stripped apart; a little of what they had concealed from me became apparent; an idea came into my mind which had not existed for me a moment earlier, framed itself in words in my head. . . ." And: "I turned my head and caught sight of them again, quite black this time. . . ." Third, Hausman notes: "I take it for granted that the creative activity which at bottom is in question is that of an agent who is responsible for Novelty Proper by virtue of some conscious effort." But he then adds a moderate proviso: "Whatever direction is present may be unrecognized by consciousness until the creation appears to be complete. The sudden occurrence of a whole musical composition, or a substantial part of it, to the consciousness of Mozart can hardly be called consciously directed or ordered before it appeared."[7] Still, this is compatible with Marcel's apparently semiconscious awareness of some of his process: "Without admitting to myself that what lay buried within the steeples of Martinville must be something analogous to a charming phrase, since it was in the form of words which gave me pleasure that it had appeared to me. . . ."

If these are necessary conditions of Novelty Proper, however, they are surely not sufficient conditions. An assumption that Hausman fully acknowledges must be added to his analysis of a created product, namely, the presence of "value" that is of a positive aesthetic nature. He finds this value to be of two kinds, the first of which is inherent in the very process of making something intelligible. Borrowing from a distinction of Nicolai Hartmann of "ideal being," the second value hinges on the first. The inherent value in the process of working out what Hausman calls the "Form" and "structure" of Novelty Proper carries with it a judgment that this is the way the new kind of object "ought to be."[8]

Now we have some problems. If Hausman has given us an explanation of the first kind of value, it is stipulative of what is taken to be inherent in controlled cognitive activity, rather than being an explanation by reference to antecedent conditions. With this we need not quarrel. After all, it is commonly enough assumed, perhaps never doubted. For example, we probably will answer the question "What is wrong with a cliché?" not only by saying that there is nothing new in a cliché but that it is a mindless, idle repetition of what is established, thus showing no evidence of its utterer's independent observations or ratiocination. This surely implies that there is value in novelty that results from independent cognitive activity. Such value, however, does not condition judgment of the way the product "ought to be." In his analysis of Novelty Proper, Hausman does not give sufficient reason to ground judgments of the way any "creative" product "ought to be." *This* value is not stipulated, as is the first one, in controlled cognitive process. To be sure, Marcel evidently found both kinds of value in completing his little fragment, sufficient to cause him to sing at the top of his voice. In the general analysis of value in creative acts, however, something is here unfinished.

We have been given an analysis of Novelty Proper primarily in terms of its "Form" and "structure." Yet we are provided with no detailing of cognitive process such that the way a creative work "ought to be" might not derive from an unconscious past that originally had nothing to do with the present Novelty, yet which, at least in certain cases, might possibly lend that Novelty all the aesthetic value it has. Suppose a composer decides to "create" a lullaby. In order for his composition to be identified as a lullaby, he will be working within a distinctive genre or paradigm. This will probably require that his composition, one way or another, constantly returns to the little diastolic tone figure detailed in Chapter 3. Still, we might find something in the result that is different enough from other lullabies to place it within the composer's distinctive, inimical style. This is Brahms's "Lullaby," we say, not Chopin's "Berceuse" or Fauré's "Berceuse." If each of these compositions has Novelty Proper, then each is the way it "ought to be." This tells us almost nothing. Moreover, if the way any lullaby ought to be depends upon its determination within a paradigm, then it does not have to that extent Novelty Proper. It is not of a different kind, with its own distinctive "Form" and "structure." Hiding behind the distinction of the second kind of value in terms of what a thing "ought to be" appears an assumption that this value is somehow determined by an individual structure (e.g., the particular tonal and rhythmic structure of Brahms's "Lullaby"). This evidently is what will give Novelty Proper to that composition which no other composition has, yet that contains a value within it that is the way it ought to be.

II

It is, of course, far from new to suggest that the aesthetic value of any work of art is to be found—if it is to be found anywhere at all—in its form or structure. If such works are always regarded as having been "created" by one or more individuals, then what aesthetic value they have must reside not only in newness, but in newness of structure. Creativity alone is not revered if it only means an ability to present what is bizarre. Hausman seems to be perfectly correct in adding the condition of positive value to his account. Creativity, correctly understood, is revered because its products are positively, not negatively, valuable. If we cannot catch the mercurial life of feelings and emotions as clear conditions of art production, then there is apparently nowhere else to look for the roots of this value than in its formal structures. Perhaps the charm of Marcel's little fragment lies primarily in his apt use of metaphor. But even metaphors have an internal structure, as philosophers and literary critics who are still trying to ferret that structure out attest.

With respect to music, W. I. Matson has expressed this quite succinctly: "Music has a just claim to the title of highest of the arts, for it demands that the listener perceive how its intrinsically meaningless data comprise wholes with an entirely self-contained meaning. Music has meaning, but it does not mean anything. That is why we like it."[9] If Matson means here that this is the *only* reason "we" like it, his statement appears to be false. "Self-contained wholes" without "meaning" in the usual sense are surely not the only attraction of an art that some devotees say makes "life worth living." But if Matson means that this is why we *ought* to like it, then he reveals sympathy with those who, now almost de rigueur, affirm what has been fashionable for a long time in judgments of this most abstract of arts.

When we analyze structures of different arts, our principles of analysis vary. Even in the case of music, analysis does not always come from the technical distinctions of music theory. Those distinctions, however, lend a precision and authority to analysis of musical notation, much as the distinctions of symbolic logic lend precision and authority to analysis of ordinary language. So let us look at one brief analysis of Schubert's C Major Quintet by H. Christopher Longuet-Higgins, of a passage that he describes as "one of the most magical passages in all music." We will notice along the way another aesthetic evaluation in his reference to a "pair of heavenly cadences." The analysis relies almost entirely upon distinctions in harmonic music theory, although a dash of metaphor at the end relates it to the points of the compass. None of this technicality, however, serves to explain the "magical" or "heavenly" qualities to be found in the music.

> I cannot resist analysing . . . what to me is one of the most magical passages in all music—the opening section of the slow movement of Schubert's C major Quintet. In the first twenty-eight bars Schubert takes us on two successive excursions away from the tonic and back again. But where exactly, and how?

Bar 1 states the tonic key, E major, and bar 2 the chord of the dominant, B major. In bar 3 we suddenly find ourselves in F# minor. But this is not the true supertonic minor; it is the relative minor of the subdominant (A major). The first violin makes this plain by insisting on C#, the submediant of E major. If we wanted to beat a cowardly retreat to the tonic the easiest way back would be via the subdominant, A major. But Schubert has us by the arm, and leads us further afield—upwards and to the left in our map of notes, not to the right. In bars 4 and 5 he transforms F# minor into its major form, in which C# and G# are the only notes that remain from the original tonic key. Bars 6–9 consolidate F# major with a pair of heavenly cadences, and in bar 10, after this refreshment, we set out for home by a more devious route. In bar 11 a remote chord of B minor has not a single note in common with the original tonic, but the first violin maintains that by holding to F# we may hope to find our way back. And so it turns out; in bars 12 and 13 we realize that the conspicuous F# was none other than the submediant of A major, the subdominant of the original key. Having found our bearings, we are back home in two strides (bars 14 and 15).

But Schubert gives us no rest. In bar 16 we find ourselves suddenly in the dominant minor, and a moment later in its relative major key—D major. Consulting our map we find we have travelled east-south-east, in the opposite direction to our first journey. But in bar 19 the first violin discovers a familiar note, B, in the chord of G major, and by harping on this note persuades the party to return home (bars 19–24), calling in at the subdominant on the way (bar 22). We are then allowed a few moments' respite (bars 25–28) before being buffeted by a south-westerly storm of flats.[10]

Judging from Longuet-Higgins's description, we cannot deny that Schubert's C Major Quintet has "Novelty Proper." It clearly qualifies itself as establishing its own "kind" that is unique. We have in this description, however, no clue to its magic.

Well, then, perhaps this is the wrong method for describing musical structure when positive aesthetic value is found in it. Let us try another kind of description, one offered by Douglas Hofstadter of Chopin's *Etudes* (Op. 10). Hofstadter is dazzled by the visual patterns found in the notation of these pieces. He concentrates on Etude No. 1, presenting both a reproduction of the score and a graphic representation of the directions of the notes by Donald Byrd through the SMUT music-printing system at Indiana University. It is as though Hofstadter has here transferred the structures that would be heard in a performance of the Etude to a visual structure, perhaps hoping to find in the latter a key to the emotional attraction of the composition. No sooner has he presented these structures, however, than he recognizes a difference between "head pattern" and "heart pattern," or between patterns he also terms *syntactic* and *semantic*.

> The notion of a syntactic pattern in music corresponds to the formal structural devices used in poetry: alliteration, rhyme, meter, repetition of sounds, and so on. The notion of a semantic pattern is analogous to the pattern or logic that underlies a poem and gives it reason to exist; the inspiration, in short.
>
> That there are such semantic patterns in music is as undeniable as that there are courses in the theory of harmony. Yet harmony theory has no more succeeded in explaining such patterns than any set of rules has yet succeeded in capturing the essence of artistic creativity. To be sure, there are words to describe well-formed patterns and progressions, but no theory yet invented has even come close to creating a semantic sieve so fine as to let all bad compositions fall through and to retain all good ones. Theories of musical quality are still descriptive and not generative; to some extent, they can explain in hindsight why a piece seems good, but they are not sufficient to allow someone to create new pieces of quality and interest. It is nonetheless fascinating, if not downright compelling, to try to find certain earmarks of greatness, to try to understand why it is that one composer's music can reach in and touch your innermost core while another composer's music leaves you cold and unmoved. It is a mystery.[11]

Recognizing the failure of analytical methods of music theory, Hofstadter admits that his own auditory-visual pattern comparisons have not succeeded, either. He ends his essay by noting that "Chopin's music is universal, so that even his most deeply Polish pieces—the mazurkas and polonaises—speak to a common set of emotions in everyone. But what *are* these emotions? How are they so deeply evoked by mere pattern? What is the secret magic of Chopin? I know of no more burning question."[12]

We now appear to be at an impasse. Rather than having unlocked the "mystery" of creativity through the distinction of Novelty Proper, with its inherent or intrinsic positive value, we are once more left with an understanding of creativity not only in Hausman's terms as paradoxical, but as essentially incomprehensible. With Chapter 3 behind us, perhaps now we can solve the mystery in a way that retains recognition of the importance of novelty, yet also answers, at least in part, Hofstadter's "burning question."

It should be clear at the outset that no individual or group of individuals creates profundity. They find it. But how? If we find profundity in Beethoven's Ninth Symphony or in Buddhist mandalas, that quality is indeed traceable to structure, in the one case auditory, in the other visual. By the argument and observations in Chapter 3, however, these structures are universal to humans at the origin of life. This explains the comprehensive appeal of certain artworks that are yet clearly created by their authors. It seems to be features of a particular novel structure that are universally shared—even though unconsciously—that solve the puzzle. Dust-jacket comments on a recording of Haydn's Symphony No. 88 describe the largo movement as "a large-scale set of variations on one of the religious-sounding themes that Haydn was fond of using, and the entry of the harsh-sounding trumpets gives shape to this piece whose superb quality prompted Beethoven to say that he 'would like his ninth symphony to sound like that.' " Indeed, all movements of Beethoven's Ninth Symphony, and especially the third, sound in basic thematic structure very like that. So also does the final movement of Beethoven's last piano sonata (No. 32). This arietta, marked *Adagio molto semplice e cantabile*, is in its main theme and its four variations strongly reminiscent of the Haydn largo. And the very points of similarity move around the little diastolic figure. To be sure, there are differences, one especially in Beethoven's meter markings in the arietta. Beginning with a meter marking of $9/16$, Beethoven moves at Variation 3 to $12/32$ in an incredible development that sounds in performance (depending to some extent on the interpreter) like jazz. Whatever the differences, however, the similarities between these compositions and the Haydn largo are such as to suggest that the "universality" of their appeal comes from the same source—one that is, to be sure, structural, but that is universally known and universally positively valued. Certainly Haydn and Beethoven created their compositions and were responsible for the manner in which they executed that universal structure. Since the manners differ in many respects, we cannot name the compositions as the same work with variations. The styles of Haydn and Beethoven are sufficiently individual to allow us to identify each of the pieces as having Novelty Proper. But it is this distinction of Hausman or others, which includes as a necessary condition a value of how the compositions "ought to be," that appears to be the source of the difficulty we run into in trying to define creativity. The newness, then, of the compositions *is* determined by their authors, as well as the details of their structures. And the different ways of different artists, such as identify their individual styles, appear to be the source of preferences among individuals for works of one artist over those of another. Thus, some people "like" Mahler better than Beethoven, or string music better than brass, or red better than green, or Christian mandalas better than Buddhist mandalas. None of this implies, however, that the value or the judgment of how the work ought to be is created by the author. Rather, it suggests a revamping of the understanding of creativity so that it now appears to be an ability to find new or individual ways to execute the same thing.

It should not be forgotten, however, that we are concentrating on the quality of profundity. Where certain cultures show a penchant for great complexities in some of their art forms—for example, in African poly-rhythmic drumming or in western European contrapuntal fugues—other values that are closer to those of complex reasoning appear to be more dependent upon the individual techniques of their authors. This is how we identify the master drummer in Africa or Haiti, or the "genius" in Bach's *Art of Fugue*. Such complexities cannot, at some time or other in human life, have been known and appreciated by everyone, anymore than the complexities and edifices in some logical or mathematical systems can be grasped by every human mind. Thus, they cannot provide a source of value to answer the question of the origin of universal understanding in human art. Thus also, values found in complexities of some art forms appear more clearly to have been created by their authors than does the value of profundity or its close associates.

The rather refined differences that have come to light here and in Chapter 3 appear uniformly to have been ridden over roughshod by pragmatists, hermeneutists, deconstructionists, and Marxists. Their gen-eral analyses of human cognition find a congenial ally in the idea of creativity so long as the differences we have pointed to here are not uncovered. Creativity is now in philosophical vogue and goes hand in hand with valuational relativism. Nietzsche has been a prime forerunner and champion of creativity as the power behind the master morality and the overman. And it is this, rather than his doctrine of eternal return, that seems still pertinent in the guise of more recent philosophies. Yet where creativity is championed today, it is by philosophers who likely confess that they cannot figure out what creativity is.

The vogue of creativity extends also to common parlance. In this regard its current popular use is most uncreative. It has become a cliché. Anything and everything is said to be "creative"—new marketing strategies, "therapy" for the bored housewife, or "creative learning" to put children in college-track classes. A character in Garry Trudeau's comic strip, "Doonesbury," says to her consort: "Michael, I've decided I want to have this baby creatively. You know, make it a piece of performance art. . . . I'd like to give birth live on cable." What goes under the mask of creativity is good old stereotyped thinking. What will the neighbors think? What will people say? Remember Mother on the calendar-designated day. Decorate with red and green at Christmas and orange and black on Halloween. Then there are the big ones: Nature, Environment, God, and Great Ideas. To Henry David Thoreau or John Muir, the only creator, whose marvelous works must forever be protected, is God. No tinkering with the environment! No Christo-"creative" wrapping of Florida islands, fencing of California coastlands, or planting of umbrellas in Japan and along California Interstate 5. It destroys the profundity of God's work. Preserve the natural species! No "creative" genetic engineering. Our natural makeup should remain as only God's creation had it. Pray! Facing each other, as over a fence, are Creativity and the Establishment. Within these clichés, all too seldom does the shallowness and superficiality of the "creative" artist's sensory setup allow profundity—to speak in the words of Plotinus—to "shine through."

Aesthetic value has been clearly linked to sensory experience, yet a part of what links "creativity" to process philosophies has been recognition that there is apparently nothing intrinsically valuable about empirically observed states of affairs. Even taking the primary valuational criterion handed down by Aristotle of structural unity (in the *Poetics*, unity of plot in tragedy), we may notice that there is nothing intrinsically valuable about structural unity. What is unified may easily be a crashing bore. We may add the two other criteria promoted by Monroe Beardsley: complexity and intensity of quality.[13] There is nothing intrinsically valuable about these, either. It stands to reason, then, that what of value is found in an artist's product is created by the artist out of initially aesthetically neutral material. Thus, the clear division between science and art remains unchallenged, and the creative artist sits on top of the valuational totem pole.

But there *is* something intrinsically valuable about the quality of profundity, and the artist does not create profundity. And there *is* something intrinsically valuable about Jung's mandala and the auditory pattern I have isolated. In their evident connection with biological beginnings of intrinsic value to newborn humans, these patterns provide the empirical link that aestheticians have sought over the centuries and never found: two sensory models to frame the legion sensory analogues of human art.

5

Memory, the Unconscious, and Neurophysiology

I

Understanding memory by introspection necessarily limits that understanding to what an "I" or a "self" remembers. Concentrating on past experiences, it presupposes that consciousness of some feature of the past has been self-reflexive. "I" was aware of that experience in the past as my own, as I am now aware of my memory of it as my own. Otherwise, so it seems, I could not remember that past experience *as* my own. Now, where we assume that there are no past experiences that are universal, of which each and every human being is aware *reflexively*, we then conclude that any and every memory can only be the memory of a particular individual, and that no memory can be shared by two or more persons. Each memory is unique to the person who has it.

When newborn humans are said to function by "instinct" or when animals are said to learn by "rote memory," it is not assumed that in these functions humans and animals are not conscious. It is only assumed that they are not reflexively conscious of themselves as functioning so-and-so. If we wish to understand the nature of their "memories" we cannot consult any one of them to tell us by introspection, since they have no self-awareness into which they might probe. Whether this is so because they have no language need not distract us.

In the preceding chapters I have not, of course, been considering "unconscious memory" in Henri Bergson's sense of a "pure memory" that is spiritual and retains the whole of a human past; and I do not think that my distinction is subject to criticisms that have been made of his concept. Although I have used *unconscious memory* to refer to something that is universal among humans, I have regarded it as a function in only a part of human memory—that is, as what relates certain present experiences to the earliest human experience, taken to be initially exclusively auditory or in a minimal way tactual, although very soon postnatally also visual. Still, looking at memory as it is understood through introspection, my distinction appears to be a misnomer. In positing that audiences at a concert are conscious of a universal bond with humanity, such as to cause them consistently to say that music is a universal language, then it cannot be something each of them remembers individually. And if we say that the audience *is* remembering a universal experience, however vaguely, but that they are not conscious that this is what is happening, then they can give no introspective report of it—thus it is improperly called a memory. Whatever the audience is conscious of cannot be of a memory.

It becomes evident that if memory of animate and conscious creatures who are not self-reflexively aware is to be understood at all, or is a distinction to be justified, this must be by "external" means. It will not do to deny such creatures all memory. But if they *have* memory, we must assume that it can only be understood "from without," as a psychologist understands other minds. What might have been an understanding of *my* memory via introspection, then, becomes now an understanding of such-and-such memory. In *Ethics and Language*, Charles L. Stevenson observes: "The continual variation of our psychological make-up leaves nothing unaltered, including the basis of meaning. But only marked changes are of practical importance."[1] Looking introspectively at our "stream of consciousness," we are inclined to agree with Stevenson, but viewing our "psychological make-up" from without, his statement looks patently false. "Objective" knowledge of our psychological makeup as such and such must be of a great deal that is unaltered.

When the evangelist arrives at a deathbed and speaks "in tongues" (nonsense speech sounds) to the dying one, we may interpret his speech as an attempt to defeat death by reviving, via memory, a will to live, through a return to a time of vigorous life so early that heard language did not yet make sense. We might note that human speech sounds are, from the start of postnatal life, of focal importance to the neonate and are probably indelibly connected with the positive dynamics of life prior to any comprehension of language meaning. At our suggestion that he does not really know what he is doing, the evangelist may well be incensed. Judging from his own interior feelings, he will say that he knows full well what he is doing. To give such a "cold" explanation of what he knows with real religious fervor is insulting. He knows introspectively what the significance of speaking in tongues is, and you are a mere outsider, an unbeliever, looking in. You are a destroyer of all that is good and holy.

Those attempts of philosophers to understand the nature of memory that have apparently come from an initial "inward look" have concentrated on identifying memories as "images." This seems to have been the case, for example, with John Locke, David Hume, and Bertrand Russell. Alexius Meinong apparently derived his understanding of memory as images that are based in sense perception similarly.[2] These and other philosophers evidently have primarily had in mind visual images, although their distinction may apply to auditory and even tactual experience as well (as in Braille images of letters and words). When philosophers have voiced objections to this approach to memory, they have mainly been with reference to questions in philosophy of mind and epistemology—specifically to the mind-body problem and to questions of the corrigibility of memory in relation to knowledge and beliefs. It has also been observed that not all memories are properly thought of as images, as, for example, when I remember correct dates in my history exam. We may assume, however, that analysis of memory as image is most relevant to our particular inquiry and will probably maintain better than other approaches a continuity between introspective and "objective" understanding of this very elusive subject. Some memory may well be correctly understood as image, whatever other considerations may be added in broader definitions.

Our problem here of explicating "unconscious memory" is compounded by our concentration on valuational rather than epistemological judgments. To the extent that value judgments are always taken to be made individually, and generally in consort with more or less strong emotions that are only *felt* by the particular judge, it is assumed that

valuations, too, like introspective memories, prohibit discovery of anything universal in their human origin. From this route, we become
valuational relativists almost by necessity. But the route to explanation
of memory via images based in sense perception appears to be our best
way of finding more extended reason for our previous analysis of *some*
valuational process. What we need is an analysis of memory in valuational
matters that retains some kind of connection between introspective
accounts and general accounts of particular states of affairs. In this we
shall once more part ways with epistemology and emphasize a split
between origins of human knowledge and origins of at least some human
value. Those philosophers, for instance Thomas Reid or Ludwig Wittgenstein, who have rejected analyses of memory in terms of image in favor of
understanding memory as knowledge can be set aside.

Philosophers have written comparatively little about memory in general, but when we look for analysis of memory specifically related to
valuational rather than epistemological questions, we look almost in
vain. The primary question of Mary Warnock's recent book, *Memory*,
stands out as a long-neglected one: Why do we value memory so highly?
In answer, Warnock concentrates on experiences of which we are and
have in the past been reflexively aware, and on the basis of which each of
us establishes an idea of personal identity. Warnock finds her answer by
combining past philosophical analyses of memory in acquisition of knowledge and beliefs with recent inquiries into the origin and nature of
personal identity. Through philosophies that have been concerned in a
primary way with the corrigibility of memory, rather than with its
(especially emotional) value, she finds an intimate connection between
memory introspectively (thus self-reflexively) understood and what she
takes to be positive value inherent in establishing the identity of a unique
person through time. *Presupposed here is that in order for memory to have
human value, that memory must be self-reflexive.*

> We can accept that a powerful sense of, and interest in, his own
> identity, continuous through time, is a normal feature of the
> species man. This interest is necessarily and inextricably bound
> up with man's capacity for memory, and the pleasure in remem-
> bering that the species as a whole displays.[3]

Warnock uses almost interchangeably several valuational terms, most
often *pleasure*, but also *joy* (especially in observations of Proust), *happiness*, and notably in one passage *profundity*:

My sole concern with the philosophical theories of personal
identity has been to show how memory is interwoven with the
concept of self. But since we do, as things are, feel deeply about
our own identity over time, we, equally, value memory as part of
this identity. Insofar as we value the one, we value the other. . . .
However patchy and incomplete my memory may be, no concept
of bits of me surviving without memory, or of my memory
surviving someone else's body . . . would be a substitute for the
profundity of my interest in identity, being the same person from
birth, through all vicissitudes, till death. (M, 73)

Warnock notes in a quoted passage from his autobiography that W. H.
Hudson lays special stress on "the child in us, the lost or foresaken youth"
(M, 77). She herself, however, does not place memory of early life as
particularly more important than memory of "anything that is *over*. . . .
We shall never *have* it again. It is a lost *possession* even though at the time
it was experienced it lacked the value that memory itself now bestows on
it" (M, 77).

Tracing extended illustrations in excerpts from the poetry of Words-
worth and the narrative of Proust, Warnock finally likens our understanding of personal identity and its aesthetic value to the telling of a story or
the working out of a narrative. Thereby, she does not, however, explain
what negative value is also lamentably found in some personal memory—
of a life wasted, a narrative ill conceived, a story poorly told. Perhaps, by
implication, then, she *does* really give credence to that special positive
value in memory of very early life, of a time in which the disasters would
not yet have been met, the mistakes not yet made, the wrong turns not
yet taken. If this is so, however, Warnock does not recognize that, in
very early childhood, experiences may not yet clearly be self-reflexive and
that the joie de vivre to be found built into them may well be established
prior to clear awareness of a *separation* (however vaguely defined) of one
conscious individual from an existence within a general humanity.
Surely, for example, love of life is likely known before a neonate clearly
identifies itself as an entity separate from its mother, or even from other
of its near or constant associates. Yet by Warnock's understanding, any
value in a memory of this state would have to have been established prior
to self-reflexive memory, thus in a memory—if it properly be called
such—that her analysis could not, then, explain.

Warnock *does* recognize a universalization of personal human experiences, as when she notes: "A good story has been worked on so that it

conveys a truth. It speaks this truth to the world in general, not just to its author. And so the memory of an individual, encapsulated in autobiography, or in an autobiographical novel, has a general and universal meaning. . . . The imagination, especially as it is exercised in the creative arts, is that which can draw out implications from individual instances, can see, and cause others to see, the universal in the particular" (M, viii). Such grasp of the universal cannot, however, be directly known through introspection. It is, rather, a result of ratiocination or thought, and takes its place within general understanding of a world of such-and-such human values.

This, then, is the disturbing upshot of Warnock's answer to her primary question of why we value memory so highly. Human values must be justified primarily introspectively in reflexively felt experience. Thus understood, however, the answer reduces the original question to, Why do I value memory so highly? An answer to the universal or general question concerning all of human valuation remains inaccessible to the introspective search. In this respect the shift required from reflexive introspection to an intellectual understanding of such-and-such a human value is self-defeating.

Warnock's account seems wisely to press beyond the most obvious pragmatic answer to her question—that "we" value memory only as it "feeds," in Dewey's terms, present activities in resolution of present problems. William James would have answered the question by reference to the "cash value" of memory, but this excludes what Warnock seems to be acknowledging as another, and perhaps primary, value of memory, found independently of whether it has cash value in the present or not. In the latter regard, after all, we may sometimes value memory positively, sometimes negatively, or sometimes remain neutral. Warnock wants to know why memory always is valued independently of the individual varying circumstances of persons. Yet she pursues her answer by concentrating precisely on the self-reflexive introspection of individuals as though she can lift those particular introspections out of their present context to yield an abstract picture, via narrative, that stands universally above that context. Thus, she seems to recognize a location of primary human value in what is universal to humans, but yet one that can only be known to one individual at a time. Broad philosophical problems with her demonstration, however, need not distract us further. We need only bear in mind the problem of how a universal value held by all humans can be demonstrated piecemeal solely through individual introspective awarenesses.

Warnock's recounting of Proust's distinction between "involuntary memory" and "ordinary memory" provides a description of what Jung might have taken to be unconscious, but of what by Proust's analysis "is certainly not experienced at the level of the unconscious. For it essentially consists in the relating of a present felt experience to another similar experience in the past, which brings to the surface with it, when it is recalled, a whole train of related experiences and emotions. . . . Although the beginning of the memory sequence is involuntary, and cannot be abstractly sought, *it will hardly count as memory at all* [italics added] unless it is followed up, quite deliberately, and the associated feelings, the conjoined explicit recollections of the past, dragged up to the surface of the mind" (M, 94).

In Jung's understanding of the mandala, in contrast, the very "dragging up" of what might have been "a whole train of related experiences and emotions" not previously grasped self-reflexively would destroy an originating power of the unconscious in the now self-conscious making of mandalas. Once more, the very conjoining of memory with the distinction of the unconscious, posited as a source of often intense or profound human value, is open to question. Although Warnock's concentration on valuational rather than strictly epistemological aspects of memory takes a positive step in a long-needed philosophical direction, it remains restricted in such a way as to leave experiences had prior to development of self-reflexive consciousness unable to account for observations like those of Jung, and at worst devoid of value. We should like to demonstrate universality of at least some human value in a shared *experience*, rather than solely as a result of intellectual generalization following introspection. Therein, so it seems, lies a major key to identifying intrinsic value. But if we restrict bona fide memory to self-reflexive memory, then there is a problem relating it as well to anything "in the unconscious."

II

Our approach to grounding the particular value of profundity by demonstration "from without" is still compatible with introspective accounts of memory in terms of images. Our concentration on the prenatal sound pattern and on Jung's "mandala," however, reduces the reference of *image* to that of *pattern*—in the one case auditory, in the other, visual. This is surely a more limited meaning than Warnock has in mind in speaking of images of narrative within a literary medium. It also restricts the origin of aesthetic value in profundity to universal experience so grossly simple that it could not, by itself, produce any picture of an individual life "from birth, through all vicissitudes, till death." Images coming together through memory in narrative, to yield a concept of a uniquely self-reflexive and complex person, give way to images of origin that encapsulate future complexities in one major value that stands opposed only to one other: death. The more we add details and complexities that identify the personal life of one over that of another, the more we blur differences that may be found between *profundity, happiness, pleasures,* or *likings.*

Methodologically, our problem is to find a way to connect early nonreflexive consciousness of the most rudimentary dynamics of life with later self-reflexive experience that takes its place within a complex and variable chain of events, thoughts, and emotions that form separate individual perspectives. If we look at the progress of human life from birth to death as one of accumulating ever more variables that are remembered in greater or lesser detail, then human values will be viewed in turn as themselves variables. Thus, when we find audiences at a musical performance making statements indicating that many individuals among them are each self-reflexively aware of an emotion of human love or sympathy for anyone whosoever, wheresoever, from a pragmatic or hermeneutical view we must regard their statements as misreadings or unwarranted extrapolations from the structural details of the abstract sounds that have just passed their ears. On the other hand, in tracking down an origin of their content of consciousness from "the outside," we may find that origin in once nonreflexive conscious content that has now become a part of present self-reflexive content through analog or resemblance of tone-rhythm pattern and that may carry with it something like "a whole train of related emotions." This explanation is analogous to Sigmund Freud's identification (in the calling up in dreams of "distortions") of unconscious content, although it is more appropriate to count the gestalt experience of the present musical performance as a transfiguration, rather than a distortion of the original and probably far simpler parent gestalt. The explanation does, however, rely on a concept of the unconscious, thought of as a resource of future conscious content that, rather than having been "repressed," has universally simply been forgotten.

In a similar way, we have suggested a far simpler and less murky explanation of mandala making than Jung's account by positing a universal, though this time postnatal, visual experience in which the circular image of a mother's breast appears merged in a gestalt with a whole ball of emotions centering on nurturing, love, and sustenance of a central dynamic force of life. In later years, in meditation, while one sits (probably cross-legged) and stares at a simple circle mandala with a center, one may repeat the experience of having been brought to a breast—almost to immersion in it—and say that one now has "revealed" an "awareness" that our usual perception of spatial distances between an observer and an observed object is illusory and that a "true" sensory visual experience wipes out spatial differentiation. Thus we say, in what may be called mystical contemplation, that we are spatially "at one with the One." This appears to be a plausible way to explain Jung's observation of Buddhist use of mandalas to assist meditation and contemplation.

It may seem strange that this simple analogy apparently did not occur to Jung. Part of the reason may lie in his familiarity with Freud's expansive, almost grandiose understanding of the unconscious. But the analogy enables us to dispense with much of what has exercised students of Jung, particularly in the shady distinction of "archetypes" biologically built into the human brain and their determination of mythologies and religions via a mysterious process of symbolism. From our explanation via unconscious memory, we do not need to invoke any symbolic process at all, and thereby we surely lose what many have taken to be Jung's or Freud's weighty insights for humanity, with all their trappings of "genius" and "greatness."

Our need to invoke the "unconscious" in order to explain judgments of profundity at the concert varies in significant ways from Freud's establishment of a heterogeneity between the conscious and the unconscious. We are not bound to defend any universal connection between these psychic functions, or indeed to identify "the unconscious" as anything like a constant "level" of the human mind. We may find compatibility with Freud's distinction of "memory traces" in conscious experiences and his establishment of the unconscious as prelinguistic. But his initial determination of the unconscious as a kind of receptacle of painful or unacceptable thoughts, received through their "repression"—indeed, his whole establishment of a pleasure-displeasure principle—seems either irrelevant to our own observations or diametrically opposed to our suggestion of an unconscious source of one major, positive aesthetic value. If early nonreflexive conscious experience of certain simple sensory patterns is read in later reflexive experience as unconscious, this has apparently been a result of universal forgetting of all humans quite independently of any pleasure-displeasure attached to the experience or of any social taboos and censors such as might have caused it to be repressed and to remain repressed. For what seem to be solely biological reasons, it has simply either been forgotten or in some cases lost entirely.

III

We are in the difficult position of claiming the existence of a uniform psychosensory makeup in all humans immediately postnatally, but also of affirming that, throughout any individual human life, differences from others appear, such that many individuals in adulthood have completely lost any auditory- or visual-pattern memories that a significant number of others apparently retain in unconscious memory. It is clear that our explanation of profundity judgments is biologically based. Yet if we seek neural-physiological analyses of memory that are compatible with our observation of certain memories as variable in humans at one time but not at another, we have difficulty. We have seen that our explanation does not fit well analysis of artificial intelligence, primarily because it presupposes that the human brain has a *life*, a history of variable as well as constant process, *that* depending upon particular *times* in development of all humans as well as of different individuals. By reference even to a computer program of parallel processing, we thus have no basis to explain why, for example, some humans apparently completely lose memory of the prenatal sound pattern in *any* sense of memory, while a significant number of others do not. Broadly, we cannot explain, through such a model, how many humans "scoot along the surface" of life, preoccupied with its disconnected details, while others try, through a variety of means such as meditation, to hold on to fleeting images of what they may call God, and vainly to lead those tone-deaf, rhythm-dumb, and pattern-blind people to "ask the big questions" and to grasp the "Truth." Why are there always those, as Spinoza complained in *On the Improvement of the Understanding,* who seek only those limited values of "Riches, Fame, and Pleasures of the Sense" and never, by whatever means, the love of God?

   The inappropriateness of AI explanatory models has been observed in much broader terms than our own of specific auditory and visual patterns. But what we need for our own present purposes is a general neural-physiological theory of memory and sense perception that can explain variability of brain function in different human individuals at different times. In a recent article in the *New York Review of Books*, Israel Rosenfield observes that "in 1895, Sigmund Freud made his last attempt to explain the neurophysiological basis of the way the brain functions." Freud's understanding of memory as a "fixed record" did not explain well why memories are rarely recalled in their original form. "It is the inaccuracy of recollection that Freudian psychology evokes so well," and Rosenfield suggests that Freud's failure in his hope to find a neurophysiological explanation of this lies in a mistaken understanding of memory as a fixed or constant process. Rosenfield then recounts a new theory developed by Gerald M. Edelman, director of the Neurosciences Institute at Rockefeller University, "that gives us powerful reasons to revise our ideas about how we think, act, and remember."[4]

There are good biological reasons to question the idea of fixed universal categories. In a broad sense, they run counter to the principles of the Darwinian theory of evolution. Darwin stressed that populations are collections of unique individuals. In the biological world there is no typical animal and no typical plant. When we say a salt molecule has a specific size we are giving a measurement which, allowing for error, is true for all salt molecules. But there is no set of measurements that will universally describe more than the one example of a plant or animal we are measuring. Qualities we associate with human beings and other animals are abstractions invented by us that miss the nature of the biological variation. The central conception in Darwinian thought is that variations in populations occur from which selection may take place. It is the variation that is real, not the mean. It was Darwin's recognition of this profound difference between the biological and physical worlds that led to the rise of modern biology. The mechanisms of inheritance through genes create diversity within populations; selection from these populations allows certain organisms to survive in unpredictable environments. . . .

The theory of the brain Gerald Edelman proposed in 1978 sought to explain neurophysiological function as a Darwinian system involving variation and selection. Although his theory is confined to neurobiology, implicit in this work is a bold attempt to unify the biological and psychological sciences, one that

strongly depends on the ideas of evolution and the facts of
developmental biology. ("ND," 22)

One primary claim of Edelman has been that "after birth, a pattern of
neural connections is fixed in each individual, but certain combinations
of connections are selected over others as a result of the stimuli the brain
receives through the senses" ("ND," 22). Further, "such selection would
occur particularly in groups of brain cells that are connected in sheets, or
'maps,' and these maps 'speak' to one another back and forth to create
categories of things and events" ("ND," 22). Without going into detail
of Edelman's understanding of the neuronal groups of which "maps" are
made, Rosenfield notes that in Edelman's theory "mappings *can be* [italics
added] related to one another without any preestablished instructions.
. . . This suggests that memory is not an exact repetition of an image of
events in one's brain, but a recategorization. Recategorization of objects
or events depends upon motion as well as upon sensation, and it is a skill
acquired in the course of experience. . . . We do not simply store images
or bits [of information] but become more richly endowed with the *capacity
to categorize* in connected ways" ("ND," 27).

Edelman's theory, then, yields an explanation of individual differences
in terms of a process of selection, "in a re-working, recategorization, and
thus generalizing [of] information in new and surprising ways. . . . Such a
view reinforces the idea that no two brains can be, or ever will be, alike"
("ND," 27).

Here we have a sophisticated account of human brain function that
answers a part of our primary question, but still only a part of it. We have
a basis to explain how a "mapping" determined by certain early auditory
and visual patterns can, in subsequent human development, change in
ways that may modify or even obliterate the original neuronal groupings.
But we do not thereby have suggested how—especially in certain unexpected circumstances—we can revert or even partially return to the
grossly simple original mapping of early brain development. In an explanation consonant with the Darwinian theory of selection, we have a basis
for understanding permanent differences between individuals, but no
basis for understanding *retention* of certain original fixed patterns of neural
connections that may, so to speak, pop out when some unknown
neurological "unconscious" guard is down. From this account, how do we
explain momentary "wipings out" of current complex and variable "mappings," in a return—perhaps through meditation, drugs, auditory experience at a concert, or mandala making—to a primordial mapping of a

whole "existential" gestalt that at one time *was* "fixed" in all humans, just as Freud and Jung took it to be?

Edelman's theory does not find in prenatal development sense perception as he sees it immediately postnatally, but rather looks at "the development of the brain in the embryo [as forming] a highly variable and individual pattern of connections between the brain cells (neurons)" ("ND," 22). Nonetheless, were he to modify this picture, were he to bring prenatal and early postnatal sense perception more in line with each other, we would yet not have in his otherwise constructive account of variable neural mappings suggestion of what might be viewed as an undoing-redoing or a backward process sufficient to explain what appears to us actually happens, indicating that in probably a majority of humans fixed "neural mappings" are only totally lost in death.

None of this, of course, suggests how strong emotions may or may not be involved in neurological brain mapping, nor how they may centrally dominate any prenatal or immediately postnatal patterns that may carry (unconsciously?) throughout human lives. None of this suggests how mandalas, in some especially valuable manner, assist Buddhist meditation, or aid the schizophrenic in ways probably not adequately explained by Jung. None of it serves to distinguish a ground for the selection by theologians of those "big questions" that "bring men closer to God," nor settles for philosophers once and for all the difference between profound and shallow insight. What conceivable neurological mappings indelibly tied to sense perception (be it auditory, visual, or tactual) can point the way to uncovering the primary value found in certain of these—precisely the ones that appear from the start to remain grossly simple and fixed throughout human conscious life?

6

Profundity and Religion

I

We may relate the quality of profundity to religion from two primary sources, established religious doctrine and religious experience. Although the value of the former may often originate in the latter—that is, doctrine may emerge from certain religious experiences—different aesthetic values may appear more or less appropriate to different features of doctrine. For example, the understandings of God of the Jews and of the Christians have been sufficiently divergent as to suggest that the quality of profundity as we have so far analyzed it may more easily relate to one of these views than to the other. In the words of Paul Johnson, "what [the Jews] could not accept was the removal of the absolute distinction they had always drawn between God and man, because that was the essence of Jewish theology. . . . By removing that distinction, the Christians took themselves irrecoverably out of the Judaic faith."[1] The God of the Jews was in control of moral law and natural events quite independently of man.

Rather than relating to the quality of profundity, then, this doctrine most obviously attaches to Kant's distinction of the "dynamically sub-lime," to an aesthetic awe in witnessing unbridled power. The Christians, on the other hand, believed that God is in every man. "[Christianity] believed in one God, but its monotheism was qualified by the divinity of Christ. To solve this problem it evolved the dogma of the two natures of Christ, and the dogma of the Trinity—three persons in one God."[2] This doctrine of God relates far more clearly to experiences of human origin in universal love, which, through the person of Christ, is identified with God and provides a clearer basis of profundity in religion. As we shall see in Chapter 8, *profundity* and *sublimity* are not synonyms. This fundamen-tal difference between Judaism and the early Christian church stands in spite of other more minor features of doctrine and ceremony with which aesthetic evaluations might have been quite compatible:

> While differing on the essential, the two faiths agreed on virtually everything else. The Christians took from Judaism the Pentateuch (including its morals and ethics), the prophets and the wisdom books, and far more of the apocrypha than the Jews themselves were prepared to canonize. They took the notion of the Sabbath day and feast-days, incense and burning lamps, psalms, hymns, and choral music, vestments and prayers, priests and martyrs, the reading of the sacred books and the institution of the synagogue (transformed into the church). They took even the notion of clerical authority—which the Jews would soon modify—in the shape of the high-priest whom the Christians turned into pa-triarchs and popes. There is nothing in the early church, other than its Christology, which was not adumbrated in Judaism.[3]

Such details, however, are comparatively superficial. It is precisely the study of "Christology" that promises to uncover what is profound in this religious doctrine. In the history of Christian theology, that study has been persistent and of central importance. In his excellent article "Who Do Men Say That I Am?" Cullen Murphy observes that "this is one of the most resonant questions in the whole of the New Testament. . . . Though rooted in the past [the study of Jesus] is among the least antiquarian of historical or theological pursuits."[4]

Murphy's article recounts interviews with prominent theologians and a philosopher that are interspersed with extended observations of his own on Christology viewed "from above and below," what can be fairly reliably

known about Jesus historically, and a background of textual scholarship
that has not even today among Christians produced any agreement as to
what the real message of Jesus was. Murphy notes that many methods of
study, including speculative, historical, anthropological, and existential,
are now pursued, but that

> historical studies, broadly defined, remain disproportionately in-
> fluential. The Jesus that people can try to know as they would any
> other person, the Jesus of history—and why he is important, and
> what his place should be, and how and when and in what way he
> should matter—is the Jesus to whom modern scholars keep return-
> ing. . . . Most Christologies today are "from below"—beginning
> their reflections with the humanity and ministry of Jesus, and
> necessarily concerned, if not preoccupied, with the Jesus of
> history, with Jesus insofar as, embedded in human history, he
> moves *somehow* [italics added] toward God. ("WD," 43)

Clearly all Christology is a product of interpretation. Murphy's interviews with the theologians David Tracy, Hans Küng, and Edward Schillebeeckx, and with the philosopher Thomas Sheehan, yield for the most
part inconclusive opinions about extremes of historical studies in relation
to faith. As Tracy puts it: "It's important to get the prepositions right. *In*
Jesus Christ: this has to mean that one has had an experience of God
that one identified as an experience of this historical figure, Jesus of
Nazareth, who is believed to be the Christ—that is to say, minimally, the
anointed one, maximally, the disclosure of God's own self" ("WD," 43).
Murphy quotes Küng: "Would it not perhaps correspond more to the New
Testament evidence and to modern man's historical way of thinking if we
started out like the first disciples from the real human being Jesus, his
historical message and manifestation, his life and fate, his historical
reality and historical activity, and then ask about the relationship of this
human being Jesus to God, about his unit with the Father" ("WD," 50).
And Schillebeeckx observes: "The first thing to remember is that there
are limitations to what we can know by using the historical-critical
approach" ("WD," 54). Murphy adds that "Schillebeeckx describes a
conversion process in which the disciples, upon recollecting the Jesus
they had known, and what he had done and said, came one after another
to a kind of illumination: a palpable sense of forgiveness and renewal,
and a conviction that fellowship with Jesus—a risen Jesus who was
actively present—remained possible" ("WD," 56).

Of Murphy's interviewees, only Thomas Sheehan wants to remove all myth and faith from an understanding of the importance of Jesus:

> Jesus is a symbol of human liberation. I believe that, sure. The real issue is that Jesus didn't come to proclaim himself. He didn't come to proclaim any particular interpretation of himself. He came to proclaim the Kingdom of God—something that in itself is problematic, couched as it is in an apocalyptic, eschatological language.
>
> To say I believe in Jesus means, first of all, that I want to take Jesus at his word. To take Jesus at his word means to step behind Christology and take the content of the message as it was actually preached. We can find out through scholarship what that message was. What is the message of the Kingdom of God? The future is now present—where the future means the eschatological coming of God—granted, present in an incipient, inchoate way, but present and soon to be fulfilled. That's the bottom line. Translate that into terms we recognize: the incarnation of God among his people, God refusing to make a distinction between divinity and humanity. Translate that: religion is over; religion that draws distinctions and tells you how to get from the human to the divine is over. Eschatology is converted into the tasks of justice and mercy. It's as simple as that. ("WD," 57–58)

Sheehan's interpretation of Jesus as a symbol of human liberation either wipes out his divinity or suggests that what has been taken in Jesus to be divine is wholly explainable in naturalistic terms. None of the three theologians quoted suggests that the divine or religious import of Jesus is reducible to purely human terms. Indeed, each has been quite clear that a strictly historical account of Jesus in naturalistic terms falls short of the mark. Moreover, Sheehan's locating of value in the person of Jesus in human liberation restricts it to the value of ethics, almost to the exclusion of any features that are more clearly identified as aesthetic. We have difficulty relating his presentation to Tracy's observation that "*in* Jesus Christ . . . has to mean that one has had an experience of God that one identified as an experience of this historical figure."

Perhaps the most important aspect of Sheehan's interpretation, how-ever, that fairly preserves the schism between it and those of the theologians, is in his suggestions that the value or *import* of what Jesus said lies in particular applications, at particular times, and at particular places. This is compatible with the pragmatic, existentialist, or phenomenological understandings of the origin of human value that we have looked at before, and precludes what Sheehan seems initially to affirm in his general reference to "human liberation"—that the value symbolized by Jesus somehow resides within himself, independently of particular applications of his "message." Thus, Sheehan says:

> There's nothing absolutely foundational in Christianity that is obligatory for anybody—for the Salvadoran guerilla, the Evanstonian bourgeois Catholic, David Tracy, or me. What you have is always the slippery ground of hermeneutics, of the need to interpret. Frankly, I don't think that there's a definable orthodoxy any longer even within Roman Catholicism. . . . I think what we have today is an explosion of pluralities. All efforts to reduce to unity are over. . . . That doesn't mean that we've lost anything. Everything is still available for retrieval—for pulling from it some kernel of truth, depending on the interest of the group looking back into it. If you break down the surfaces of positions you can still find something in the most speculative fourth-century Cappadocian Greek Fathers that is useful today for liberation theology. ("WD," 58)

Pulling together the above three features of Sheehan's answer, then— that the divine reduces to the natural and human, that the value found in Jesus is primarily or exclusively ethical, and that it is not a universal that stands established independently of human circumstance—we fail to uncover an alternative possible interpretation that lies somewhere between Sheehan's and that of the theologians. This would make far more explicit how the historical Jesus can, in Murphy's terms, "move somehow toward God." We need not reiterate features of profundity as the idea has been analyzed in the preceding chapters, but it seems clear that the felt quality lurks behind the persistence of Christological studies of the past and present. In recent times, especially, an exclusive disjunction has consistently been presented that increases the pressure to answer in a conclusive way the original question that Jesus put to his disciples: "Who do men say that I am?" Either our answer, now made with full recognition of tremendous complexities of culture, is given in totally naturalistic and historical terms—thus ignoring what primary value theologians have found in the relation of Jesus with God—or we are faced with an incompatible supernatural explanation that seems tacked on by those who, for one reason or another, cannot rest without it. Perhaps, however, we have now an explanation of deep schisms in Christology on entirely naturalistic, biological grounds. Whether these are primarily or exclusively aesthetic, ethical, or in some fundamental way both remains to be considered later on. But it seems that one way to cut through much of the diversity that marks academic study of Christology lies in drawing connections between observations wedded to text and history, and human activities observable cross-culturally, especially those now most commonly called "art."

We are reminded in religious devotions of changes in body stance in prayer, anywhere from near total return to the fetal position, to at least head bowing (with eyes closed) and forward-hand marrying, to outright prostrations before the One. We are reminded, too, of cross-legged Buddhist contemplation of mandalas and "quaternities," or of the minimal fingertip sensations of telling beads in Christian service (plausibly traced to imitation of prenatal tactual sensations). And what was it in all of the doctrine and ceremony that early Christians took intact from Judaism that might cause the devoted to recall in some vague way a very early time of "being at one with the One" or a "Higher Power"?

Murphy is dissatisfied with Sheehan's answer to the question. "Thomas Sheehan is a layman. He is a philosopher, not a theologian, and he stands at the modern end of a long, uneven, tradition: of secular writers who have ventured into Jesus territory. His book will probably hit a nerve in some educated Christians, who will suspect that Sheehan is saying what many theologians don't dare to say but deep down really believe. I think that perception is wildly incorrect" ("WD," 58). Acknowledging a probably permanent diversity of interpretations of Jesus, Murphy ends his article giving special credit to mythology. Having spent a day near Christmastime "talking with various scholars about Jesus research, . . . at times I had the distinct impression of being present at some sort of clinical procedure. Walking up Michigan Avenue in the early evening through a light snowfall, I came to the Water Tower, brightly lit. On the pavement nearby was a Salvation Army band, which, as I approached, began to play 'O Little Town of Bethlehem.' And I must say that it was quite a thrill" ("WD," 58). Thus, Murphy clearly implies that more is needed in addition to text and history than the Sheehans among us can provide. Yet even in the case of mythology, Jung made available an explanation in naturalistic terms of mental "archetypes" that, although far from clearly presented or demonstrated, obviated the need for supernatural explanation of religious experience.

Perhaps the need for understanding religious profundity through religious experience, as well as through religious doctrine, is most evident in the increasingly popular use of "gospel music" in Protestant (usually Baptist) services. Augustine and those he influenced may still in large measure determine what is acceptable or appropriate for religious worship. But the African-derived dynamics of united, percussive hand clapping and body swaying, combined with texts of little more than "Jesus, Jesus, Jesus, Jesus," punctuating the diastolic phase of prenatal pattern imitation, provide as good a reason as we can find for turning to religious experience for an understanding of religious profundity. A recent newspaper article is titled "Black Gospel Music Wows Italian Holy City." Its author, Jesse Hamlin, begins:

> For 800 years, pilgrims have flocked to the holy city of Assisi to feel the mystical spirit of St. Francis, il poverello, the little poor man who befriended criminals and beggars. . . . On Thursday night, the basilica shook with a sound unlike anything heard here in eight centuries—the gospel of black America. . . . It was the opening concert of the Umbria Jazz Festival, a 10-day musical feast that draws musicians, students and tourists from across Italy to Perugia, an ancient fortress city perched atop a huddle of rolling green hills in central Italy. . . .
>
> Three gospel groups were imported from New Orleans to praise the Lord in one of Christendom's holiest shrines. . . . The acoustics, as in any cathedral with high ceilings, were not ideal. But it did not matter; the surging power of the music came rumbling through the basilica with an emotional intensity that blew the crowd away. Most of them had never experienced the raw feeling of testifyin' gospel.
>
> And they heard the real thing—the First Baptist Church Choir of New Orleans, the Famous Zion Harmonizers and the Gospel Choralettes. These groups annually perform in the gospel tent at the New Orleans Jazz and Heritage Festival. They make you feel like the whole tent is going to lift off the ground. . . .
>
> They jumped and jived and danced. They got 1,000 sophisticated Italians to drop their cool and wave their arms as if they were in some backwoods church. Young Franciscan priests rocked like Deadheads in monks' robes. . . .
>
> Even with the TV crews and the muddy acoustics, gospel at Assisi was unforgettable. How often do you hear "Swing Low,

Sweet Chariot" and "Oh Happy Day" sung by 105 great voices in
a magical basilica?

The crowd flowed out of the basilica to find the word PAX—
Latin for peace—aflame in giant letters, spelled out by lanterns
on the huge lawn in front of the church.

The lights of Umbria, stretching out to the plains of Spoleto,
flickered in the hot, still night.

"It felt like a Baptist church, like I was singin' at home," said
Famous Zion Harmonizer bass Louis Jones. "But I must admit, oh,
it was a heck of a high!"[5]

II

As suggested before, what is "high" and what is "deep" may be viewed as
two sides of the same coin. The "profound" has a solemnity to it that joie
de vivre overwhelms. Yet their source seems to be the same: recognition
in an immediate "moving" experience of the intrinsic and primary worth
of all human life, an experience also frequently termed "knowing God."
Thus PAX appears here as a literary expression of this, rather than as an
ethical injunction, such as "Make love, not war." There is no question
that ethical injunction or "law" is a primary feature of religious doctrine,
and we should think that to "black America" the force of Christian
"salvation" would derive directly from the clearly immoral circumstance
of past slavery and of continuing social suppression. Yet in the musical art
of black Americans, the force of recognition through it of the intrinsic
worth of human life and of the immanence of God in us all, regardless of
social circumstance, appears to derive from African modes established
long before enslavement. Indeed, the rudiments of most Christian "fun-
damentalist" doctrine provide the least reason for finding "profundity" in
it. Whether in details of moral injunction, or in "literal," nonmetaphor-
ical readings of scripture, Christian fundamentalism relates almost exclusively to the ethical issues of the day, or to the "facts" perhaps disclosed
by the most recent archaeological diggings. It will not, then, be expected
that the depths of religious understanding will have been gleaned from
doctrine, but rather—if they are tapped at all—from religious experience.

The quotation on the cover of the Macmillan Collier Books paperback
edition of William James's classic The Varieties of Religious Experience
notes: "I believe that no so-called philosophy of religion can possibly

begin to be an adequate translation of what goes on in the single private man." When it came to judging the impact of Martin Luther's "faith" on Protestantism, he found that the more "vital" source was not "faith in a fact intellectually conceived of," but rather in "something . . . immediate and intuitive, the assurance, namely, that I, this individual I, just as I stand, without one plea, etc., am saved now and forever."[6] With regard to the history of religions, James found that "the original factor in fixing the figure of the gods must always have been psychological. The deity to whom the prophets, seers, and devotees who founded the particular cult bore witness was worth something to them personally. They could use him" (VRE, 263). James was careful to distinguish the value that may be found in religious experience from the truth of doctrine that may be based upon it, or the veracity of particular interpretations of what religious experience reveals. He delayed until the very end of his book a consideration of the extent to which believing in the truth of religious doctrine determines, at least in part, the value of religious experience. The focus of his description and analysis of religious experiences through-out is on their subtleties, variations, and intrinsically emotional character, along with an explanation of their value independent of particular religious doctrines that they might or might not be taken to verify.

A great deal of the value that James found in religious experiences, especially in conversion, mystical experience, and prayer, almost coincides with our analysis of profundity. Certain words and turns of phrase are characteristic of the most important experiences he examines: peace, joy, assurance, security, love, immortal love, "sweet calm" (VRE, 203), "fear and egotism fall away" (VRE, 368), justification and unification of all past experiences, "a monistic insight in which the *other* in its various forms appears absorbed into the One" (VRE, 306), beyond the rational, "a gradual but swiftly progressive obliteration of space, time, sensation, and the multitudinous factors of experience which seem to qualify the Self" (VRE, 303), increasingly intense sense of underlying or essential consciousness, and "insight into depths of truth unplumbed by the discursive intellect" (VRE, 300).

James gleaned most of this language from testimonials. Longer phrases include: "I felt myself in a new world" (VRE, 178); "It seemed to come in waves and waves of liquid love. . . . I wept aloud with joy and love" (VRE, 208); [there were] "floods of light and glory" (VRE, 204); [a sense of] "higher control" (VRE, 199); and (in James's own account of Tolstoy's faith) "a force that re-infuses the positive willingness to live" (VRE, 159).

Especially in cases of sudden conversion, "voices are often heard, lights seen, or visions witnessed; automatic motor phenomena occur; and it always seems, after the surrender of the personal will, as if an extraneous higher power had flooded in and taken possession" (*VRE*, 188). The strength of sound, light, and such motor stances as characterize prayer (including outright prostration) were acknowledged by James as strengthening beliefs. "Incursions [of automatisms] from beyond the transmarginal region have a peculiar power to increase conviction. The inchoate sense of presence is infinitely stronger than conception, but strong as it may be, it is seldom equal to the evidence of hallucination. Saints who actually see or hear their Savior reach the acme of assurance. Motor automatisms, though rarer, are, if possible, even more convincing than sensations. The subjects here actually feel themselves played upon by powers beyond their will. The evidence is dynamic; the God or spirit moves the very organs of their body" (*VRE*, 372).

Mystical experiences are generally more somber and less personality shaking than are those of sudden conversion. Moreover, rather than occurring unexpectedly, they are deliberately courted by Hindus, Buddhists, Muslims, and Christians alike. James summarizes four characteristics of mystical experience: an immediate "ineffability" that defies expression; a noetic quality found in "states of insight into depths of truth unplumbed by discursive intellect"; transciency (i.e., a temporal limit of occurrence); and passivity, found in "abeyance of the will" and a "profound sense of importance" of memory of past mystical experiences (*VRE*, 299–301). What is perhaps most gratifying in the light of our previous analysis of profundity, however, is James's following observation:

> In mystical literature such self-contradictory phrases as "dazzling obscurity," "whispering silence," "teeming desert," are continually met with. They prove that not conceptual speech, but music rather, is the element through which we are best spoken to by mystical truth. Many mystical scriptures are indeed little more than musical compositions.
>
> [Quoting from H. P. Blavatsky]: "He who would hear the voice of Nada, 'the Soundless Sound,' and comprehend it, he has to learn the nature of Dhâranâ. . . . When to himself his form appears unreal, as do on waking all the forms he sees in dreams; when he has ceased to hear the many, he may discern the ONE— the inner sound which kills the outer. . . . For then the soul will hear, and will remember. . . . And now thy *Self* is lost in SELF,

thyself unto THYSELF, merged in that SELF from which thou first didst radiate. . . . Behold! thou hast become the Light, thou hast become the Sound, thou art thy Master and thy God. Thou art THYSELF the object of thy search. . . . (*VRE*, 330)

James's interpretation of this and other passages is that "music gives us ontological messages which non-musical criticism is unable to contradict, though it may laugh at our foolishness in minding them. There is a verge of the mind which these things haunt" (*VRE*, 330).

How, then, is the significance of religious experience to be judged, and how is it to be accounted for? Although James made no attempt to explain his comments on "the verge of mind that [music] haunts," he did suggest a general psychological explanation of religious experience that is once more very close to ours. In this account, however, he did not manage to find either a source of value of religious experiences or a verification of what they have been consistently taken to reveal. "You see," he notes, "the existential facts are insufficient for determining the value" (*VRE*, 24). He *did* think that he could explain how such experiences occur, and in that explanation he found the roots of what he termed spiritual profundity. Strangely, this did not connect clearly with "aesthetic satisfactions"; thus, his explanation of the psychological origin of "profound" religious experience does not relate well to art forms that may be found in religious practice as well as independently of it.

Working with the distinctions of his contemporary psychologists of a "field of consciousness" and of a "subconscious" and of "subliminal experience" that are close to Findlay's distinction between fulfilled and unfulfilled consciousness, James found that "there is not only the consciousness of the ordinary field, with its usual centre and margin, but an addition thereto in the shape of a set of memories, thoughts, and feelings which are extra-marginal and outside of the primary consciousness altogether, but yet must be classed as conscious facts of some sort, able to reveal their presence by unmistakable signs" (*VRE*, 191). What some have called a "faith state" James found to be "a biological as well as a psychological condition" (*VRE*, 301). "The normal waking consciousness" of humans, James found, or "rational consciousness as we call it, is but one special type of consciousness, whilst all about it, parted from it by the filmiest of screens, there lie potential forms of consciousness entirely different. . . . They may determine attitudes though they cannot furnish formulas, and open a region though they fail to give a map" (*VRE*, 305).

Much of what appears to be sudden in religious conversion may in fact be a result of "subliminal incubation" over a long period. It likely emerges from a "transmarginal or subliminal region" that is to be distinguished from

> the level of full sunlit consciousness. Call this latter the A-region of personality, if you care to, and call the other the B-region. The B-region, then, is obviously the larger part of each of us, for it is the abode of everything that is latent and the reservoir of everything that passes unrecorded or unobserved. It contains, for example, such things as all our momentarily inactive memories, and harbors the springs of all our obscurely motivated passions, impulses, likes, dislikes, and prejudices. Our intuitions, hypotheses, fancies, superstitions, persuasions, convictions, and in general all our non-rational operations, come from it. In it arise whatever mystical experiences we may have. . . . (VRE, 375–76)

In this understanding of levels of consciousness in which there are "whole systems of underground life, in the shape of memories" (VRE, 193), James yet failed to consider the possibility that certain of earliest memories, universal to humans, provide the key to finding a "profound" value in so-called religious as well as nonreligious experiences that is intrinsic, and avoids a reduction in the explanation of experiential value simply to biological-psychological facts or states of affairs. This would make certain "existential facts" sufficient for "determining value," contrary to James's opinion.

On the basis of his psychological analysis, James seems almost to have forced himself into drawing a dichotomy between "spiritual profundity" and "aesthetic satisfactions," although he did acknowledge that in religion "the aesthetic motive must never be forgotten" (VRE, 358). He found that Protestantism has "an admirable congruity with the structure of the mind" (VRE, 200) that is either lacking or lost in the aesthetic attractions that Catholicism spreads before its flock. Its grasp of the deeper functions of mind endows Protestantism with a "spiritual profundity" that is weak in Catholicism. In the following passage it appears, then, that James did not attribute aesthetic value to spiritual profundity.

> How many emotions must be frustrated of their object, when one gives up the titles of dignity, the crimson lights and blare of brass, the gold embroidery, the plumed troops, the fear and trembling,

and puts up with a president in a black coat who shakes hands with you, and comes, it may be, from a "home" upon a veldt or prairie with one sitting-room and a Bible on its centre-table. It pauperizes the monarchical imagination!

The strength of these aesthetic sentiments makes it rigorously impossible, it seems to me, that Protestantism, however superior in spiritual profundity it may be to Catholicism, should at the present day succeed in making many converts from the more venerable ecclesiasticism. The latter offers a so much richer pasturage and shade to the fancy, has so many cells with so many different kinds of honey, is so indulgent in its multiform appeals to human nature, that Protestantism will always show to Catholic eyes the almshouse physiognomy. The bitter negativity of it is to the Catholic mind incomprehensible. (VRE, 358–59)

If "whatever mystical experiences we have emerge" from "whole systems of underground life," and if music is as central to mystical experience as James agreed that it is, then his account of sources of spiritual profundity that are congenial with Protestant aesthetic asceticism appears to be inconsistent. Or, if it is not inconsistent, then his explanation appears to be incomplete. We may, of course, question the claims of mystics to priority of music in mystical experience, but a closer look only seems to add to James's examples evidence that confirms them. In one case, James observes that "in the Mohammedan world the Sufi sect and various dervish bodies are the possessors of the mystical tradition. . . . We Christians know little of Sufism, for its secrets are disclosed only to those initiated." He offers, then, a translation of Al-Ghazzali's autobiography, beginning: "The 'Science of the Sufis' aims at detaching the heart from all that is not God, and at giving to it for sole occupation the meditation of the divine being" (VRE, 316). We need only to add to this a back reference to the above-listed recording of music of the "Islamic Mystical Brotherhood" that helps the Sufis on this road to God and that provides one of the best examples of dynamic imitation of the entire prenatal sound pattern.

In general, James's positing of the source of religious experiences in a subconscious underground and "subliminal incubation" fails to explain the primary and apparently indelible connection of the most important of those experiences with aesthetic concerns of art. However many details, variations, and complexities of aesthetic concern may be found in religious art and religious programs that one might find counter to profundity in religion, it is difficult to avoid looking at the former as embellishments on the latter, or perhaps more accurately as audiovisual aids to regaining those elusive, transient experiences of maximum value that we call mystical. In 1988 the *New York Times* reported the creation of a Buddhist mandala at the Leonhardt Center at the American Museum of Natural History. We may have been astonished at the refined intricacy of the process. Dennis Hevesi writes:

> Amid the clamor and clatter of the city, a pinpoint of pure calm—a "gateway to bliss"—is being created.
>
> On pillows, under a pagoda-like structure draped with ornate brocade linens, three robed Buddhist monks will spend the next six weeks sifting incredibly fine grains of multi-hued sand into an intricate pattern that, when it is done, will represent "the abode of the gods. . . ."
>
> The monks—one of them a personal attendant to the Dalai Lama, spiritual leader of the world's Tibetan Buddhists—were brought from the Namgyal Monastery in the foothills of the Himalayas by a private foundation called Samaya. . . .
>
> The mandala that the monks are creating is called Kalachakra, "The Wheel of Time," and while they work, the monks must invoke the blessings of 722 deities.
>
> Creating the mandala, said the Venerable Lobsang Samten, who is one of four attendants to the Dalai Lama, "manifests peace, and even a person who simply sees it will feel peace from deep inside."[7]

Surely, if the words of this venerable monk are correct, there must be some indelible connection between the fine grains of sand or the 722 deities and a "feel[ing of] peace from deep inside." Can it be the simple mandala form?

III

In two primary ways, James's explanation of the origins of religious experience failed to free all value of such experience from religious doctrine. Some of this James himself acknowledged. The first way relates to ethical value.

If James did not attribute aesthetic value to spiritual profundity, he apparently did not attribute ethical value to it, either. Ethical value clearly depends upon ethical doctrine, articulated in a certain language. To the extent that a preponderance of examples cited by James of religious experiences (especially conversions) has been attributed to a release and pardon from all past sin, we have retained a relation between experience and doctrine that James's psychological explanation of religious experience does not clearly accommodate. Indeed, James criticized the work of one Professor Leuba as "making too exclusive" an interpretation of conversions as "purely ethical" (VRE, 170). This is a criticism similar to that made by Murphy of Sheehan's interpretation of Christology. James quotes from Leuba's description of one conversion experience: "The Spirit of God [was shown] me in ineffable love; there was no terror in it; I felt God's love so powerfully upon me that only a mighty sorrow crept over me that I had lost all through my folly; and what was I to do? . . . From that hour drink has had no terrors for me: I never touch it, never want it. The same thing occurred with my pipe. . . . So with every known sin, the deliverance in each case being permanent and complete" (VRE, 183–84).

James's objection to exclusively ethical interpretations of the value of religious conversion seems to have lain primarily in an implicit recognition that the state to which one is brought by conversion—call it divine grace, eternal love, or universal brotherhood—is not clearly a moral state. As we have seen before, recognition that "all men are brothers" is not recognition of a peculiarly ethical principle. Similarly, it appears that tortured conditions of morally "sick souls" are exchanged in conversion for a state of "peace" and "freedom" that not only escapes the torture but at once also removes its ethical dimension. But James did not demonstrate that no value of religious experience is ethical in character.

This brings us to the second way in which his explanation of religious experiences does not completely separate their value from religious doctrine. James acknowledged that his psychological and pragmatic understanding of religious experience provides insufficient explanation of a primary value that consistently attaches to (indeed, that appears to be biologically and psychologically built into) humans and that posits a *belief* in something transcendentally existent, in a "something More." To put James's point in a different way: take away all such transcendental conviction and you have seriously damaged the value of all religious experience.

Let me . . . propose, as an hypothesis, that whatever it may be on its *farther* side, the "more" with which in religious experience we feel ourselves connected is on its *hither* side the subconscious continuation of our conscious life. Starting thus with a recognized psychological fact as our basis, we seem to preserve a contact with "science" which the ordinary theologian lacks. At the same time the theologian's contention that the religious man is moved by an external power is vindicated, for it is one of the peculiarities of invasions from the subconscious region to take on objective appearances, and to suggest to the Subject an external control. In the religious life the control is felt as "higher"; but since on our hypothesis it is primarily the higher faculties of our own hidden mind which are controlling, the sense of union with the power beyond us is a sense of something, not merely apparently, but literally true.

Although the religious question is primarily a question of life, of living or not living in the higher union which opens itself to us as a gift, yet the spiritual excitement in which the gift appears a real one will often fail to be aroused in an individual until certain particular intellectual beliefs or ideas which, as we say, come home to him, are touched. These ideas will thus be essential to that individual's religion;—which is as much as to say that over-beliefs in various directions are absolutely indispensable. . . .

A good hypothesis in science must have other properties than those of the phenomenon it is immediately invoked to explain, otherwise it is not prolific enough. God, meaning only what enters into the religious man's experience of union, falls short of being an hypothesis of this more useful order. He needs to enter into wider cosmic relations in order to *justify* [italics added] the subject's absolute confidence and peace. (VRE, 396, 398, 400)

Well, James got pretty far with it. Had he gone a little farther, linked up sensory experience (especially auditory) with the subconscious, recognized more clearly that "subliminal incubation" may not be only a one-way street—that is, may "slough-off" as well as "add-on"—and identified certain primordial sensory patterns as those very "starting points" that are now pragmatically forbidden, he might have found a key to value in religious experience that is entirely independent of religious doctrine. At the same time, in linking sensory experience with subconscious as well as conscious life, he might then have arrived at an explanation of religious profundity that maintains a clear connection of the religious and the sensory, indeed an intimate aesthetic dependency of the former on the latter. And freed as it would be from doctrine, he could have shown in this way an independence of the value in religious experience from ethics that he seems only, at least sometimes, to have assumed but not demonstrated. That would have given the edge to the theologians interviewed by Murphy over the Sheehans among us who consistently interpret "human liberation" strictly in terms of "justice and mercy."

James distinguishes between the "once-born" and the "twice-born." The former are those who have never seen ill of the world, who are "healthy-minded," and, as we now say, are always "upbeat." The twice-born are those who find again what they have lost through living in "this vale of tears," grappling with their diabolical sins. Conversion cleanses them of the soul's "sicknesses," and thus they are born again through postnatal life in the space-time world. If James had pushed subconscious memories back to before life in the space-time world or to a subconscious perinatal memory of being born, he might have reached another more fundamental and clearly biological understanding of the twice born. From a prenatal floating in "water" (to be mimicked later in baptismal ceremony) and minimal tactual perceptions through it (to be repeated later in the telling of beads), it was then, after all, that one emerged stretched out, face down (to be repeated later before the altar or the queen) into what must have been an almost blinding first-seen light. It was then that one emerged through a dynamic sound pattern (repeated later in infinite subtleties of music and drumming sequences), crying aloud, to a circle of sustenance and overwhelming peace (later exuded in the painting, modeling, and dancing of mandalas), to a total dependency and safety in an enveloping love from a "being" larger but somehow identical with a self, yet "above" it in power—a Self. "For then the soul will hear and will remember . . . merged in that SELF from which thou didst first radiate. . . . Thou art THYSELF the object of thy search." From this interpretation, when we are twice born, *all* of us are twice born, healthy and sick souls alike.

To get back to such an immediate memory experience is, indeed, to be born again, and is, so we see it, the primary source of religious profundity, as well as of profundity found elsewhere. How, then, in the postnatal world can this profound experience that has been forgotten be got at once more? And how if it is in some sense recaptured is it to be interpreted by conscious minds that now distinguish Subject from Object?

Why, by sensory-motor means, of course. But art, we say, is the creation of different humans at different times and in different cultures. Look at all the hues in all the million grains of sand. Do they not, then, *create* their masterpieces? Of course they do. But what endows primary value to those masterpieces is like what is *given* in algebra or geometry—a y or an axiom—not made, but found in universal memory.

7

Profundity in Literature

When we enter the "world" of literary art, we should do so in fear and trembling, for we shall be looking for a quality heretofore analyzed as prelinguistic, lacking in subject-object distinction, and even at its earliest point previsual. It seems obvious that judgment of profundity in literature must be in an art linguistically dependent and derived, from a space-time world of subjects and objects that is, epistemologically speaking, primarily visual, and that may emerge from the pen of one who is in motor matters "all thumbs" and in auditory matters tone deaf or—at least in prose writing—rhythm dumb as well. (There are novels that are judged profound whose sentences read like a series of trainwrecks—Theodore Dreiser's, perhaps?) Literature *can* succeed more nearly in the way that philosophy succeeds, without a tactual or auditory dimension, and perhaps even without a visual one. Visual features of descriptive prose often, indeed, take second place in judgment as "comparatively superficial," however adept at this descriptive art the author may be. And translation of novels into motion pictures often so highlights the purely visual aspects of the original as to bring forth negative aesthetic judgments of the transferred product. How, we may ask, could anyone have hoped to translate Marcel Proust's *Swann in Love* into a motion picture (or, for that matter, *The Great Gatsby*, by F. Scott Fitzgerald) and retain any of the depth of the original?

We can, however, pick out certain features of profundity as it has previously been analyzed to see how well they relate to major analyses of literature that is not only judged "great," but "great" in point of its profundity. One of these is, obviously, memory. Another is recognizing the universality of the brotherhood of man. Another is acknowledging a relation of music to poetry, recognized by Plato and Aristotle and, in refined form, by contemporary theory of the importance of word sound.

Cast in the postnatal world of mortal humans, the underlying subject of profound literature will be that of life versus death, often brought to particular detail in peace and war, or in any portrayal that celebrates a fundamental worth of human life. Especially in relation to Chapter 6, a primary problem that cannot be dodged is the central, almost indelible connection of literature with ethics. If there ever were an art form whose value cannot be separated from ethics, it is that of literature—especially prose. We have in literary art a far more socially complex situation than we have in pure music, or even in visual arts of geometrical patterns, such as circles, quaternities, or triangles.

We must pick and choose. The wealth of literature on literature is so enormous that we must sample, thereby leaving the central question open ended.

I

We may as well meet the ethical problem head-on, and start with the stickiest of samples: analyses of tragedy. There may be no other literary art form to which *deep* or *profound* are more commonly attributed than that of tragedy, whether ancient or modern. Yet whole treatises have been given over to demonstrating that the source of this quality stems from conflict between ethical laws—mainly, if we follow G.W.F. Hegel, between "natural" ethical law and social ethical laws. Thus, Antigone's determination to bury the body of her brother comes into conflict with Creon's law that forbids burial of anyone who is an enemy of the state.

> Creon, the king, as ruler of the state, by a decree couched in the severest terms, forbade the right of burial to the son of Oedipus, who had proved himself an enemy of his country by bringing an army against Thebes. This proclamation was so far justifiable that it expressed care for the weal of the entire city. Antigone, however, is animated by an ethical principle of equal authority, in other words by her love for her brother, whom she finds it impossible to leave unburied, the prey of carrion birds. To leave such a duty unfulfilled would be in direct opposition to the sacred instincts of her personal relationship. She consequently violates the decree of Creon.[1]

Ethical conflicts between relations of blood relatives and laws of a particular state must be expressed, in Hegel's opinion, through the "form of independent individuals," rather than "in their inherent universality." If we are looking for an origin of pathos in tragedy in decrees of the gods we look in the wrong place. "It is impossible to say that the gods possess pathos. They are merely the universal content of that which is the stimulating energy in the resolves and actions of human individuality."[2] Yet in other passages it appears that the law that Antigone follows has a universality to it that Creon's laws lack. Thus, Hegel writes in *The Philosophy of Right*:

> Piety in the "Antigone" of Sophocles is most superbly presented as the law of the woman, the law of the nature, which realized itself subjectively and intuitively, the law of an inner life, which has not yet attained complete realization . . . the eternal law, of whose origin no one knows, in opposition to the public law of the state. . . .
> Since the phases of the ethical system are the conception of freedom, they are the substance or universal essence of individuals. In relation to it, individuals are merely accidental. Whether the individual exists or not is a matter of indifference to the objective ethical order, which is alone steadfast. It is the power by which the life of individuals is ruled. It has been represented by nations as eternal justice, or as deities who are absolute, in

contrast with whom the striving of individuals is an empty game, like the tossing of the man.[3]

If the "pathos" of tragedy lies in portraying individual conflicts between ethical principles, then it seems unlikely from Hegel's analysis that we shall find profundity explained in other than relativistic terms of human societies. On the other hand, if Antigone's "law" is one of "nature" and of "an inner life" that is "subjective and intuitive" and yet is moral, the *justification* of her law stands above Creon's—that is, it derives from an "eternal law" that, in consequence, must wipe out the source of tragic pathos.

The problem that Hegel presents, and the inconsistency of his analysis of tragedy between *The Philosophy of Fine Art* and *The Philosophy of Right*, highlights the problem to be found in any contrast between social and natural law. Through our initial detailing of profundity, we have been looking for the basis of a universally experienced quality, rather than for any universal law or universal concept linguistically articulated. We have made considerable progress in analysis of a single word, a metaphor, whose vagueness alone has apparently frustrated elucidation for many. But our problem now in relation to human ethics forces us to look more closely at the concept of natural law as it has functioned in analyses of tragedy. The idea persists in many such analyses, but in some of the most successful attempts it has not been identified as peculiarly ethical or moral in character. Indeed, Jane Ellen Harrison could not understand how the idea of "natural law" could have become connected with the moral goodness of nature or of God. Both her comments and those of Gilbert Murray come far closer to our analysis of profundity in the preceding chapters than does Hegel's. What is most important for our purposes here is that they free the source of profundity or depth in tragedy from ethical interrelations. In the second and third sections of this chapter, we shall see in examples from Proust and Gerard Manley Hopkins a similar differentiation between sources of profundity in literature and human morality.

Jane Harrison concentrates on ancient Greek religion, especially as expressed in ritual and myth. But she states in the preface to her book *Prolegomena* that her primary incentive had been to comprehend better certain forms of Greek poetry. "I have tried to understand primitive rites, not from love of their archaism, nor yet wholly from a single-minded devotion to science, but with the definite hope that I might come to a better understanding of some forms of Greek poetry." Her analysis of

these rites yields a general opinion that "the religious impulse is directed
. . . primarily to one end and one only, *the conservation and promotion of
life*. This end is served in two ways, one negative, one positive, by the
riddance of whatever is conceived to be hostile and by the enhancement
of whatever is conceived of as favourable to life."[4] It remained for Gilbert
Murray to show in detail how these observations connect with tragedy.
Harrison's concentration was on rituals and myths of survival. But in her
concluding remarks she notes:

> Man's first dream of a god began, as we saw, in his reaction
> towards life-forces not understood. Here again we begin with the
> recognition of, or rather the emotion towards, a truth. There *is* a
> mystery in life, life itself which we do not understand, and we
> may, if we choose, call that mystery by the name of god, but at
> the other end of the chain of evolution there is another thing, a
> late human product which we call goodness. By a desperate effort
> of imagination we try to link the two; we deny evolution and say
> that the elementary push of life is from the beginning "good,"
> that God through all his chequered career is immutably moral,
> and we land ourselves in a quagmire of determinism and teleology.
> Or, if we are Greeks, we invent a Zeus, who is Father and
> Councillor and yet remains an automatic, explosive
> Thunderstorm. . . .
>
> To any rational thinker it is at once clear that Dike, Natural
> Order, and Themis, Social Order, are not the same, and even
> they are not mother and daughter; they stand at the two poles
> remote and even alien. Natural Law is from the beginning; from
> the first pulse of life, nay even before the beginning of that
> specialized movement which we know as life, it rules over what
> we call the inorganic. Social Order, morality, "goodness" is not
> in nature at the outset; it only appears with "man her last
> work. . . ."

The mystic will claim that life is one indivisible movement, one,
if he prefers it, ever accumulating snowball. We gladly agree. But
to say that Alpha is Omega, the end is as the beginning, that life
and force are the same as moral good, and to label the mystical
marriage of the two "God," is to darken counsel. It is to deny that
very change and movement which *is* life, it is to banish from a
unified and sterilized universe "l'Evolution Créatrice."[5]

How can such understanding of natural law that is stripped of ethical value relate to a tragedy in which particular individuals play out their roles within a particular moral society? We may suggest that the love of a sister for her brother, or of a son for his father, is natural but not intrinsically ethical, but that filial love forms the basis or reason for the ethical determination to give a brother's body a "decent" burial or to avenge the murder of a father. Can we, however, separate these two functions when they are personified in tragic characters?

Here is how Gilbert Murray tried it. Looking at details in the characters of Orestes and Hamlet, and at the female characters (both Greek and Scandinavian) of Gerutha, Amba, Hermutrude, Gormflaith, Gaia, Rhea, and Jocasta, Murray found rudimentary relationships between them deriving from "the primitive religious rituals on which the dramas are ultimately based."[6] The similarities between the characters of Orestes and Hamlet that Murray observed are detailed and striking. We need not repeat them here, but initially he noted that Orestes appears in seven extant Greek tragedies: Aeschylus, *Choephoroe* and *Eumenides*; Sophocles, *Electra*; and Euripides, *Electra, Orestes, Iphigenia in Tauris,* and *Andromache*. Not only is he always the same character, but "we must realize that before any of these plays was written Orestes was a well-established character both in religious worship and in epic and lyric tradition" (*CTP*, 206). Similarly, Murray traced the origins of the Hamlet character to English sources antedating Shakespeare's extant three main forms of his play, and notes that "before it was an English play, it was a Scandinavian story: a very ancient Northern tale, not invented by any person, but just living" (*CTP*, 208). From his comparisons between Orestes and Hamlet, Murray adds: "I think it will be conceded that the points of similarity, some fundamental and some perhaps superficial, between these two tragic heroes are rather extraordinary, and are made the more striking by the fact that Hamlet and Orestes are respectively the very greatest or most famous heroes of the world's two great ages of tragedy" (*CTP*, 224).

With regard to the female characters, Murray found them all, with the exception of Clytemnestra and perhaps Gormflaith, to exemplify the "Queen Mother" or "Earth Mother." "There is something strangely characteristic in the saga treatment of this ancient Queen-Mother, a woman under the shadow of adultery, the shadow of incest, the shadow of murder, who is yet left in most of the stories a motherly and sympathetic character. . . . Gaia and Rhea are confessed Earth-Mothers, Jocasta only a few stages less so." After having clearly tied the moral circumstances of adultery, incest, and murder to these characters, Murray thus frees them by observing that "one cannot apply moral disapproval to the annual remarriages of Mother Earth with the new Spring-god; nor yet possibly to the impersonal and compulsory marriages of the human queen in certain very primitive states of society" (CTP, 232). Murray draws his conclusion:

> What does our hypothesis imply? It seems to imply, first, a great unconscious solidarity and continuity, lasting from age to age, among all the children of the poets, both the makers and callers-forth, both the artists and the audiences. In artistic creation, as in all the rest of life, the traditional element is far larger, the purely inventive element far smaller, than the unsophisticated man supposes. . . .
>
> It seems only natural that those subjects, or some of those subjects, which particularly stirred the interest of primitive men, should still have an appeal to certain very deep-rooted human instincts. I do not say that they will always move us now; but, when they do, they will tend to do so in ways which we recognize as particularly profound and poetical. . . .
>
> In plays like *Hamlet* or the *Agamemnon* or the *Electra* we have certainly fine and flexible character-study, a varied and well-wrought story, a full command of the technical instruments of the poet and the dramatist; but we have also, I suspect, a strange, unanalyzed vibration below the surface, an undercurrent of desires and fears and passions, long slumbering yet eternally familiar, which have for thousands of years lain near the root of our most intimate emotions and been wrought into the fabric of our most magical dreams. How far into past ages this stream may reach back, I dare not even surmise; but it seems as if the power of stirring it or moving with it were one of the last secrets of genius. (CTP, 239–40)

Here once more we have a tracing of profundity in tragedy that moves back in time to something that is not properly called ethical and that derives, as Jane Harrison put it, from the universal human end of the conservation and promotion of life. As we have assumed, accomplishment of this end may be considered aesthetic in its various modes, but even in its literary forms it predates any ethical norms relative to different societies. If there is such a thing as natural law, it is biological, not ethical. And as Alasdair MacIntyre has put it:

> The subject-matters of moral philosophy . . . —the evaluative and
> normative concepts, maxims, arguments and judgments about
> which the moral philosopher enquires—are nowhere to be found
> except as embodied in the historical lives of particular social
> groups and so possessing the distinctive characteristics of historical
> existence: both identity and change through time, expression in
> institutionalized practice as well as in discourse, interaction and
> interrelationship with a variety of forms of activity. Morality
> which is no particular society's morality is to be found nowhere.
> There was the-morality-of-fourth-century-Athens, there were the-
> moralities-of-thirteenth-century-Western-Europe, there are nu-
> merous such moralities, but where ever was or is *morality as such?*[7]

MacIntyre's relativistic and most persuasive account comes, as have
others, exclusively from a concern with ethics. Yet the concept of natural
law has been prominent in philosophy and history for more than two
thousand years. To be sure, as A. P. d'Entrèves observes, it has been
roundly criticized as ambiguous, "even in the days when it was considered
self-evident," and both as "critically unsound and as historically pernicious."[8] We might note in addition to d'Entrèves's introductory comments, however, his later observations on the Nuremberg Tribunal:

> I strongly suspect that the boundaries of legal positivism were
> overstepped, and had to be overstepped, the moment it was stated
> that the trials were a "question of justice." The principle *nullum
> crimen sine poena*, on which the sentences were grounded, was a
> flat contradiction of one of the most generally accepted principles
> of positive jurisprudence, the principle *nulla poena sine lege*.
> Whether or not the assertion of that principle constitutes a
> dangerous precedent is not for me to judge. All I suggest is that
> the words used by the Court ("So far from it being unjust to
> punish him, it would be unjust if his wrong were allowed to go
> unpunished") are clearly reminiscent of old natural law argumen-
> tations.[9]

I suspect that a good part of the persistence of the concept of natural law
stems from a hidden feature in it that may be identified as aesthetic—a
feature that has been inextricably mixed with its ethical base—and that
this accounts for a great deal of its ambiguity, as well as for its persistence
in spite of what in it may be unsound or pernicious. It is this feature that

is the mark of profundity, or, if you will, pathos in tragic literature.
D'Entrèves gives a clear statement of this mixture of the ethical with the
aesthetic from Sir Ernest Barker's *Traditions of Civility:* "The origin of the
idea of natural law may be ascribed to an old and indefeasible movement
of the human mind (we may trace it already in the *Antigone* of Sophocles)
which impels it towards the notion of an eternal and immutable justice;
a justice which human authority expresses, or ought to express—and
must pay the penalty for failing to express by the diminution, or even the
forfeiture, of its power to command. This justice is conceived as being
the higher or ultimate law, proceeding from the nature of the universe—
from the Being of God and the reason of man."[10]

II

Clearly not all profundity in literature is linked to tragedy, nor is it taken
to be inextricably related to ethics through a concept of natural law.
What did George Duncan Painter have in mind when he named Marcel
Proust's novel, *A la recherche du temps perdu,* "one of the profoundest . . .
achievements of the human imagination"? Not only was Proust not
writing tragedy, he was centrally concerned with the joy and happiness
to be found in what he termed involuntary memory of a lost past. From
Proust's detailing of past experiences as those of individual characters,
rather than of society in general, and from his concentration upon their
interrelations as members of the French aristocracy and bourgeoisie, we
should think that nothing of universal import might be found in the
novel, such as would now lead us to attribute profundity to it. How is
that quality present in *this* sort of thing?

Indeed, early critics of the novel did not generally so praise Proust's
work. That is not to say that it was not lauded, only that the praise did
not characteristically center on profundity. For example, in 1929, Lewis
Galantière made the following observations:

> That Odette's daughter (even more than Swann's) can become
> Mme de Saint-Loup marks a social revolution, it is almost the
> "moral" of the novel. . . . More than one critic has compared
> Proust with the enchanting Provençal entomologist, Fabre. The
> parallel is as pretty as it is facile. Proust observed human as Fabre
> insect society. . . . There is in these pages a density of character-

isation, in the portraits particularly of Mme Verdurin, Odette, and Swann, which Proust equals elsewhere certainly, but which to me is unsurpassed and rarely paralleled by any other novelist. . . . [Proust] was limited essentially in his interest to the movements inspired in man by considerations of love and vanities of the world of fashion; but here, in this field, itself immense and fertile as is no other, he stands higher than any novelist I have ever read.[11]

Central to Proust's concerns in the society he portrayed were homosexuality, snobbishness, vanity, and cruelty, all of which he saw as moral vices. With respect to his own homosexuality, Harold March has observed that "he felt that he could and should conquer his inclination. He did not, and from 'Avant la nuit' in 1893 to *Sodome et Gomorrhe* in 1921, he rationalized homosexuality, without ceasing to consider it a vice and without convincing himself by his own arguments."[12] In March's analysis of the "two worlds of Marcel Proust," however, it is quite unclear how such moral concerns connect with the search for lost time through involuntary memory.

No sooner have we been introduced in the first approximately sixty pages to almost all of the characters to be followed throughout Proust's novel than we are also introduced to what March simply terms "the madeleine incident"—the "prototype" disclosure of involuntary memory. This and other unexpected disclosures later on of involuntary memory are all sensory in nature: visual, auditory, tactual, or gustatory. Rather than yielding "intellectual" knowledge of the world of voluntary memory—and, we might add, *justification of ethical judgments*—they yield a joy and happiness that is prelinguistic and alluded to in frequent references to "visceral depths" and "primitive existences." Generally the courting of involuntary memory (and also contemplation) has been described as a search for lost time, but the Marcel of the novel also finds it to disclose a "reality" that the ordinary sensory-intellectual content of voluntary memory does not grasp. As we saw in Chapter 4, he observes in the steeples of Martinville a mystery, a "something else . . . which they seemed at once to contain and to conceal."

Mary Warnock notes that "it is precisely because real memory comes involuntarily and by chance, that we can be sure that it is true. There is nothing in it that is invented or factitious." She then quotes from Marcel:

I had not gone to see the two paving stones in the courtyard against which I had struck. But it was precisely the fortuitousness, the inevitability of the sensation which safeguarded the truth of the past it revived . . . since we feel its effort to rise upwards to the light and the *joy of the real recaptured.* That fortuitousness is the guardian of the truth of the whole series of contemporary impressions which it brings in its train, with that infallible proportion of light and shade, of emphasis and omission, of memory and forgetfulness, of which the conscious memory or observation are ignorant.[13]

Although the effectiveness of the little phrase in the Vinteuil sonata is not given as disclosure of involuntary memory, Marcel wonders

whether music were not the single example of what—but for the invention of language, the formation of words, the analysis of ideas—might have been the communication of souls. It is like a possibility that has no sequel; humanity set out on other roads, on that of spoken and written language. But this return to the unanalyzed was so intoxicating that, on coming out of this paradise, contact with more or less intelligent beings seemed to me of extraordinary insignificance.[14]

In such passages as this we find what ethical concerns as would attend "contact with more or less intelligent beings" to be divorced from the significance of "the communication of souls" that we have found marks the profound. Paul Ricoeur observes that "Swann's mistake . . . was to have assimilated the happiness afforded by the phrase of the sonata to the pleasures of love: 'he was unable to find in it artistic creation.' "[15] We might add that Swann's musings about his relation to the cocotte Odette de Crécy do not center on her moral licentiousness. Ricoeur adds: "It is as someone who has fallen in love with the musical phrase" (I, p. 231) that Swann clings to his memory. And this memory, henceforth, is too closely tied up with his love for Odette to provoke the interrogation contained in its promise of happiness. The entire field is occupied by a more pressing interrogation, pushed to the point of frenzy, one which is constantly generated by jealousy. The apprenticeship in the Verdurin salon to the signs of love, interwoven with that of the signs of society, is alone capable of making the search for lost time coincide with the search for truth, and lost time itself coincide with the defection that ravages love (*TN*, 139).

Before considering the unifying relations that may be found between

Time Regained and *Remembrance*, we may find compatibility of judgments of profundity in the latter and in our previous analysis of the quality in other arts and in religion. We have a quality that derives from what we have termed unconscious, and Proust termed involuntary, memory. The disclosures of memory are again prelinguistic, retreating to childhood, and distinctly sensory in origin. And since Vinteuil has been thought by some to have been modeled after César Franck, we may even wonder whether that "little phrase" was entirely fictional, and how closely some real music, perhaps by Franck, that may have moved Proust himself coincided with our little diastolic figure.

Proust was critical of visual perception as especially closely linked to intellectual grasp and as especially vulnerable to the habit and sensory fatigue inherent in voluntary memory. This is compatible with our understanding of the metaphor of depth as nonvisual. And although Proust's narrative is couched in the individual characters of the novel, he saw in and through them life "that is simply our life, true life . . . the life which, in a sense, dwells at every instant in all men, and not in the artist alone."[16] Still, the connection of morality with what "dwells at every instant in all men" is unclear.

Ricoeur finds in Proust's novel an intimate structural unity between *Remembrance* and *Time Regained* that requires their rereading over the more common interpretation of March in terms of two separate "worlds." March writes:

> Social panorama, character creation, style, psychology—all these aspects of Proust's individuality acquire significance only in rela-tion to his basic philosophy, his report on experience. Here what Proust has to say sifts down to this: there are two worlds, one the world of time, where necessity, illusion, suffering, change, decay, and death are the law; the other world of eternity, where there is freedom, beauty, and peace. Normal experience is in the world of time, but glimpses of the other world may be given in moments of contemplation or through accidents of involuntary memory. It is the function of art to develop these insights and to use them for the illumination of life in the world of time.[17]

We may look at Proust's view of the artist as one of "developing" views of two worlds, however, more broadly and subtly. We have not yet through such an interpretation as March's exhausted the sources of profundity in Proust's work. It is not only to be found in the search for lost time in involuntary memory and contemplation that brings that time momentarily into the present; it is also to be found in "time regained," through which in Ricoeur's interpretation it becomes the "vocation" of the artist—in Marcel's case the literary artist—to disclose an intimate relation between time lost and time regained.

Ricoeur's superb analysis is entirely too detailed and subtle to recount here. But we may pick up certain features of it that should clarify and justify his interpretation. Ricoeur warns against "equating time regained with involuntary memory" and states that there is a "symmetry between the beginning and the end [that] is revealed to be the guiding principle of the entire composition" (TN, 236–37).

> What does the narrator mean by time regained? To attempt to reply to this question, we shall take advantage of the symmetry between the beginning and end of the great narrative. Just as the experience of the madeleine in Swann's Way marks a before and an after, the before of the state between waking and sleeping and the after of the time regained with respect to Combray, the great scene in the Guermantes library demarcates, in its turn, a before to which the narrator has given significant amplitude and an after in which the ultimate signification of Time Regained is discovered. (TN, 141)

There is a recognition of the "hero" that "one must give up an attempt to relive the past if lost time is ever, in some as yet unknown way, to be found again. This death of desire to see things again is accompanied by the death of the desire to possess the women he had loved." The first part of the novel, by far the longest, "is made up of a mist of events that are poorly coordinated among themselves . . . but which all bear the double sign of disillusionment and detachment."

> All of the events recounted, all the encounters reported in what follows are placed under the same sign of decline, of death. Gilberte's narrative of the poverty of her relations with Saint-Loup, now her husband; the visit to the church in Combray, where the power of what endures accentuates the precariousness of mortal beings; and especially, the sudden mention of the "long years" that the hero has spent in a sanitorium, contributing a realistic aspect to the feeling of separateness and of distanciation required by the final vision. The description of Paris at war adds

to the impression of erosion that affects everything. The frivolity of Parisian drawing rooms has an air of decadence about it. The campaigns for and against Dreyfus have been forgotten, Saint-Loup's visit, home from the front lines, is that of a ghost; we learn of Cottard's death, then of the death of M. Verdurin. The chance encounter with M. de Charlus in a Paris street during the war places on this sinister initiation the seal of a deadly abjection. From the degradation of his body, of his loves, rises a strange poetry which the narrator ascribes to a complete detachment, something the hero is not yet able to attain. The scene in Jupien's bordello, where the baron has himself whipped with a chain by soldiers on leave, reduces the painting of a society at war to its quintessence of abjection. The interconnection in the narrative between Saint-Loup's last visit, rapidly followed by the news of his death—evoking another death, that of Albertine—and the narrative of Charlus's ultimate turpitudes, leading to his arrest, give these pages the tone of a funereal maelstrom, which will again prevail, although with an entirely different signification, in the symmetrical scene that follows the great revelation, the scene of the dinner surrounded by death's-heads, the first test of the hero converted to eternity. (TN, 142)

What had been regained from involuntary memory in the first "locus" of the novel had not been created, but was recognized. Creating "at this level is translating" (TN, 145). The "great revelation" preceding the dinner scene was of time not in the sense of something regained from what had been lost, but in the sense of its suspension, of *eternity*, "or to speak as the narrator does, 'extra-temporal' being." Through this, the narrator realizes that his vocation as a writer is one of intellectual construction, primarily through interpretation of "signs" and framing of metaphor. By these means he brings what would remain "transcendent" without his vocation: "the character of eternity that mysteriously circulates between present and past, out of which it creates a unity" (TN, 144).

Within an understanding of Proust's novel so much broader than that expressed by March, the primary ingredient of the novelist's "creation" is precisely humans, not just in terms of their individual "lost" memories, but in terms of their interrelations, interpreted within some (regained) time frame. The novelist cannot play the role of the mystic and commune with eternity alone on a mountaintop. That is not just because language fails him and he cannot on that account pursue the writer's vocation. More important, it is because he has taken himself out of the domain of social communication. It seems, then, that if we expand the source of profundity in literature beyond the "depth" of memory lost, but somehow regained, to retain the recognition that this is interpreted in worlds of humans who can never shed their ethical mores, we can no longer plausibly separate out the ethical domain from profundity in novel writing, as Harrison and Murray managed to do in tragedy. We might add that not only does Ricoeur's interpretation of Proust's novel appear to be the more insightful one; there are even well-respected contemporary analyses of tragedy that still maintain an indelible connection between "universal justice" and "human destiny." For example, Richard B. Sewall observes: "Historically, literary tragedy has always appeared at the mature period of a culture, not at its beginning. Although it retains the primitive sense of terror at what Joyce called 'the secret cause' of suffering, it is in another sense highly sophisticated. It puts to the test of action all the formulations of philosophy and religion. In the three major western cultures—Hebrew, Greek, and Christian—there have come times (our present era may be one of them) when for reasons internal and external, spiritual and sociological, the questions of ultimate justice and human destiny seem suddenly to have been jarred loose again."[18]

There are details, however, in this general picture that cannot be overlooked. The *value* that Proust put in the novelist's vocation stressed the creativity of the writer and the unity of structure that he forges. As Ricoeur notes, "time regained is also death regained" (*TN*, 152). Thus our past grounding of profundity in the celebration of life and the lamenting of death lies essentially outside the primary source of value in novel writing determined by Proust (and evidently also by Ricoeur). Disillusion, depression, and finally death are evaluated as structural means to unify a novel that otherwise might remain bifurcated between time lost and time regained. This is, of course, a created product of the author. But from our own perspective, this moves the aesthetic significance of all human death in the wrong direction. It is, of course, almost a cliché to assume that value in the novel lies in its structural unity. There is nothing, however, of intrinsic value in unity—even if we include the now-mandated "variety" to accompany it. On the other hand, there is something intrinsically wrong about death, as life has intrinsic value. If Proust was going to place the value of the novel in the creativity of the writer, he could not, then, have praised what is recognized but not created in "time regained."

Critics praise Proust for his creativity and imagination, as witness that his masterpiece is not autobiographical. Yet this fails to explain the repeated invoking by critics of profundity as the final arbiter. Recognition of the "depths" and the "primordial" does not result, so it seems, from an imaginative or creative mind, but rather from one who is able to observe in unusual and unexpected circumstances something that has been there all along—a subjective universal. However deftly and subtly Proust wove this into a unified fabric that married time lost with time regained—that surely *was* creative—does not change the source of the value. It remains a value intrinsic and built in, a source that is other than the unified structure in which it is found. Looked at in relation to the quality of profundity, the ethical concerns in the novel—the homosexuality of M. de Charlus, snobbishness, vanity, and cruelty—*can* be set aside. Looked at as valuable because of the novel's unified structure, they cannot be.

Pin this down to the case of Swann in love. We may interpret Swann's relating of the little phrase of Vinteuil to his love of Odette, such that he heard in the phrase nothing creative, in a way that is independent of the structural fit that Ricoeur finds in it in the quotation cited above. Such an interpretation is admittedly at the expense of a well-founded value judgment based on unity of the entire narrative. It will, however, more clearly elucidate a profundity that Swann undoubtedly may be taken to have found in the music, of a similar quality as that which he found in the love of another human being—regardless of her moral character. To be sure, Swann was beset with jealousy and other psychological ills. But there must have been something in the music as he heard it that was valuable in itself, and which he then later attached to his love. If he found in it nothing creative, it could well have been because he was observant enough to realize that profoundly affecting music is discovered, not created. In other words, we *can* separate whatever moral problems Swann had with Odette from what might have been profundity of the little phrase. But if we give Ricoeur's interpretation in terms of Swann's motives as fitting narrative structure, we cannot.

In this inquiry into Proust's novel, then, the main difficulty of separating profundity from human mores has stemmed from an admixture of profundity with structural unity. It seems that if we simultaneously judge Proust's "masterpiece" in terms of profundity *and* in terms of its structural unity, separating or even distinguishing profundity from ethical concerns is not warranted. If, on the other hand, we take different incidents and characters separately and perhaps then come up with an interpretation of the novel like March's—in terms of two different "worlds"—the separation becomes much easier. In the case of analysis of tragedy, the difficulty of such separation has been traced to the persistence of the concept of natural law. However implausible or undemonstrable that concept may be, its persistence raises questions concerning dependence upon certain language use as a starting point for analyzing *profundity* in the first place. It seems that a certain aesthetic feature of "natural law" should be recognized as buttressing its clearly ethical connotation. But it is the question of separability, or even of distinguishability, in the use of *natural law* that gives us pause. At any rate, in these particular phases of literature, tragedy and the novel, we have the hardest time maintaining a separation that has in the case of auditory and visual arts appeared to be far easier.

III

I shall argue, however, that the separation in certain short forms of poetry between literary profundity and ethical concerns can be quite clearly maintained. Although this requires the presentation of an entire short poem, which is nowadays frowned upon as irksome to the reader and generally unnecessary, in this particular case no demonstration of my extreme claim can be made without it. I shall not rely on others' analyses of this poem or of any other poem, but shall provide my own assessment of this example in "direct confrontation." This will suggest that where word-sound is prominent in effecting judgments of profundity in literature—and that will include religious texts—the question of structural unity of an especially long and complex text, such as that of Proust, takes second place. As we have just seen, this seems in the case of the novel to be the primary source of difficulty in keeping profundity judgments clear of ethical entanglement. This, of course, has been our aim in order to keep our analysis of profundity in literature consistent with that of profundity in the preceding chapters.

Beyond the well-known relations drawn by Plato and Aristotle between music and poetry, as well as older specific comments made on the importance of the chorus in Greek tragedy, more than one contemporary philosopher has found special importance in word-sound, both in secular and religious literature. Hans-Georg Gadamer has emphasized spoken language in the hermeneutics of understanding, and in his special consideration of lyric poetry he has found heard language not only to

determine the identity of a poem, such that it cannot be translated into
another language, but also its "form" and "unity." These features by
themselves do not clearly connect with aesthetic judgment—that is,
identifying a poem as itself and none other, and determining its unity,
need not constitute any aesthetic judgment at all. However, Gadamer
brings in aesthetic considerations when he notes:

> Poetic language stands out as the *highest fulfillment* [italics added]
> of that revealing *(deloun)* which is the achievement of all speech.
> For this reason it seems to me that an aesthetic theory that
> interprets the poetic word simply as a combination of emotional
> and signifying moments added onto everyday language is thor-
> oughly misleading. That may well be the case, yet it is not *because*
> [italics added] of this that a word becomes a poetic word, but
> because it acquires the power of "realization. . . ." The word is
> true in the sense that it discloses, producing [a] self-fulfillment.
> . . . The decisive thing is that the word summons up what is
> "there" so that it is palpably near. The truth of poetry consists in
> creating a "hold upon nearness."[19]

Clearly this result is primarily dependent upon what is heard spoken.
Thus Gadamer concludes his essay: "This is not a romantic theory, but a
straightforward description of the fact that language gives all of us our
access to a world in which certain special forms of human experience
arise; the religious tidings that proclaim salvation, *the legal judgment that
tells us what is right* [italics added. *Pace* natural law in tragedy] and what is
wrong in our society, the poetic word that by being there bears witness
to our own being."[20] From Gadamer's remarks, we might add that word-
sound has apparently not been of concern in translation of Proust's novel.
The lack of ability to repeat sounds of the words or sentences in the
original French has not frustrated attempts to translate the novel, and in
such translations to capture whatever "profundity" has been found in it.

In the essay "Aesthetic and Religious Experience," Gadamer extends
his observations on word-sound to interpretation of religious texts, such
that "linguistic articulation communicates a content and elevates that
content into a vivid and tangible presence so that it entirely fulfills us"
(*RB*, 144). In religious invocation, he also mentions its repetition in
some cases "again and again" (*RB*, 145) and that "the sermon is unique
in being the word of an individual who certainly subscribes to the belief
of the Church, but who bears witness as an individual and speaks publicly

as a helper of the word. That is why the sermon is the real acme of ecclesiastic rhetoric in which one individual speaks to many and seeks to communicate to them the message of salvation" (RB, 150).

William James finds similar roles of word-sound in "mystical" matters: "Most of us can remember the strangely moving power of passages in certain poems read when we were young, irrational doorways as they were through which the mystery of fact, the wildness and the pang of life, stole into our hearts and thrilled them. The words have now perhaps become mere polished surfaces for us; but lyric poetry and music are alive and significant only in proportion as they fetch these vague vistas of a life continuous with our own, beckoning and inviting, yet ever eluding our pursuit." Again, James notes that "intoning" the "list of scholastic attributes of the deity . . . [carries] these exalted and mysterious verbal additions just as it enriches a church to have an organ."[21]

Undoubtedly Gadamer has been influenced by Roman Ingarden's *Das literarische Kunstwerk*, in which he defines the literary work as having four "strata." The first of these he calls the "word-sound" stratum, and his analysis of it brings out many of Gadamer's points. Indeed, Gadamer refers to Ingarden's work as "very important." In a distinction between word-sound and word-meaning (the second stratum), Ingarden observes that "the cogivenness of the manifested psychic states makes precise, often only at the very moment they are spoken, the meaning of the sentences, whereby this meaning either attains full development or is modified in specific ways."[22]

I need not pursue in greater detail the philosophical authority that can be lent to my following venture in analyzing the short poem "Felix Randal," by Gerard Manley Hopkins—one of the world's most "musical" poets, and one of its most gifted. Here is a case, as I read it, of profundity made immediate in a brevity of presentation that is so dependent upon word-sound as almost to bring it into equal partnership with the poem as a priest's (Hopkins's) vision of human death and redemption. The two merge in an indelible unity that indeed bears out the observations of Gadamer and Ingarden.

In 1880, a blacksmith named Felix Spencer died in Liverpool of pulmonary consumption after a long illness. Gerard Manley Hopkins, then serving as a Catholic parish priest in Liverpool, had known Spencer for two years and had given spiritual comfort to him in the last stages of his illness. It is a matter of conjecture why Hopkins changed Felix Spencer's last name in the poem, and why he picked the name "Randal."

There were probably more subtle reasons than simply that *Randal* rhymes with *sandal*, the last word of the poem.

Consider a general statement by Fr. Alfred Thomas:

> [The poem] is about many things—the death of Felix Spencer, his anointing by Hopkins, the working of grace in the soul, the contrast between the secular and the sacred, between the temporal and eternal, the dignity of human labour, the situation of every-man, and man's relation to the mystical body of Christ. For in itself this sonnet assumes all the main beliefs of the Christian faith—the doctrines of man, sin, the Incarnation and Redemption, the Church, the sacraments, sanctification and eschatology, while the doctrine of God underpins the whole sonnet. . . . In thought the sonnet progresses from question to affirmation, from abstract to concrete, from earth to heaven, from physical to spiritual, from temporal to eternal. Felix has died yet nothing is discarded of the sensuous or human. The beginning is transcended, not obliterated.[23]

Although Thomas acknowledges that some have seen Hopkins's sonnet as "no more than a pious clergyman's sentimental reflection on the death of one of his parishioners, rounded off with a picture of the smith as he used to be," Thomas's own judgment is surely closer to majority opinion: "[Hopkins] has left us an elegy and an exultation, a superb and marvellous celebration of the Christian victory over death."[24] Once more, what is surely a profound piece of literature is linked directly to recognition of the intrinsic worth of all human life, portrayed in the death, through "some fatal four disorders," of one individual, once a "hardy-handsome" farrier. Thomas's judgment is only a shade less extreme than that of the authors he names (Gardner, Hunter, Mariani, Orwell) who have found "Felix Randal" to be "the best short poem in the language."[25]

Unfortunately, such general appraisals as these do not bring out the main point I wish to make. Thomas's list of the "many things" the poem is about places "sin" in apparently equal partnership with the others. Yet in the "narrative" second stanza it now appears not to matter whether Felix Randal had been a big sinner or a small one. We do not know what his confessions to the priest had been, whether he had confessed fully, and, if so, whether all of his sins had been only minor ones. But we do know that, whatever they were, to the priest they are now of no concern.

"Ah well, God rest him all road ever he offended!" surely indicates that
Felix Randal has now been absolved of all sin, "since I had our sweet
reprieve and ransom tender'd to him." What shines through Hopkins's
"elegy and exultation, . . . superb and marvellous celebration," is Felix
as a child of God, who, *as* a child, is due all that every child is due ("Thy
tears that touch'd my heart, child, Felix, poor Felix Randal"). We are
back once more to a state of the innocence of "everyman" known prior
to all sin, to a state of unconditional love that allows no reason to
withhold it for any possible moral transgression.

Memory here is crucial ("How far from then forethought of"), to yield
a comparison of this man and one who was once so stalwart. But it is
needed to bring the question of the poem's first stanza to full force: How
can it be that Felix Randal is dead ("My duty all ended?")? We have here
essentially the same concern as that of tragedy and of Proust in *Remembrance*, couched in a primary recognition of the intrinsic worth of human
life. But the subject, the concern in full force of one individual's question,
in this lyrical form of poetry brings the profundity quite without ethical
or moral concern. Here alliteration and symmetry of phrase beat marries
with memory. We find the dynamic analog of the priest's memory of Felix
Randal at the "random grim forge" in the mimicking of the sound of the
blacksmith's anvil with the *a-a-a*-beat in "great grey drayhorse" and in
"and battering sandal," driving through the priest's memory of earlier
days of a full life, "powerful amidst peers." Now the rhyming of *sandal*
with *Randal* returns the memory ending to the beginning—"Felix Randal
the farrier, O he is dead then?"

FELIX RANDAL

FELIX RANDAL the farrier, O he is dead then? my duty all
   ended,
Who have watched his mould of man, big-boned and
   hardy-handsome
Pining, pining, till time when reason rambled in it and
   some
Fatal four disorders, flesh'd there, all contended?

Sickness broke him. Impatient he cursed at first, but
   mended
Being anointed and all; though a heavenlier heart began
   some
Months earlier, since I had our sweet reprieve and ransom

Tender'd to him. Ah well, God rest him all road ever he
offended!

This seeing the sick endears them to us, us too it endears.
My tongue had taught thee comfort, touch had quench'd
thy tears,
Thy tears that touch'd my heart, child, Felix, poor Felix
Randal;

How far from then forethought of, all thy more boisterous
years,
When thou at the random grim forge, powerful amidst
peers,
Didst fettle for the great grey drayhorse his bright and
battering sandal!

IV

We have looked in this chapter at illustrations of three forms of literature,
to each of which profundity is commonly attributed. And through each
illustration runs a common theme: the recognition of the intrinsic value
of human life. In the case of tragedy we have lament at the loss of life,
but also highlighted in Gilbert Murray's interpretation "a strange, unanalyzed vibration below the surface, an undercurrent of desires and fears
and passions, long slumbering yet eternally familiar, which have for
thousands of years lain near the root of our most intimate emotions and
been wrought into the fabric of our most magical dreams." In Proust's
novel we have joy and happiness found through involuntary memory of
vivid sensory experiences of early life. And in the poem of Hopkins, a
priest's elegy on the death of Felix Randal through "some fatal four
disorders, flesh'd there, all contended," once more illustrates the common
theme.

In earlier chapters we have identified profundity as an exclusively
aesthetic value that in origin predates ethical judgment. We have mainly
been concerned in this chapter to determine how plausible such a
separation is between profundity and ethics in literature. In Murray's
interpretation, "one of the last secrets of genius" maintains the separation
quite well, and in Hopkins's lyric poem again morals are quite beside the
point in Felix Randal's redemption in the love of God.

The question becomes more complex in the case of Proust's novel. We found inconsistency of results, depending upon whether we mixed the criterion of profundity with Ricoeur's admittedly Aristotelian criterion of structural unity. The latter standard requires an integral relationship between *Remembrance* and *Time Regained*, such that the joys and happiness of full early life meet as equally important the scene "surrounded by death's heads" to afford the hero a glimpse of eternity. Looking at the unity of the entire novel as Proust evidently intended it makes death no longer a cause for lament, but yields a glimpse of what might be called the other side of time.

It may be noted here that the classical Aristotelian criterion of literary evaluation is Ricoeur's sole criterion for judging Proust's novel, and that this criterion has apparently been by far the most influential over the centuries in the evaluation of all forms of literature. This may be one major reason, together with Plato's identification of Beauty, that the profound in aesthetic judgment has been virtually ignored.

8

Repercussions

I

It is easy enough to acknowledge that there is no objective basis for valuational judgments, that there are no human values in existence independently of humans who find them. This, however, does not warrant the common corollary assumption that there are no valuational universals. From the point of view of process philosophies, or of any philosophy that traces origin of human values to interaction between subjects and environments, an aesthetic judgment of beauty, for example, must be a product of particular circumstances of particular judges. Hence, the ages-old dictum that "beauty is in the eye of the beholder." Products of artists heralded as beautiful are taken to be results of artists' interpretations of materials at hand—tones, beats, pigments, and so forth—which in the objective world are valuationally neutral. There seem to be among us no Platonists or Neoplatonists any more. Thus, we put great stress on creativity, on a capacity of some individuals somehow to make highly valuable things from what initially has no objective existence.

In a major way, the whole history of Western philosophy has let us down in aesthetic inquiries. Largely due to Plato, the center of inquiry in aesthetics has been taken to be beauty. Many philosophers have treated beauty as another general name for "aesthetic value." Other aesthetic predicates, such as sublime, lovely, magnificent, exquisite, and so forth, have typically been assumed to be subsumable under the general predicate beautiful, as species of a genus.

Largely due to Aristotle, the second stress of aesthetics has been on form or structure, and the identification of unity as the primary basis of judgments of the beautiful. Kant's recognition of a "moment of universality" in *Analytic of the Beautiful* brought to the fore a primary feature of aesthetic vocabulary that neither the stress on beauty nor on formal structure can well accommodate. Claims to universality of aesthetic quality cannot entirely be explained by linking an imperative function to the form of a declarative statement, "that thing is beautiful." Perhaps, indeed, the judge is making a demand that all men shall find it so, but couched within that demand there appears to be a conviction that this thing really *is* beautiful. Yet if we are not Platonists, where can that quality reside?

The general history of aesthetics leaves us at an impasse. Beauty is in the eye of the beholder, yet searching for its origin in form or structure reduces a primary human evaluation to a description of a state of affairs that has no intrinsic value. Perhaps, then, we have not looked carefully enough at an aesthetic predicate that has played in and out of the pages of philosophy at least since primary judgments of ancient Greek tragedy, but has never been recognized, or isolated and analyzed, as "beauty" has been. Perhaps the profound has been ignored because it seems to fit uneasily under the general heading "beauty." There is a universal connotation of *profundity* as a quality that is grasped, understood, felt by all humans all the way back to "primitive man," to what is "primordial." Perhaps the Greek stress on reason and the acquisition of wisdom has blocked recognition of such a quality as philosophically important. Then, too, no artist can create an aesthetic value that is universal. That is not only technically impossible; it is logically impossible as well.

Success in tracing and analyzing profundity in this inquiry has depended upon treating its locus as biological, not logical. In agreement with Kant's general assessment of aesthetic judgment as based on feelings rather than concepts, we have treated the particular quality of profundity as based on feelings and sense perceptions that feelings most often accompany. The biological relation between sensory patterns and their attendant feelings here detailed is clearly not one of logical entailment. Yet an analogy can be drawn between similarities of simple sensory patterns to one another and the relation of universal rules of inference to justifying steps of proof on a logical base.

Thus, looking at the prenatal sound pattern as a parent pattern that has been imitated in human auditory art in myriad ways in all cultural periods, we can also justify a judgment of musical profundity by back reference to the universal parent pattern in a way that is analogous to deductive logical justification. Similarly, we can justify and explain production of mandalas and their consistent feeling-description as one of "peace deep inside" by back reference to the visual image of the universal source of sustenance of human life. Thus, we can also find a corollary with current analyses of artificial intelligence in terms of logical pattern matching by analysis of *some* aesthetic judgment in terms of biological pattern matching.

Within the biological domain, we have thus had two primary tasks: to distinguish among any two sensory analogues one of them as a pattern that is universal to humans; and, second, to suggest how this parent pattern comes to be intrinsically aesthetically valuable. That is a tall order, but if the theory of this book is incorrect or not plausible, I cannot see how otherwise these two eminently worthwhile tasks could be accomplished. In the end, however, following out the account presented here corresponds with something about human artistic activity that all around us seems in fact to be true. In tracing sensory and sensory-motor functions to perinatal experience, what has been observed about artistic and religious activities yields an essentially simple explanation, free from diversities of context and the differences in possible interpretations those diversities entail, and exposes primary forces behind the repeated recognition that all men are brothers. Either in celebrating the value of unimpeded life in joie de vivre or in the lament of its loss when death finally defeats it, we find what may be the only locus of intrinsic aesthetic value. Thus, this inquiry not only allows philosophers to solve at least some of the mysteries of creativity and the justification of certain aesthetic convictions; it fills in a deep hole in the entire history of Western philosophy.

Three issues emerge from this that are unrelated to one another but that require some further clarification. These are identified in the next three sections by subtitles.

II: The Profound, the Beautiful, and the Sublime

There may yet be doubt that it is inappropriate to consider profundity as an extreme degree of beauty. This may make the above-mentioned deep hole look a little less cavernous. I do not think, however, that the entire preceding analysis of profundity should be looked upon as a misidentification of a quality that is really an extreme form of the beautiful or of the sublime.

The technique of pinning down word use or typical usage is admittedly a slippery business. Especially in analysis of aesthetic vocabulary we wonder what becomes of identifying use or usage in general parlance. I may say that most consistently I term melodies beautiful (rather than profound) that I now analyze as taking diastolic form, and that I want to call profound those pieces that I now analyze as imitating the entire prenatal pattern. This is my use of these words and I am assuming also that of others, whether they recognize it or not, whether they agree with my analysis or not. Then, of course, I can think of my own exceptions, and I can extend such exceptions to others. A Buddhist monk may say that the public viewing the New York sand mandala will be moved "deep inside," yet others may rather find the mandala "beautiful" or "sublime." It is easy enough to dismiss the opinion of those who find nothing in it at all. Perhaps most disturbing, however, when we are looking for traits of general usage, are the apparently significant numbers of people who go with what must simply be fashion, and who find profundity in such things as black-velvet paintings.

Fashion may be distinguished from tradition, however, by resurrecting Hume's condition of the qualified judge as one who is sensitive to and knowledgeable of the field he is judging. There is something lacking in breadth of experience, or perceptiveness, or both, in those who "merely" follow fashion. Mothers who find the ugliest of babies "beautiful," or "we" who find "our love sublime," however, may base such judgments on more than fashion—that is, upon a wedding of certain biological experiences to traditional word usage. Indeed, tradition in terms of "our" language use has been brought to bear more than once in criticism of past and present attempts to define beauty.

Neither Plato's definition of Beauty as a Form, nor Plotinus's identification of it as "Soul shining through," allows us to distinguish between objects, both of which are beautiful, but one of which is more beautiful than the other. The best we can do to accommodate such cases to Plato or Plotinus is to say that these objects "partake" of Beauty more or less completely, or allow Soul to shine through more or less clearly.

Donald Crawford has recently made similar criticism of Kant's analysis of aesthetic judgments: "that Kant's aesthetic theory does not admit of there being degrees of beauty."[1] Although his development of this claim is based primarily on immediate aesthetic experiences of variations in degree of beauty in different objects, his criticism also seems to imply that the word beauty itself denotes a quality that varies in degree. Thus, his criticism is in line with understanding of the word as it has been characteristically used in the Western world since the nineteenth century. What is perhaps most interesting, beyond Crawford's immediate concern, is Kant's evident recognition of the dependence of analysis of beauty on language function such as might identify him as a discerning precursor of twentieth-century language analysis. Kant telescopes much of this in the frequently quoted passage from the *Critique of Judgement* in his account of what the aesthetic judge *says*: "He [the judge] says the *thing* is beautiful, and he does not count on others agreeing with his judgment of pleasure because they did so occasionally in the past; rather he *demands* this agreement from them. He censures them if they judge differently and denies them taste, which he yet demands they should have."[2] Surely Kant's grasp of aesthetic predication stands in stark contrast to his analysis of predication in his refutation of the ontological argument in the *Critique of Pure Reason*.[3]

The authors of two recent theories of beauty, Guy Sircello and Mary Mothersill, both assume that beauty varies in degree, and in that respect they imply that they wish to keep their analyses compatible with standard usage of the word. In spite of this, however, Sircello's *New Theory of Beauty* has been criticized for not providing an analysis compatible with "normal use" of the words *beauty* and *beautiful*. In his review of Sircello's book, Haig Katchadourian repeats a list of adjectives given by Sircello as descriptive of the beauty of music and as examples of what Sircello counts as "properties of qualitative degree (PQDs)" of any complex whole. Many of these Khatchadourian finds not to be "beautiful properties, even when they are found in 'objects' in a very high degree, as we normally use the words 'beauty' and 'beautiful.' (Indeed one may wonder whether *any* 'aesthetic features' exist that are not PQDs.)"[4] Once more, common or "normal" language use has determined judgment of the adequacy of aesthetic theory.

In *Beauty Restored*, Mary Mothersill seeks a definition of beauty such that it functions as a generic term that others may simply call "aesthetic

value." Her objections, especially to Kant's distinction between judgments of the beautiful and judgments of the sublime, are based on her
own distinction between language that has been fashionable only during
a certain historical period and language whose historical place is "fixed
and secure." She speaks of theories of the sublime as having "a great
though relatively short-lived vogue."[5]

> A philosopher who borrows a term from the popular literary
> culture of his day is apt to get both more and less than he
> bargained for—more in the way of expressions of contemporary
> taste, less in the way of clarity and coherence. The concept of
> beauty, like the concept of knowledge or of right, is a "standing"
> concept. Whether it should be counted an *a priori* concept has
> yet to be determined, but whatever its status, its place in our
> repertory is fixed and secure. Plato and, let us say, Croce, differ
> on many basic issues, such as the relation of art to nature. . . .
> Yet there isn't (it seems to me) any question but that they are (to
> put it crudely) talking about the same thing. The "sublime," by
> contrast, picks out a collection of ideas which is historically local;
> the components hang together for a while (in this case for a little
> over a hundred years) and are then dispersed. A philosophical
> theory that places any weight on such a collection will come,
> sooner or later, to look *dated* and to resist interpretation. (BR,
> 232–33)

Although Mothersill finds that Kant's distinction of the sublime drew
attention to things of "soul" that observations of the "beautiful" might
seem to skirt or overlook, she thinks that he

> should have kept the "sublime" under the rubric of the
> "beautiful. . . ." (BR, 237)

> Kant has no generic aesthetic predicate, and the disjunction, "*x*
> is either beautiful or sublime," is unsatisfactory, since in fairness
> to the relevant convention of usage, the disjunction ought to be
> extended: ". . . *or* picturesque or pathetic or natural, etc.," and
> then there would be a question about what ties the disjunction
> together. . . . (BR, 243)

> A better way is to recognize that on Kant's own account, the
> beautiful and the sublime can be seen as falling under a single

concept and that where there is a concept, there is a place for a general predicate. If that is true, then the strongest candidate is "x is beautiful." (BR, 245)

Now, if Mothersill holds that beauty is a quality that varies in degree, then it seems that all qualities falling under the general predicate "beautiful" should also vary in degree, else they do not belong there. Considerable question can be raised about whether Kant's understanding of the "sublime," or that of others during those 100 years, was of a quality that varies in degree. If Kant was consistent on this with Crawford's analysis of his understanding of the beautiful, then he regarded neither the beautiful nor the sublime to vary in degree. In this respect, Mothersill's suggestion obfuscates certain points that Kant was evidently trying to make about judgments of the beautiful and the sublime. What of importance is "fixed and secure" in usage of *beauty* from Plato forward, if inherent in it is reference to what varies in degree, when Plato did not see it that way at all and apparently neither did Kant?

Traits of sublimity traced in brief review by Mothersill are of "intrinsic grandeur" (Longinus), "cosmic majesty, dignity, and power" (Johnson), and "seeming omnipotence of nature" (Kant). Experiences of the sublime feature "melancholy and terror" (Burke) and being "astounded and terrified" (Kant). We should note in addition Kant's exclusively visual illustrations of the sublime: "Bold, overhanging, and, as it were, threatening rocks, thunder-clouds piled up the vault of heaven, borne with flashes and peals, volcanoes in all their violence of destruction, hurricanes leaving desolation in their tracks, the boundless ocean rising in rebellious force, the high waterfall of some mighty river, and the like" (quoted in BR, 235).

In almost all of this vocabulary, it is difficult to think of the sublime as varying in degree. In Kant's general distinction of the "mathematical sublime" and the "dynamical sublime" we do not regard mathematical infinity as varying in degree, nor is it likely that we think of unbridled natural power as something we can have more or less of. If we have less of such a power then it is bridled. We do not generally think of "cosmic majesty, dignity, and power" as qualities that we have more or less of, nor anything that has "intrinsic grandeur." How, then, is it possible to fit these qualities into a generic definition of beauty that is taken to vary in degree?

Suppose we extend this question to the possible inclusion of profundity as a feature of beauty. Profundity then looks like a marker of an extreme point of beauty, and not itself an aesthetic value. At the opposite extreme would be superficial or shallow beauty, again forcing superficiality as a marker of a degree of beauty that is not itself an aesthetic value (though a negative one). Yet if we are starting our inquiry into beauty by noting language usage as "fixed and secure," surely the valuational use of *profound* and *shallow* or *superficial* is as fixed as beauty, and in its failure to vary in degree even more so. It is only a pity that the quality of profundity has not in the history of Western aesthetics been singled out for separate treatment as something evidently not reducible to a degree of beauty.

Is the meaning of *profundity*, however, reducible to at least part of the meaning of *sublime*? We might have a better chance of showing this than we have of relating profundity to beauty, since during its heyday the sublime was apparently not taken to be a quality that varies in degree (even though at the time beauty was not, either). Even though the sublime is now out of fashion, we might be able to argue that it ought to be resurrected (is it still not the case that "our love is sublime"?)—if only it were not for the sophisticated(?) opinion of twentieth-century aestheticians that *no* aesthetic qualities are invariant in degree.

There are several reasons indicating that it would be inaccurate, at best, to link profundity with sublimity. These reasons also extend the above argument against its connection with beauty. The first relates to the consistent identification of beauty and sublimity (at least in Kant) with experienced *pleasure*. Mothersill notes that many would not describe *Guernica*, *King Lear*, or *Oedipus at Colonus* as beautiful, but she explains this through a use of *beauty* that is restricted from the sublime (BR, 241–42). We may, however, suggest that neither appellation is suitable, because *pleasure* is an inaccurate word to denote the "depth" of experience that these works elicit. We have drawn a close relation between the experience of profundity and that, however briefly glimpsed, of mystics. It is surely inaccurate to describe the mystic's experience as simply one of *pleasure*. The term does not go "deep" enough.

Considering especially Kant's analysis of the sublime, there is a second reason that profundity does not fit well. As we noted, Kant's illustrations of the dynamically sublime were almost exclusively visual. True, we do not *see* mathematical infinity, but even in the case of the "mathematically sublime" we can visualize galaxies upon galaxies as impetus to think that they "go on forever." Consistent usage of *profound*, on the other hand, discloses a meaning that is nonvisual, of something that is hidden from view. This is closely connected with another and broader difference.

What is visible is so in the space-time world of subjects and objects. There is not a suggestion in theories of the sublime or of the beautiful that the very distinction between observing subject and object observed is lost. Kant was astute to observe a discrepancy between what the judge says and what he intends. But this goes on, in his opinion, within a social world of many intending subjects, such that the judge, aware of the social context of his judgment, attributes to anyone whosoever (*jedermann*), indeed *demands* of anyone whosoever, agreement with his own judgment of the beautiful. This early form of language analysis does not suggest that the judge at certain moments is more nearly "at one with the One" in a perception that makes profundity interchangeable between a quality of an object and a feeling of its finder. Where a judgment of profundity erases, or almost erases, a difference between observer and observed, it goes beyond understanding of either judgments of the beautiful or of the sublime, taken as made within a social environment of many judging subjects.

There is yet another difference between judgments of profundity and those of beauty or sublimity. In analyses, past or present, we do not find in references to beauty or sublimity a backward reference to memory. In neither of these do time distinctions appear important when we "find" beauty or sublimity. Keeping in mind our beginning analysis of *profundity* in terms of usage, however, *depth* not only goes hand in hand with "being moved deeply," it also goes hand in hand with the "depths of memory." Thus, it is not just that we do not want to call Sophocles' *Antigone* "beautiful" because we are operating with a limited understanding of *beauty* that does not encompass what Kant meant by *sublime*. It would not be all right if we added sublimity to our judgment and would then be satisfied with a judgment that it is beautiful in an expanded sense. An expanded understanding of the beautiful *still* does not get at the inadequacy of that appellation.

From the point of view of language analysis, however, perhaps the most telling indication that it is inappropriate to link beauty with profundity is found in references to artistic creativity. Consistently over the centuries, the artist is said to create beauty, but the artist is *not* said to create profundity. Because of its connotation of universality, profundity appears in an artist's work not as something that he has created but rather as something that he has found. And because of the domination of beauty in past theories of aesthetics as definitive of the "aesthetic" mode of human experience and action, it is likely, and a pity, that profundity will remain in historical aesthetic studies unrecognized, unisolated, and unanalyzed. Yet there it will have been all along, waving at us through the centuries, a quality whose analysis may finally prove to have far more explanatory power of what is intrinsically aesthetically valuable than have all the theories of beauty and sublimity combined.

III: Where Ethics and Aesthetics Meet

Defenses of valuational relativism in philosophies mentioned at the beginning of this inquiry have not just depended upon a conviction that there is no human "starting point" that is sensory in nature or that is precognitive or prelinguistic. In one way or another, they have as well depended upon recognition of complexities in human experiences that may produce unpredictable consequences. The more complexities are stressed in scientific or artistic processes and the more any *value* in these processes is traced to such complexities, the less appropriate or relevant is a judgment in any of them of profundity. We may take exception to one or another feature in the breakdown of *profundity* use or usage in Chapter 1. But surely the major feature of universality of reference to what all humans "know" is on target, and it is this general feature that in the name of total valuational relativism must be denied.

Defenses may be worked out logically in terms of predicate calculus, where use of profundity all but wipes out a required distinction between subject and predicate. Or, at least within certain interpretations of Wittgenstein, "ordinary use" of *profundity* as a reference to universal human understanding having universal human value must be judged to be a "misuse." No more than we are able by ordinary language analysis to find universal conditions of "knowledge" should we be able to find out by this means what a universal quality of "profundity" is. Nor, in current neurophysiology, with its analysis of brain "mappings" that are ever changing, ever more complex, and ever marking *differences* between individuals, is the suggestion made plausible that there can be found retreats to universal maps of earlier and simpler pattern, as well as advances to diverse and permanent differences.

In such defenses some assumptions must be made at the beginning whose restrictions effectively crowd out *profundity* either as some kind of misnomer or as the name of a quality that cannot exist. Yet there they are in all their persistence: the claims in auditory and literary criticism, in philosophy itself, in defenses of religious experience and religious doctrine, in sociological polemic of sameness through diversity of human cultures, all standing in stubborn defiance of what the most extended philosophical, scientific, and logical analyses disclose.

It will not do simply to say that we have here pictures of two "possible worlds" that cannot be reduced, the one to the other. It should be quite possible to identify unnecessary assumptions that can be corrected in any one analysis, such as may bring perspectives of cognitive science closer in line with those of human valuation. That, in large measure, is what I have tried here to do.

There remains, however, one feature that is especially resistant to such a marriage. It centers on the relation of ethical to aesthetic value. It is now commonly accepted that ethical and aesthetic values are not of the same kind, or, as Stuart Hampshire has put it, cannot be looked at as species of a genus "value." "One may invent a kind of judgment called a value judgment, and let it be either a judgment about conduct or a judgment about Art and Beauty: a single genus with two species. From this beginning one may go on to distinguish value judgments from other kinds of judgment. But the existence of the genus has been assumed, the assimilation of moral to aesthetic judgment taken for granted." Hampshire argues that there is no comparable purpose to be found in aesthetic judgments with moral judgments and that "there are no problems of aesthetics comparable with the problems of ethics." This means that procedures for justifying ethical judgments differ from those of aesthetic judgments. Where works of art are produced "gratuitously and not in response to a problem posed, there can be no question of preferring one solution to another; judgment of the work done does not involve a choice, and there is no need to find grounds of preference." In making ethical judgments, in contrast, "it makes sense to speak of a solution of a problem" and to "ask for reasons for preferring one solution to another; it is possible to demand consistency of choice and general principles of preference."[6]

Mary Mothersill reflects Hampshire's thinking:

> All attempts to force aesthetics into the mold of ethical theory must end in paradox and confusion. The two have, as it were, different centers of gravity. The pre-theoretical intuitions for ethics are themselves lawlike: they are the elementary rules of right conduct that one ought to keep one's promises, alleviate suffering, tell the truth. . . . Ethical theory, at a higher level of abstraction, is conceived as an attempt to systematize and ration-

alize the rules of right conduct or, in the traditional phrase, to discover the "foundation of morality. . . ." In the domain of taste [aesthetic] there are no interesting laws or "good-making characteristics" and no principles or "critical features." Given even a sketchy description of Brutus's act, one can say: "He may have had reasons but nonetheless he was Caesar's *friend!*" No description, no matter how detailed, of a work of art entitles an analogous weighing of merit and demerit. (BR, 170–71)

Thinking in a similar vein, Peter Caws argues that no universal aesthetics is possible, because, unlike the possibility of a universal ethics, aesthetics can evidence no "terminal value," as contrasted with an instrumental one. "A universal ethics is possible, since there is a universal instrumental value, namely freedom. But a universal aesthetics is not possible; it would require a universal terminal value, and there is not a shred of evidence that such a value exists, nor any plausible reason for supposing that it ever could." It is in the nature of creative imagination to posit freely certain ends, but there is

no reason to suppose that, within [a certain] range, we would all have to alight at the same point. It does not require creative imagination, of course, to posit certain biological or even intellectual ends common to human beings with inherited constitutions, drives, and so forth; a descriptive study of values actually expressed might lead to the formulation of a kind of universal terminus as the state of the world an ideally rational man would prefer if confronted with the set of all possible alternatives. . . . But this does not take us as far as aesthetics. . . . What we are denying is the possibility of a universally *normative* aesthetics, that is, of a universally valid set of prescriptions about the ends to be sought by free action, including the quintessentially free actions of the artist.[7]

Caws presupposes here that all particular values identifiable as aesthetic are on an equal footing in the artist's judgment; that is, any of them *may* through "freedom of choice" determine the aesthetic value of his product. Even though Caws acknowledges a possibility of formulating "a kind of universal terminus as the state of the world an ideally rational man would prefer," he does not suggest that such biological back-reference might yield a criterion of aesthetic judgment that all men find (rather than choose), and find to be of superior value in the very fact of its human universality. In his denial of the possibility of a "universal normative aesthetics," Caws provides no basis for explaining comparative judgments of different works of art precisely on the particular ground of profundity—that is, "this is profound, that is shallow."

Consistent with Hampshire and Mothersill, it is difficult to deny that aesthetic and ethical values are of different types. This is one thing; but to account for it by denying or affirming that universal normative reasons can be found to justify aesthetic or ethical judgments is another. In deciding issues of life and death, the concept of natural law has appeared to be exclusively ethical. Yet we have suggested that it carries an aesthetic component—as in Sophocles' *Antigone*—that provides a *reason* for a final ethical judgment. We have not looked at the principle that "all men are brothers" as itself an ethical principle, as Hilary Putnam evidently did (although this is unclear). Yet if we regard the love of humanity as an aesthetic motive, "all men are brothers" is found repeatedly to function as a reason for certain specific and rudimentary ethical judgments, such as those of the Nuremberg Tribunal; that is, it is given as a reason for the judgment of "crimes against humanity." It should be noted, however, that this point at which ethics and aesthetics meet is found specifically through an aesthetic quality that is the mark of profundity. Especially where we think of aesthetic values as all under the general rubric of "beauty," "sublimity," or both, such a connection is evidently not demonstrable. This provides us, then, with the more reason to distinguish profundity from beauty and sublimity as a different or separate aesthetic quality.

A great deal of the discrepancy here seems to stem from a difference between ethics and aesthetics when they are analyzed in general terms and when they are looked at one value at a time. Undoubtedly Sircello's and Mothersill's results stem in large measure from identifying aesthetic values in general terms of beauty, even though it can be in an expanded sense that includes what Kant and others called sublimity. Our problems concerning the relation of ethical to aesthetic judgment, on the other hand, have resulted from the particular judgment of profundity, and, at that, especially in interpreting the particular art of literature. If we had been concerned with judgments of beauty—in any sense of beauty consistent with standard usage—then the question of its relation to ethical judgments might not even have arisen.

We have found a problem in explaining the persistence of the concept of natural law in relation to Sophocles' *Antigone*, the paradigm example in Hegel's opinion of a merger of rudimentary ethical and aesthetic values. We have found in Paul Ricoeur's interpretation of Proust's masterpiece an inability clearly to separate these values, although they remain in the novel distinguishable as different in type. The same concern may easily be voiced between ethical and aesthetic values in religion. If it was possible to distinguish PAX on the lawn outside the Italian basilica as an aesthetic exclamation, rather than an eclipsed ethical injunction, such as "make love, not war," it might also have been possible to read PAX with an ethical connotation, after all. We stressed the first interpretation as compatible with a general analysis of aesthetic value in pure music that is quite independent of ethics, although it might well have been that those enthused at the concert would have stressed the second as they walked out into the night. Certainly the use of gospel music in church service is indelibly connected with "man's humanity to man."

These instances are far from the only ones that we could point to. Consider judgments of the novels of James Baldwin. We cannot, in the interest of fairness, divorce their aesthetic merit from the clearly ethical base upon which they are framed, injustice to blacks in America:

> To blacks he offered dry but nourishing crusts of hope: "What white people say about you, as well as what they do and cause you to endure, does not testify to your inferiority but to their inhumanity and fear. There is no reason to become like white people and no basis whatever for their impertinent assumption that *they* must accept *you*. The really terrible thing is that *you* must accept *them* and accept them with love. It will be hard, but you come from men who, in the teeth of the most terrifying odds, achieved an unassailable and monumental dignity."[8]

How is that for a thoroughgoing mixture of ethics and aesthetics? Once more, however, the aesthetic connection is not one of beauty or sublimity. It is found in the one upon which this book has productively concentrated: profundity.

Philosophers may be confident that by now, in one way or another, they have set things straight on the relation of ethics to aesthetics. But simply drawing a difference in kind between ethical and aesthetic judgments will not tell the whole tale. Nor will a general insistence that there is no universal normative aesthetic principle or "terminus."

IV: Refuting Relativism

There may be differing opinions of what constitutes a refutation. For example, the finding of counterexamples has recently been taken to "demolish" certain general philosophical theses on the ground that they have not laid out necessary or sufficient conditions. Especially in the light of process philosophies, however, the search for necessary and/or sufficient conditions may now be regarded as misplaced and useless. If a "refutation" is of this kind of search, it may well now be looked upon as a waste of time and to have missed a primary message of contextual dependency both in epistemology and valuation. At best, typical cases and contexts ought to be explored.

Perhaps the strongest form of refutation consists of the defense of the contradictory of any premise to be refuted. This book's refutation of valuational relativism presents the contradictory of a premise that has been uniformly upheld in process philosophies: All human values or valuations are context dependent—or—No human values or valuations are context free. Our inquiry into the particular aesthetic value of profundity makes the contradictory plausible: There is one major human value (aesthetic) that is not context dependent—that is universal to humans and context free. Evidence for the truth of this contradictory is indirect and is based upon inference of a causal connection between specific sensory analogues—initially between the prenatal sound pattern and the visual mandala pattern—and cross-cultural patterns of particular auditory and visual artworks. It has been assumed that these connections, and the aesthetic value that the patterns seemingly carry regardless of contextual differences, are not coincidental or accidental.

The explanation of sensory-pattern connections in terms of unconscious memory may well not itself be refutable. But it is the close pattern analogies themselves, as well as common talk about "profundity" of certain artworks, rather than the explanation of their origin, which warrants the conclusion that, in matters valuational, process philosophies have overgeneralized. In detail, our analysis indicates that the following assumptions are either incorrect, unnecessarily restrictive, or both:

1. All sense perception begins at birth. There is no "natural starting point" in human sense perception of pattern.
2. All sensory pattern recognition is a product of interpretation.
3. If there *were* such a thing as a universal aesthetic value, this would have to be biologically determined in genetic coding.

4. All neurological brain "mappings" are highly complex, hence all human cognition is a process of interpretation.
5. "Facts and values" are inseparable, hence valuations inherent in cognition are to be understood in just the same terms as is cognition. There are no essential differences to be found in valuational and epistemological process. Facts and values are correctly understood only in terms of evolutionary and historical process.
6. All aesthetic values in "art" are a product of creativity or imagination.
7. All significance or "meaning" in auditory, visual or literary art, or religion is a product of symbolism, not of imitation.

Must we not acknowledge, however, that each and every judgment of profundity is made or evoked in *some* context or other? In broadest terms, have we not already looked at profundity as a comparatively somber quality and joie de vivre as two sides of the same coin? And the moment we have "pinned down" profundity to two specific sensory patterns, have we not overlooked their inseparability from arts whose cross-cultural differences cannot be denied? Must profundity not always be attached to a host of context-dependent perspectives, possibilities, and choices, however pressing these may be?

Looked at linguistically, aesthetic predicates that are far from synonyms have a disturbing way of mixing with one another, sometimes in seemingly random fashion, of stumbling over each other, entering or exiting at will. These are not just dependent upon bodily circumstance (perhaps we have a headache today) or upon environmental conditions (perhaps the painting is in the wrong light). It is as though aesthetic predicates are nearly always in an unsettled state even when subjective and objective conditions are optimum. And in the case of mystical experiences whose profundity is not denied, we have not only transiency of occurrence, as James observed, but also an ultimate functional failure of all predication.

It is one thing, however, to agree that all values or valuations are found in or occur within some context, and another to conclude that all of them *originate* within that context. The biographical film *James Baldwin: The Price of the Ticket* (PBS, *American Masters*) opens and closes with scenes of Baldwin's funeral at the Cathedral of Saint John the Divine in New York, dominated by continuous sequences of African drumming that form as close a reproduction, as blatant a copy, of the prenatal sound pattern as can be found in human auditory art. In the film we have heard once more Baldwin's assured statement: "All men are brothers. . . . If you can't take it from there, you can't take it at all." Certainly his "belief in a new Jerusalem—that we can all become better than we are" took its passion not only from the conflicts and controversies of his personal life but from his entrenched experience with American racism. In an interview in the film, Maya Angelou says: "Jimmie was not bitter. What Jimmie was was angry—he was constantly angry at injustice, at ignorance, at exploitation, at stupidity, at vulgarity. Yes, he was angry."

It will not do, however, to put Jimmie's cart before Jimmie's horse. Surely the *value* in recognizing that all men are brothers does not itself derive from the particular context of racism—wherever it is found, however far-reaching and devastating its consequences—but rather vice versa. At the end of the film, we see Baldwin's casket carried out of the church and down a ramp to the street, followed by the incessant beat of the drummers and a mass of silent mourners. Now we can no longer *see* the *man*. Even what remains is shrouded in a wooden box. We know its contents; we know where it is going. What now can we, the living, do but *sound* once more—again and again, undamped, loud and clear, all stops out—that incessant beat of the fully living, as in a plea: "Come back, come back among *us*." In this profound lament, what is heard brings the dynamic fullness of life into direct conflict with a picture of the finality of its loss in the everlasting human war between life and death, and brings it entirely without words. This, in the end, is not just a lament of the loss of a dynamic opponent of the devastation and blight of racism. Its profundity does not derive from that, nor from the fact that the drumming happens to be African in style. Beneath this lament of the loss of one life well worth living is the lament of the loss of any human life. This was Jimmie's horse, and the horse has independent locomotion. It is the cart that must be pulled.

Notes

Introduction

1. For example, Peter Kivy, "Platonism in Music: Another Kind of Defense," *American Philosophical Quarterly* 24 (1987): 245–52, and Jerrold Levinson, "What a Musical Work Is," *Journal of Philosophy* 77, no. 1 (1980): 5–28.

2. Terry Winograd and Fernando Flores, *Understanding Computers and Cognition: A New Foundation for Design* (Norwood, N.J.: Ablex, 1986), 75.

3. Hubert Dreyfus, *What Computers Can't Do: The Limits of Artificial Intelligence* (New York: Harper & Row, 1979), 63.

4. Richard Rorty, *Philosophy and the Mirror of Nature* (Princeton, N.J.: Princeton University Press, 1979), 367–68.

5. George Steiner, "Viewpoint: A New Meaning of Meaning," *Times Literary Supplement*, 8 November 1985, 1265, 1275.

6. Brand Blanshard, *Reason and Analysis* (La Salle, Ill.: Open Court, 1962), 370–71.

7. Ibid., 372–79.

8. Quoted by Judy Stone, "A Man of Dignified Irreverence," *Datebook, San Francisco Chronicle*, 29 August 1987.

9. J. N. Findlay, *Language, Mind, and Value* (Atlantic Highlands, N.J.: Humanities Press, 1963), 127.

Chapter 1

1. Władysław Tatarkiewicz, *A History of Six Ideas*, translated from the Polish by Christopher Kasparek (The Hague: Nijhoff, 1980), Conclusion, 341–42.

2. Herbert Blomstedt's remarks on Beethoven appeared originally in the San Francisco Symphony's June 1985 program book. They were reprinted in abbreviated form in the *San Francisco Examiner and Chronicle*, 8 June 1986, Music S-1, 2.

3. Brand Blanshard, "Wisdom," *The Encyclopedia of Philosophy* (New York: Macmillan, 1967), 8:322–24.

4. J.W.N. Sullivan, *Beethoven: His Spiritual Development* (New York: Random House, Vintage Books, 1927).

5. See *The Relevance of Charles Peirce*, ed. Eugene Freeman (La Salle, Ill.: Open Court, 1983). Putnam's Carus Lectures have been published as *The Many Faces of Realism* (La Salle, Ill.: Open Court, 1987); the quotation near the beginning of this section is from p. 80.

6. J. N. Findlay, *Values and Intentions* (London: Macmillan, 1961), 118–19.

7. Thomas Nagel, *Mortal Questions* (New York: Cambridge University Press, 1979), 212.

8. See C. I. Lewis, *An Analysis of Knowledge and Valuation* (La Salle, Ill.: Open Court, 1950), 391, ch. 14 passim, 457, 477.

9. Nagel, *Mortal Questions*, 209.

10. Richard Rorty, "Pragmatism and Philosophy," in *After Philosophy: End or Transformation?* (Cambridge, Mass.: MIT Press, 1987), 45.

11. Ibid., 54.

12. "Black Man, You Better Know Yourself . . ." (produced by W. Riley, 85 West St., Kingston, Jamaica; Techniques 92-26832).

13. Richard Rorty, *Philosophy and the Mirror of Nature* (Princeton, N.J.: Princeton University Press, 1979), 38.

14. Marx Wartofsky, "Perception, Representation, and the Forms of Action: Towards an Historical Epistemology," *Boston Colloquium for the Philosophy of Science* (Dordrecht: Reidel, 1985), 223.

15. Ibid., 237.

16. "Proust, Marcel," *Encyclopaedia Britannica*, 14th ed. (1970), 18:678–79.

17. J. N. Findlay, *Values and Intentions* (London: Macmillan, 1961), 16.

Chapter 2

1. Nelson Goodman, *Fact, Fiction, and Forecast* (Indianapolis, Ind.: Bobbs-Merrill, 1965), 42, 56–57.

2. Nelson Goodman, *Ways of Worldmaking* (Indianapolis, Ind.: Bobbs-Merrill, 1978), 2–4.

3. Ibid., 138.

4. I have made this observation more extensively in my book *Soundtracks: A Study of Auditory Perception, Memory, and Valuation* (Buffalo, N.Y.: Prometheus Books, 1986), 86–89.

5. John Dewey, *Art as Experience* (New York: Minton Balch, 1934), 175. Further references to this work, abbreviated AE, will be included parenthetically in the text of Chapter 2.

6. John Dewey, *Human Nature and Conduct* (New York: Random House, Modern Library, 1930), 40–41. Further references to this work, abbreviated HNC, will be included parenthetically in the text of Chapter 2.

7. *The Encyclopedia of Philosophy* (New York: Macmillan, 1967), 2:382.

8. J. N. Findlay, *Values and Intentions* (London: Macmillan, 1961), 93. Further references to this work, abbreviated VI, will be included parenthetically in the text of Chapter 2.

Chapter 3

1. Herbert Blomstedt, *San Francisco Examiner and Chronicle*, 8 June 1986, Music S-1, 2 (text reprinted in abbreviated form from the San Francisco Symphony's June 1985 program book).

2. Jean Gabbert Harrell, *Soundtracks: A Study of Auditory Perception, Memory, and Valuation* (Buffalo, N.Y.: Prometheus Books, 1986).

3. P. F. Strawson, *Individuals* (New York: Doubleday, Anchor Books, 1963), 61, 82, 83. A. J. Ayer, *The Foundations of Empirical Knowledge* (London: Macmillan, 1963), 253–55.

4. Eduard Hanslick, *The Beautiful in Music*, trans. Gustav Cohen (New York: Bobbs-Merrill, Library of Liberal Arts, 1957), 52.

5. *The Collected Works of C. G. Jung*, trans. R.F.C. Hull (New York: Pantheon Books, 1968), vol. 9, pt. 1:387–88. An excellent example of Islamic mandalas, both in dervish dancing and in the interiors and exteriors of mosques, may be found in the television biographical documentary "Suleyman, the Magnificent" (produced and directed by Suzanne Bauman; executive producers: National Gallery of Art and Metropolitan Museum of Art; presented on PBS by WETA, Washington, D.C.; aired 17 April 1987).

One may also note in this documentary that the musical soundtrack presents an excellent illustration of the prenatal sound pattern as it appears in typical Islamic musical style. The clear relation of dervish dancing to religious experience, belief, and ceremony comes through in the narrator's comments: "The dance brings on a trance state in which [the dancers] strive to become one with the universe. . . . [Quoting from the philosopher Rumi] 'Dancing . . . is when you rise above both worlds, tearing your heart to pieces and giving up your soul. . . .' One hand pointed toward heaven, the other extending to earth, they whirl in timeless ecstasy."

6. Jung, *Collected Works*, vol. 9, pt. 1:3.

7. Ibid., 5–7.

8. *The Encyclopedia of Philosophy* (New York: Macmillan, 1967), 4:296.

9. Jung, *Collected Works*, vol. 9, pt. 1:390.

10. Ibid., 278–79.

11. Terry Winograd and Fernando Flores, *Understanding Computers and Cognition: A New Foundation for Design* (Norwood, N.J.: Ablex, 1986), 115.

12. Ibid.

13. Ibid., 97.

14. H. Christopher Longuet-Higgins, *Mental Processes: Studies in Cognitive Science* (Cambridge, Mass.: MIT Press, 1987), 183.

15. Ibid., 185.

16. Brian Rotman, "Between Atoms and Experience," *Times Literary Supplement*, 15–21 January 1988, 424.

17. Longuet-Higgins, *Mental Processes*, 169.

18. *Confessions of St. Augustine*, trans. William Watts (Cambridge, Mass.: Harvard University Press, Loeb Classical Library, 1939), bk. 10, ch. 23, 165.

19. Heinrich Schenker, *Harmony*, trans. Elisabeth Mann Borghese (Chicago: University of Chicago Press, 1954). Quoted by Oswald Jonas, Introduction, xv.

20. Ibid., 3.

Chapter 4

1. Marcel Proust, *Swann's Way*, trans. C. K. Scott Moncrieff (New York: Random House, Modern Library, 1956), 258–61.

2. Ibid., 260–61.

3. Judith Axler Turner, "Untangling the Meaning of Art for a Special Student," *Chronicle of Higher Education*, 27 January 1988, A3.

4. From a letter to the author, 11 April 1988.

5. Carl R. Hausman, *A Discourse on Novelty and Creation* (The Hague: Nijhoff, 1975), 28.

6. Ibid., 43.

7. Ibid., 42.

8. Ibid., 50–51.

9. W. I. Matson, *Sentience* (Berkeley and Los Angeles: University of California Press, 1976), 156n.

10. H. Christopher Longuet-Higgins, *Mental Processes: Studies in Cognitive Science* (Cambridge, Mass.: MIT Press, 1987), 68–69.

11. Douglas Hofstadter, *Metamagical Themas: Questing for the Essence of Mind and Pattern* (New York: Basic Books, 1985), 181.

12. Ibid., 188.

13. Monroe C. Beardsley, *Aesthetics: Problems in the Philosophy of Criticism* (New York: Harcourt, Brace, 1958), 466.

Chapter 5

1. Charles L. Stevenson, *Ethics and Language* (New Haven, Conn.: Yale University Press, 1958), 60–61.

2. Alexius Meinong, "Toward an Empirical Assessment of Memory," in *Empirical Knowledge*, ed. Roderick Chisholm and Robert Swartz (Englewood Cliffs, N.J.: Prentice-Hall, 1973), 253–70.

3. Mary Warnock, *Memory* (London: Faber and Faber, 1987), 74. Further references to this work, abbreviated M, will be included parenthetically in the text of Chapter 5.

4. Israel Rosenfield, "Neural Darwinism: A New Approach to Memory and Perception," *New York Review of Books*, 9 October 1986, 21. Further references to this work, abbreviated "ND," will be included parenthetically in the text of Chapter 5.

Chapter 6

1. Paul Johnson, *A History of the Jews* (New York: Harper & Row, 1987), 144.

2. Ibid., 161.

3. Ibid., 145.

4. Cullen Murphy, "Who Do Men Say That I Am? Interpreting Jesus in the Modern World," *Atlantic Monthly*, December 1986, 37. Further references to this work, abbreviated "WD," will be included parenthetically in the text of Chapter 6.

5. Jesse Hamlin, *San Francisco Chronicle*, 9 July 1988, A-1, 14.

6. William James, *The Varieties of Religious Experience* (New York: Macmillan, 1961), 201. Further references to this work, abbreviated VRE, will be included parenthetically in the text of Chapter 6.

7. Dennis Helvesi, "Buddhist Isle of Peace in Uptown Manhattan," *New York Times*. Quoted in the *San Francisco Chronicle*, 11 July 1988, B-8.

Chapter 7

1. G.W.F. Hegel, *The Philosophy of Fine Art*, trans. F.P.B. Osmaston (New York: Hacker Art Books, 1975), 1:293.

2. Ibid., 293, 296.

3. G.W.F. Hegel, *The Philosophy of Right*, trans. S. W. Dyde (London: Bell, 1896), sects. 144–45.

4. Jane Ellen Harrison, *Epilegomena and Themis* (Hyde Park, N.Y.: University Books, 1962), xvii.

5. Ibid., 478, 535.

6. Gilbert Murray, *The Classical Tradition in Poetry* (Cambridge, Mass.: Harvard University Press, 1927), 226. Further references to this work, abbreviated *CTP*, will be included parenthetically in the text of Chapter 7.

7. Alasdair MacIntyre, *After Virtue* (Notre Dame, Ind.: University of Notre Dame Press, 1984), 265–66.

8. A. P. d'Entrèves, *Natural Law* (London: Harper & Row, Harper Torchbooks [The Academy Library], 1984), 13.

9. Ibid., 106.

10. Ibid., 14.

11. Lewis Galantière, Introduction to Marcel Proust, *Swann's Way*, trans. C. K. Scott Moncrieff (New York: Random House, Modern Library, 1956), xi, xii, xiii.

12. Harold March, *The Two Worlds of Marcel Proust* (New York: Barnes, 1961), 251.

13. Mary Warnock, *Memory* (London: Faber and Faber, 1987), 101–2.

14. Quoted in March, *Two Worlds of Marcel Proust*, 221.

15. Paul Ricoeur, *Time and Narrative*, trans. Kathleen McLaughlin and David Pellauer (Chicago: University of Chicago Press, 1985), 2:145. Further references to this work, abbreviated *TN*, will be included parenthetically in the text of Chapter 7.

16. Quoted in March, *Two Worlds of Marcel Proust*, 247.

17. Ibid., 251.

18. Richard B. Sewall, *The Vision of Tragedy* (New Haven, Conn.: Yale University Press, 1980), 7.

19. Hans-Georg Gadamer, "On the Contribution of Poetry to the Search for Truth," in *The Relevance of the Beautiful and Other Essays*, trans. Nicholas Walker, ed. Robert Bernasconi (Cambridge: Cambridge University Press, 1987), 112. On relations of word-sound to "form" and "unity," see Hans-Georg Gadamer, "Philosophy and Poetry," in *Relevance of the Beautiful*, 134.

20. Gadamer, "Contribution of Poetry," in *Relevance of the Beautiful*, 115. Further references to this collection, abbreviated *RB*, will be included parenthetically in the text of Chapter 7.

21. William James, *The Varieties of Religious Experience* (New York: Macmillan, 1961), 302, 357.

22. Roman Ingarden, *The Literary Work of Art: An Investigation on the Borderlines of Ontology, Logic, and Theory of Literature*, trans. George G. Grabowicz (Evanston, Ill.: Northwestern University Press, 1973), 61.

23. Alfred Thomas, "Hopkins's 'Felix Randal': The Man and the Poem," *Times Literary Supplement*, 19 March 1971, 331–32.

24. Ibid., 332.

25. Ibid., 331.

Chapter 8

1. Donald Crawford, "Comparative Judgments and Kant's Aesthetic Theory," *Journal of Aesthetics and Art Criticism* 38, no. 3 (Spring 1980): 289.

2. Immanuel Kant, *Critique of Aesthetic Judgement*, trans. J. C. Meredith (Oxford: Clarendon, 1911), ¶ 7.

3. See my more extended comparison in "Two Faces of Kant," *Akten des 4. Internationalen Kant-Kongresses* (Mainz, 6–10 April 1974), Teil II.1 (Berlin: de Gruyter, 1974).

4. Haig Katchadourian, review of Guy Sircello, *A New Theory of Beauty*, *Journal of Aesthetics and Art Criticism* 35, no. 3 (Spring 1977): 362.

5. Mary Mothersill, *Beauty Restored* (Oxford: Oxford University Press, 1984), 234. Further references to this work, abbreviated *BR*, will be included parenthetically in the text of Chapter 8.

6. Stuart Hampshire, "Logic and Appreciation," in *Essays in Aesthetics and Language*, ed. William Elton (Oxford: Blackwell, 1959), 161–62, 164.

7. Peter Caws, *Science and the Theory of Value* (New York: Random House, 1967), 134–35, 144.

8. "James Baldwin, a Manchild from Harlem, Sang the Song of Himself with a Fury That Seared Us All," *People*, 21 December 1987, 89.

Index